Building Knowledge-Based Systems

towards a methodology

John S. Ed

Aston Business School/A

Pitman

PITMAN PUBLISHING
128 Long Acre, London WC2E 9AN

A Division of Longman Group UK Limited

© J. S. Edwards 1991

First published in Great Britain 1991

British Library Cataloguing in Publication Data
Edwards, John
   Building knowledge-based systems.
   1. Computer systems. Design
   I. Title
   004.21

   ISBN 0-273-03048-5

Reproduced and printed by photolithography
in Great Britain by Biddles Ltd, Guildford

Preface

The aim of this book is to look at building knowledge-based systems (KBSs) from a viewpoint which brings together three disciplines: artificial intelligence, conventional software engineering and "soft" operational research/systems analysis. This was prompted by the belief that all three disciplines have something to offer to the builder of a KBS which is intended to address a commercial need in an organization. A particularly relevant point is the need for such a KBS to link with other systems, both computer-based and "organizational".

The material is intended to be accessible to computer-literate readers from any background, since at present it seems as if almost anyone may be called upon to develop a KBS. However, those with knowledge of one or more of the three disciplines mentioned above may be able to omit or skim through the appropriate chapters in the first half of the book. The first three chapters cover artificial intelligence in general, and what might be called "the artificial intelligence approach to knowledge-based systems" in particular. A chapter each on conventional software engineering and "soft" operational research/ systems analysis follow. The second half of the book sets out the POLITE methodology for building knowledge-based systems, including some of the work on the use of KBSs in conventional systems design which helped to stimulate its development.

The book draws on the experience gained from developing several systems of varying sizes, but particularly from the *Intellipse* project (SE057 of the Alvey Directorate) which encouraged the original links between building KBSs and structured methods for conventional software engineering. My thanks are due to all of the *Intellipse* team, at Aston University, BIS Applied Systems and British Steel Corporation Strip Products Group, especially Jon Bader; to all my other colleagues at Aston and elsewhere who have helped to shape my ideas, particularly Al Rodger, who proposed the exploratory, solution-driven and problem-driven perspectives; to the staff of Pitman Publishing for their support; and finally, but most importantly, to my family for putting up with "knowledge-based systems with everything"!

Contents

Chapter 1: Putting Knowledge-based Systems in Context

1.0 Introduction

The overall objectives of this chapter are (a) to define our view of knowledge-based systems in general and our particular type of knowledge-based system, and (b) to explain the structure of the book.

This book is primarily about knowledge-based systems, which from now on we shall refer to as KBSs, but much of what we have to say will be applicable to other types of computer system as well. The purpose of this introductory chapter is to put KBSs in their proper context, particularly as far as commercial applications are concerned. Summed up in a sentence, this is that KBSs are different from "conventional" computer systems, but not very different. The hype and exaggeration which have plagued many articles and books about KBSs or expert systems are beginning to subside, but there is a residual mystique, even amongst computing professionals, which leads to unnecessary confusion and suspicion.

We'll have to discuss the hype and mystique a little in this chapter, if only in an attempt to de-mystify the subject. However, our discussion of where KBSs came from will be a relatively brief one, since we (and, we trust, you) are more interested in where KBSs are going.

What is true is that for between ten and twenty years now there have been research KBSs, normally using substantial mainframe computing resources, and usually written in the language LISP, which come close to the performance of human experts in a very limited domain of expertise. This domain of expertise was at first normally concerned with science or medicine. DEC's R1 (later renamed XCON), an expert system in a technological domain, that of configuring computer systems, was the first to make it into the commercial arena. More recently, two other types of KBS have appeared, both with some successful commercial applications. The first stream followed the original research direction in being big stand-alone systems, but now languages such as LISP and Prolog were augmented by special-purpose development environments and artificial intelligence (AI) workstations specially configured for running AI languages. The other stream of expert systems were more modest affairs, usually based on PCs and frequently using the new "expert system shells". The cost savings or profits attributed to some of these systems, especially those of the first type, run into hundreds of thousands of pounds or dollars. However, these are the minority of KBSs; most KBSs have been built for research or to gain useful experience, not for commercial use. KBSs are not at present the answer to all management problems, or even all management computing problems, but the existence of successful examples means that the time is right for KBSs to move into widespread usage.

1.1 Artificial Intelligence: a brief overview

Artificial intelligence (AI) has been an area of active research for around 40 years, with the central theme being the possibility of producing machines which think. Figure 1.1 shows some of the "milestones" in the development of AI, which we shall now discuss briefly. At one time, in the immediate post-World War II years, there was little "distance" between AI research and the work on the first electronic stored-program computers. Indeed, it seemed possible that "thinking machines" were only a few years away. For example, the mathematician Alan Turing was involved in both the development of the Manchester Mark I computer and in the question of how to judge the intelligence of a machine. His speculations on the latter led to what is now called the "Turing test". In such a test, a person interacts with a terminal, which is connected either to a machine or to a terminal operated by another human being. If the person cannot distinguish interactions with the machine from those with another human, then the machine may be regarded as intelligent .

In 1956, a seminal conference on AI was held at Dartmouth College, New Hampshire, USA. Following this (though not directly because of it!), during the late 1950s and early 1960s, AI research increasingly diverged from the "number-crunching" and transaction processing applications which made up the mainstream of data processing. The main emphasis in AI during this period was on systems which possessed some degree of general intelligence or problem-solving ability. This led to such spin-offs as the development of the computer language LISP, which was to become one of the corner-stones of AI research.

As time went on, although both AI and mainstream computing were concerned with the storage of large amounts of data in one form or another, there was little commonality in the work done. The main concern of mainstream data processing was with structures which permitted the efficient storage and

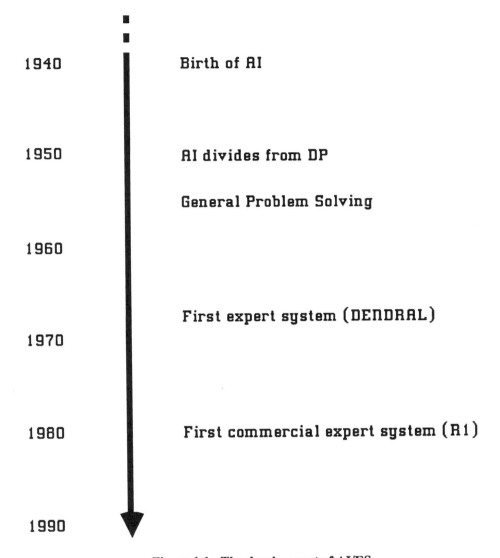

1940	Birth of AI
1950	AI divides from DP
	General Problem Solving
1960	
1970	First expert system (DENDRAL)
1980	First commercial expert system (R1)
1990	

Figure 1.1: The development of AI/ES

retrieval of data, while AI was more concerned with attempting to produce structures which represented the way in which the human brain stores data/ information/knowledge.

Only in the late 1970s did the AI work begin to bear fruit as far as potential mainstream commercial applications were concerned, in the form of rudimentary natural language understanding and of the first expert systems. It has taken a further 10 years for these developments even to come close to being

3

regarded as normal commercial practice. In the meantime, AI research has inevitably progressed still further, giving us the present situation with many potential mainstream applications but substantially fewer actual ones.

Much has been made of the phrase "artificial intelligence" in order to portray recent developments as the greatest thing since sliced bread, or indeed sliced bits! The connotations of the phrase, be they mystifying or frightening, appear to have been used (perhaps mistakenly) as a focus for marketing the related products. The implication appears to be that, unless you are steeped in AI, you cannot possibly make use of the fruits of AI research. In our view, this is dangerously misleading. After all, much of conventional computing relies on the fruits of theoretical research in mathematics. However, it is not necessary to study set theory extensively in order to use, or even write an application in, a relational database package. Just because the AI research may come from different disciplines, such as cognitive psychology, does not render the theory itself any more important from the point of view of applications. Indeed, for the applications developer, one over-riding similarity between mathematical and AI research is crucial - neither takes any consideration of the commercial purpose for which the system is being developed. We shall return to this point at length later, in Chapter 8.

We shall look in more detail at the fruits of AI research in the next sections. To close this section, we have deliberately not attempted to define AI with any precision - this is because anyone attempting such a definition at present is stepping into a minefield! Perhaps the most useful definition is that offered by Marvin Minsky: "AI is the science of making machines do things which would require intelligence if they were done by a human." We believe that much of the argument over definitions of AI which takes place elsewhere stems from the lack of agreement as to what constitutes human (or indeed any other natural) intelligence.

To illustrate this point, computer programs for calculating income tax or solving linear programming problems routinely accomplish tasks which are beyond the abilities (intelligence?) of many humans; micro-processor based "chess computers" play chess to a reasonable enough standard to sell in large numbers, if not to a standard which would worry a Grand Master - and some research machines are reaching that standard; and conventional computer systems exist which perform tasks such as working out credit ratings, tasks which are often described as requiring human expertise. Indeed, one of the findings of the last 40 or so years of work in AI and other areas of computer science is that there are tasks which humans find difficult which machines can be made to perform well, and conversely tasks which humans find easy which machines at present struggle with.

For the purposes of this book, it does not matter whether the systems under discussion are intelligent or not. Their functions will need to be considered in much more detail than the sweeping generalities of terms like intelligence. We would, however, suggest that the use of the adjective intelligent in relation to current commercially feasible computer systems is, at best, extremely misleading - and the source of much unnecessary apprehension.

In the next two sections we shall look at some of the areas of AI research which have the potential for wider application. This will be the first of many such lists of categories in this book, and so it is a good place to give an important disclaimer:

None of our categorisations should be seen in absolute hard and fast terms; we are dealing with applications in human activity systems, where the characteristics of the system depend on the opinions of the person observing it. Thus our categories may not always appear to be either mutually exclusive or exhaustive - some examples may spill over two categories, others may not fit into any category. Our intentions, whenever we set out some categories, are to give guidelines to the important features, aspects or subdivisions of the topic, not to lay down theoretical rules, and are meant to help you think, not put you in a straitjacket!

We shall distinguish six different areas of AI:

- KBSs

- natural language understanding

- pattern recognition

- intelligent computer-assisted learning

- speech recognition

- models of human cognition.

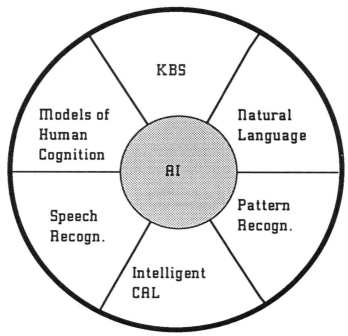

Figure 1.2: Six areas of AI

1.2 Knowledge-based Systems

1.2.1 What's in a name?

Most people would agree that what you call a system is unlikely to affect its practical usefulness. However, even if your system's name does not affect its functionality, it might just influence the way you think about it as a system. Even more importantly, it might influence the way other people think about the system. It is therefore worth discussing some of the names which might be used for knowledge-based systems.

By knowledge-based systems, we mean computer-based systems which support, or perform automatically, cognitive tasks in a narrow problem domain which are usually only carried out by human experts. The human expert performs these tasks by employing personal skills, expertise and judgement acquired and learnt over a period of time. By cognitive tasks, we mean tasks whose successful completion requires knowledge and/or expertise which is not accessible in any other organised external form.

For example, a human medical consultant will have begun by studying basic sciences, then studied the theory behind medicine (to degree level), then

6

begun to practice medicine, probably in a general area at first, and then gradually becoming recognised as being knowledgeable about a particular specialised area of medicine. Although much of the basic knowledge is available in books, the knowledge or expertise which establishes a consultant's reputation is not in the books, and can only be acquired "on the job".

Other authors use "expert systems" or "intelligent knowledge-based systems" for roughly the same concept, or use the term KBSs with a slightly different intended meaning, so let's look at these different titles and whether these differences are significant.

Expert systems was, historically, the first of these terms to be coined. The earliest AI systems were intended as general problem solvers; whilst much was learnt from these, they were not terribly successful in this activity. The emphasis thus shifted to research intended to mimic the performance of a human expert in a narrow, well-defined domain. The successful outcomes of this research were the first expert systems, such as DENDRAL (an expert in a very limited part of molecular chemistry) and MYCIN (an expert system which diagnoses microbial infections and recommends appropriate medical treatment). In both of these cases the domains were scientifically-based, and this was true of all the early expert systems; applications in business and management came considerably later.

It is important to realise that the term expert systems has been applied to a wide variety of rather different systems. This is not unusual in computing: the term database is applied to systems as diverse as all the information about the operations of a large corporation stored on a correspondingly large mainframe, and a list of a few names and addresses on a PC . Similarly, with expert systems, on the one hand we have large systems on specialist machines or large mainframes, and on the other, small systems running on PCs.

The use of the word "expert" in this context has led to some of the same problems which we have already considered with respect to the word "intelligent". Some of the expertise in DENDRAL came from two Nobel prize-winners, but expertise does not need to be at such a high level in order to be useful. In the appropriate context, a merchant bank's top investment advisor and the person in the mail room who knows the best way to send a parcel to Hong Kong to arrive by Monday both possess scarce expertise. Indeed, for many of the tasks for which this type of system appears to be useful, the term expert system seems somewhat pretentious. We would however admit that the term "expertise" sounds less inhibiting; strangely, it appears to us that for most people, the phrase "being an expert" conveys rather higher status than the apparent grammatical equivalent "possessing expertise". Some authors have therefore chosen to describe the small PC-based systems whose expertise does not equate to that of a human professional, but is at a more modest level, as "competent systems" rather than expert systems. Many have chosen to describe both of these types of system as "knowledge-based systems", to avoid the connotations of the word "expert".

One other school of thought, exemplified by Addis (ADD85), is that KBSs is a wider term than expert systems. Taking expert systems to be those which operate in the manner of a typical human consultant like a doctor, lawyer or accountant (as all the early expert systems did), he distinguishes several other types of KBS:

- question-answering systems,
- teaching systems,
- systems for machine translation,
- intelligent front-ends,
- planning systems.

We would agree with this wider definition of the field. However, we do not feel the distinction between the "narrow" and "wide" definitions to be a problem, for two reasons. First, most management or administrative applications of KBSs at present are likely to take the form of expert systems. Second, the distinctions between the various types of system, as usual, are not clear-cut; for example, the knowledge base of an intelligent front-end may rely on the expertise of a human who is used to "interpreting" for the package concerned. In such a case, it does not matter whether one calls it an expert system or an intelligent front-end; it is whether or not the system is useful that matters. As another example, where expert systems have been used to enable lower-level staff to take on a new task, it has sometimes been found that the staff learn to do the job without the system, even though it was not intended as a teaching system and would not have been labelled as such.

The acronym IKBSs for intelligent knowledge-based systems became widely known in the U.K. as a result of the industry/academia collaborative research initiative set up under the auspices of the Alvey Directorate. This "Advanced Information Technology Programme" arose from a report submitted to the U.K. government in 1982, in which intelligent knowledge-based systems was identified as one of the key areas of the programme, along with others such as software engineering and very-large-scale integration (VLSI). Since then, some attempts have been made to "lose" the adjective intelligent, but at the time of writing it still survives in the Alvey Directorate's successor, the Information Engineering Directorate(IED). As far as we are aware, the meaning given to IKBSs by the Alvey Directorate and the IED matches what we have called the wide definition of KBSs.

To summarise this section: as far as we are concerned, all expert systems are knowledge-based systems (or equivalently, intelligent knowledge-based systems); there are some (intelligent) knowledge-based systems which are not expert systems, but relatively few of them at present.

1.2.2 Examples of KBSs

In this section, we shall present various examples of KBSs (and of IKBSs and expert systems!), to give you a better idea of the sort of systems we shall be addressing in the rest of the book. You should, however, recognise that in a rapidly-progressing field such as this, existing examples can only hint at the potential for future applications.

The examples here will be presented under the following categories:
- Systems built using shells on PCs
- Systems built using shells on mainframes
- Systems built using LISP or Prolog
- Systems built using an environment and workstation.

We do not intend to give a rigorous definition of these terms here. They are discussed, and defined in more detail, in chapter 3. We also do not attempt in this section to make any judgements about the different hardware and software used for building the KBSs; this too is covered in chapter 3.

Looking first at small, stand-alone systems, there are many so-called "expert system shells" on the market which will run on IBM or compatible PCs. The term "shell" arose because such a product is the empty shell of an expert system, containing everything except the knowledge base. Indeed, the very first shell, EMYCIN, was constructed in this way from the MYCIN expert system, by removing all the knowledge specific to MYCIN's domain of expertise. Many current products can trace their ancestry back to the structure of EMYCIN. The leaders in the UK expert system shell market include Crystal, Xi Plus, and Leonardo. In the US the market leaders include Insight 2+ (also known as Level 5), Exsys (not to be confused with a very different

.British product) and VP-Expert (perhaps the cheapest of all commercially available shells). Versions of most of these products can be obtained for less than £1000, and the cheapest are around the £100 mark.

In almost all of these shells, the expertise is entered in the form of rules, written in a restricted sub-set of the English language (so restricted, that we would not regard it as constituting the natural language understanding discussed in section 1.3.1). These rules take the form IF <condition is true> THEN <take action or draw conclusion>, and so are often known as IF...THEN... rules. Product development is continuing at a rapid rate, the most recent versions incorporating features such as links to spreadsheet (typically Lotus 1-2-3) and database (typically dBASE III) packages, and better editing facilities to cope with the manipulation of the large amounts of text typically involved.

Examples of PC expert systems built using shells

1. VATIA
This is a system developed in the UK by Ernst & Whinney, one of the largest accounting and financial consultancy organisations. It is designed to help Ernst & Whinney's general auditors to assess the adequacy and compliance with legislation of clients' Value Added Tax (VAT) systems and procedures. (VAT is a tax levied on supplies of goods and services, and thus a major concern of most organisations in the UK and indeed Western Europe.) The auditors have some knowledge of VAT, but are not themselves "experts" in the field; the expertise was provided by Ernst & Whinney's VAT specialists. The VATIA system was developed using the shell Crystal, and was installed on all the portable micro-computers used on audit assignments. Some 600 copies had been installed by May 1988.

2. Burner fault diagnosis
BP International has developed a system to assist engineers to identify problems with gas burners used in their production and refining processes by analysing the burner flame. It is PC-based, and was constructed using the Xi Plus shell. It has been delivered to at least 18 BP sites world-wide.

3. Equity selection
One of the products of the ARIES "club", set up by the UK's Alvey programme to produce prototype expert systems for insurance work,

was a system for assisting with decisions on whether or not to purchase particular equities. The system is intended to be used by a fund manager or investment analyst. Although originally developed using KEE (see later in this section), the system was ported to the Leonardo shell.

4. Stockmaster
This is an expert system developed by the Swedish companies Traversum AB, a company specialising in the stock market, and Novacast Expert Systems AB. It is designed to evaluate an individual stock or future with a view to a recommendation to buy, hold or sell. The system was produced using the SuperExpert rule induction shell, and has been in daily use by Traversum AB since January 1987.

5. Polapres
This system was developed by Metallurgique et Minière de Rodange-Athus (MMRA), a steel-making company based in Luxembourg. It diagnoses faults in the process of rolling, in which heated ingots of steel are passed through cylindrical presses. It was developed using Texas Instruments' Personal Consultant Plus shell, with the twin aims of preserving the expertise of MMRA's principal rolling "expert", who was due to retire, and of reducing the number of calls on the experts during the night shift. It has been in use (by the manufacturing foremen) since mid-1987. By now the system has more than repaid the development costs of some $235000; this somewhat high figure for a PC-based system includes the considerable amount of work needed to produce the original non-expert system record of all the defects which might arise during steel rolling at MMRA.

All the above examples concern PC-based shells. In addition there are similar rule-based products available for mini-computers and mainframes. In general, the facilities they offer are broadly similar, but as with other types of applications package each different type of hardware brings its own advantages and disadvantages. We shall pursue this further in chapter 3.

Examples of mainframe or mini-computer systems using shells

1. S39XC Configurer
The UK computer company ICL used its own shell, ICL Adviser, for a system which configures Series 39 mainframe computers. Fittingly, it runs on a Series 39 itself, and may be accessed by any of ICL's sales

staff. Since its launch in 1986, ICL estimates that S39XC has saved the company over £5 million per annum.

2. 9370 Expert System Configurator

Before its release to the market, IBM used a pre-release version of KnowledgeTool, then called YES/L1, to build an expert system to help configure computers using the IBM 9370 family of processors. The Configurator (sic) runs on an IBM S/370 mainframe and is used by both marketing and manufacturing staff.

3. DIAESS

Standard Electrik Lorenz (SEL), a West German supplier of telecommunications equipment, developed a system called DIAESS (DIAgnostic Expert System Shell) for the identification of faults in printed circuit boards for telephone exchanges. It was developed using the ExTran shell, running on a DEC VAX mini-computer, and in 1986 was reported as having been in full scale use at SEL for over two years.

The next category of system, requiring somewhat more specialised software expertise, consists of systems written in a special-purpose "AI language", of which LISP and Prolog are far and away the two leading candidates. LISP was developed in the USA, and has always dominated the market there. It is much the older of the two, and indeed pre-dates many "conventional" languages such as Pascal and C, being only about a year "younger" than FORTRAN. (Both LISP and FORTRAN date from the late 1950s.) Prolog was developed somewhat later, in Europe, and has always fared correspondingly better in the European market-place than in the USA. However, Prolog received a considerable boost when it was chosen as the language for the Japanese Fifth Generation Computer project; this stimulated interest not only in Japan, but world-wide. Note that all the examples which follow are PC-based. This is because the performance/price ratio of mainframe LISP or Prolog versions has been relatively poor, and thus for those with budgets running beyond a PC, a special-purpose workstation (see later) would often be a "better buy" than a mainframe implementation.

Examples of PC systems written in LISP or Prolog

1. Spinpro

This system was commissioned by the US firm Beckman Instruments, to advise its customers on the use of its centrifuges. Setting-up a modern centrifuge in a chemical laboratory to produce the best results is a complex process, particularly as the meaning of "best" depends on the preferences of the user. The system was written by the LISP vendor Gold Hill, to run on an IBM PC XT.

2. Tipi

This system was developed jointly by the French bank Caisse D'Épargne and the consultants Arthur Andersen. It advises on applications for "controlled loans" to purchase houses. The bank's experts on this government-subsidised loan scheme are at Head Office. The use of Tipi enables bank branch staff to give an immediate decision to an applicant in many cases, and in the remainder to ensure that all the necessary information is passed on to Head Office. The system is written in Le_Lisp and runs on an IBM PC.

3. GATES

This system was developed for the US airline TWA to help in gate management at John F.Kennedy airport in New York. It is used by airport ground controllers, and was written in Turbo Prolog to run on a PC. Originally it was used to produce quarterly gate schedules; a daily scheduling version following later.

4. Betting shop manager trainer

Ladbroke's, the bookmaker, together with Kingston College of Further Education (both in the UK) produced a PC-based system to train potential betting shop managers in the "marking-up" of bets, i.e. the calculation of the customer's winnings. It was written in LPA's Prolog Professional, and also incorporates tests of the trainee's performance.

The specific differences between LISP and Prolog we shall not discuss here; suffice it to say that each has some useful attributes from the point of view of constructing KBSs. Each also has its quota of "champions" and detractors!

It is also worth noting that it is perfectly possible to write a KBS directly in a conventional language. As an illustration, while some of the expert system shells or development tools are written in LISP or Prolog, a greater number are written in conventional languages; for example, Crystal, Exsys and VP-Expert are written in C, SAGE and 1st Class are written in Pascal, ExTran and TIMM in FORTRAN 77, etc.. Indeed, ExTran actually generates FORTRAN 77 code. There is no reason why a conventional language should not be used for a KBS, although in some cases the special-purpose languages will have advantages, as with other computer applications such as simulation.

Carrying on up the scale of complexity brings us to the use of specialised workstations such as those manufactured by Symbolics or Xerox, or the Explorer from Texas Instruments. Essentially these are machines which deliver the power of a mini-computer to a single user and are specially designed and/or configured to run LISP efficiently. It isn't surprising, therefore, that the performance achieved with such systems is remarkable compared to that of a PC or a time-sharing system on a mainframe. In many cases, the machine comes together with a purpose-built software environment for creating KBSs; most of the environments need a specialised machine to support all their features, and so the two go hand in hand. Given the price of both the hardware and the software involved, it is clear that while this is certainly a technologically viable way to develop a KBS, the expense would often rule out such a project. This would be particularly true of systems which needed several such machines/environments for delivery of the working system.

Examples of systems developed using environment+workstation

1. COMPASS
The US company GTE developed its Central Office Maintenance Printout Analysis and Suggestion System to aid in the maintenance of telephone switching systems (exchanges, etc.). It reads the data from remote monitoring stations over the telephone lines, and can advise switch maintenance personnel of various skill levels about the maintenance requirements of the equipment. It was developed using the environment KEE and the language Interlisp-D (a version of LISP) on a Xerox 1108 workstation, the development taking about 3 person-years. In 1986 it was reported that it was being put into field use after a successful field trial, and it is now in use at hundreds of remote sites across the USA.

2. Expert Cabling
This system was developed by Ferranti in the UK to help engineers in the drawing office to configure computer cabling. It was developed in a period of 7 calendar weeks, using the Inference ART environment running on a Symbolics workstation.

3. Portfolio Management Advisor
A system produced by the Athena Group, which specialises in financial expert systems. It is intended to help a professional portfolio

manager construct and maintain investment portfolios for his/her clients. The system was written in ART, and is sold by Athena as a "package" comprising the basic generic expert system plus a period of management consultancy to customise the product to the individual portfolio manager's requirements and integrate it with other computer systems.

4. Authorizer's Assistant

American Express commissioned this system to help with the task of authorizing credit card transactions - over one million such transactions take place per month. The system was developed by the Inference Corporation, using ART running on a Symbolics workstation, and is now in use. A major element in constructing the system was interfacing the expert system with American Express's existing transaction processing and database systems, running on IBM mainframes.

The gap between the PCs and the workstations is, however, closing quite rapidly. Two specific developments in the last couple of years have been:

• The advent of general purpose micro-computers based on the faster 80386 chip. This has enabled cut-down versions of the environments incorporating a limited subset of the features of the workstation-based products to be made available on PCs. Machines based on the even faster 80486 chip are at the time of writing just beginning to become available, although it appears that they are being marketed as workstations rather than as PCs.
• The introduction of micros specially intended for AI/ES work. Texas Instruments now offer the micro-Explorer, which includes a LISP chip in addition to the standard technology of a Macintosh SE. This combines the user-friendliness of the Mac's interface (and normal Mac software) with a fast LISP processor for AI software.

Two other sub-categories of KBSs need to be mentioned, namely those using the language OPS5, and those integrated with the vast number of existing mainframe applications, as opposed to merely sharing the same machine.

OPS5 is in a class of its own, somewhere between the special-purpose languages like LISP and Prolog and the shells, being described as a "rule-based programming language". It was developed for and by DEC in association with Carnegie-Mellon University in the USA, and has been used for many of DEC's extensive range of internal KBS applications. The hardware used, not surprisingly, is a DEC VAX mini-computer.

15

At the mainframe level, proper integration into the usual mainframe systems development environments, especially those of the so-called "fourth generation" type (see section 1.3.1), is also beginning to be seen. Products on offer here include Cullinet's Application Expert (now called Enterprise:Expert) and Top-One from Telecomputing. This is also the best category in which to put IBM's ESE(Expert Systems Environment), a rule-based tool designed to integrate with other tools familiar to the IBM mainframe systems programmer. Fully operating practical examples are, however, hard to find in the literature - except for IBM's own internal ESE applications, which include KBSs for claiming capital allowances and diagnosing problems in disk drives.

In much the same way that the mainframe computer hardware market dominates the PC hardware market in financial volumes, despite the noise made by and about the latter sector, we expect the mainframe market to be a vital direction for the development of future KBSs. This is one of our reasons for writing this book from the perspective we have chosen.

We do not intend to ignore the other aspects though, especially as PC to mainframe (and indeed workstation) communication is becoming ever more straight-forward.

Whatever "technology" is used for a KBS, two other aspects of the system are worthy of careful consideration. One is the balance of roles between the KBS and the people using it, and the other is the extent to which the KBS is integrated with other computer systems.

1.2.3 Style of KBS

A KBS can act in a number of different roles:

• *assistant* - invoked by the user to perform a specific task as part of a wider exercise

• *critic* - reviews work already completed and comments on accuracy, consistency, completeness, etc.

• *second opinion* - executes task and compares its results with those of the user, perhaps critiquing the user's choice

- *expert consultant* - offers advice or an opinion based on information given by the user

- *tutor* - trains the user to perform an "expert" task

- *automaton* - completes task automatically and independently of the user and reports result.

The roles at the top of the list are those in which the user has more expertise in the relevant domain than the system has. As we move toward the bottom of the list it is the KBS which has the greater expertise, and also the KBS which takes more of the initiative in a consultation. It is of course possible for a KBS to operate in more than one of these roles.

KBS as Assistant
The Ferranti cabling system already mentioned is an assistant-style KBS, since it covers only part of the designer's duties, and is used by the designers themselves. Another example is the UK Department of Health's Performance Indicator Analyst, developed by Coopers and Lybrand using the shell Crystal. This is used to look at the performance of, for example, a district health authority; again this task is only part of the job of the person using it, who might be on the staff of either the district concerned or its "parent" regional health authority.

KBS as Critic
This type of system is altogether less common, being probably the rarest of the six roles. One KBS which does operate in this role is NOEMIE, a computer configuring system developed by Arthur Andersen for Honeywell Bull (as it was then called) in France. One of the options in NOEMIE is to validate configurations which were not originally generated with NOEMIE. Another feature is that the salesperson can add, delete or change elements of any configuration produced, and then NOEMIE validates any changes automatically. (NOEMIE also functions in the expert consultant KBS role.)

KBS as Second Opinion
An example of this role is the Market Timing System, developed by Criterion Software and available in the UK and Europe from Financia Ltd. This carries out technical analysis of market indices, and signals when the market is about to go up or down. An experienced technical analyst can use this as a second opinion; it can track more indices than the analyst can, but does not have the same access to informal sources of information.

KBS as Expert Consultant

Not surprisingly, this is far and away the most common role, corresponding to what we might term the "classical" model of an expert system, if it's reasonable to use the adjective classical at all in such a young field! Of those mentioned in section 1.2, VATIA, Stockmaster, Polapres, Spinpro and Tipi, amongst others, all operate in this role.

KBS as Tutor

We have already pointed out that it is often possible to learn from a KBS, even if that was not the purpose for which it was designed. However, some KBSs have been designed to operate primarily as tutoring systems. One such example is the betting shop manager training system (see section 1.2). Another is the recovery boiler tutor, a system to teach a student how to control recovery boilers used in the pulp and paper industry. As well as the knowledge based part, the system incorporates a simulation model of the boiler. Its development was supported by the American Paper Institute, Inc.

KBS as Automaton

This is probably the second most common of the "pure" KBS roles, partly because it is not easy for a system to combine this role with any of the others. Operating as an automaton sometimes involves the KBS being incorporated in a piece of hardware, thus making direct interaction with a human user rather difficult. SPE (Serum Protein Electrophoresis diagnostic program) is a long-standing example of this. It is incorporated in a piece of medical equipment called a scanning densitometer, and distinguishes between the various possible causes of inflammations in a patient. Even where the KBS is still in the form of software, it will probably have been set up to receive all its data inputs automatically, either from sensors or other computer programs; again, there is often no provision for human input. COMPASS (section 1.2) operates in this role, as does ACE, which is another telephone maintenance system, this time for cables. Linkman is another example, being a knowledge-based real-time process control package running on a DEC mini-computer or MicroVAX, originally developed for the control of the temperature of cement kilns at Blue Circle Cement. It has now also been sold to several other companies, including some outside the cement industry. Finally in this role, the Sumitomo Bank in Japan has a KBS which automatically handles telexes dealing with the transfer of funds, covering all the processes between receipt and banking.

1.2.4 Modes of interaction with other computer systems

There are three ways in which a KBS can perform its chosen role: these are illustrated in Figure 1.3.

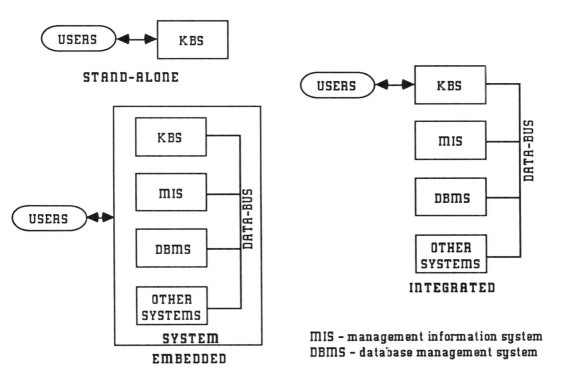

Figure 1.3: KBS modes

• *standalone* - interaction is with the user only

• *integrated* - interaction is with company databases, management information systems or PC-based tools such as spreadsheets and database packages. The operation of the KBS involves the exchange of data between the KBS and other systems as well as dialogue with the user,

• *embedded* - complete absorption within an information system, so that the user does not interact directly with the KBS but indirectly through the user interface of the host system; the latter handles the interaction with any KB components. Thus the operation of the KBS may be triggered without the direct intervention of the user at all.

Choosing again from some of the systems mentioned in section 1.2, VATIA and Stockmaster are completely standalone KBSs, as are most systems written using shells running on PCs, and indeed most KBSs.

The Authorizer's Assistant is perhaps the classic example of an integrated KBS, having to interface to more than one large mainframe for transaction processing and customer account information, and to operate within very tight real-time performance standards. The DoH Performance Indicator Analyst is another highly integrated KBS , for which the only human input required is the name of the Health Authority about which the report is to be produced; the KBS itself retrieves all the other data required. The recovery boiler tutor KBS is also integrated with a FORTRAN model which simulates the boiler itself.

Embedded systems are less easy to find. This is not surprising, as they are more difficult to build. Most of the automaton KBSs are embedded in something, but not always an information system. For example, the only function of COMPASS from the user's point of view is to advise about maintenance requirements, so we would call it a standalone system. The mainframe systems are usually advertised, and indeed demonstrated, as being ideal vehicles for embedded systems, but the operational examples- which as we have said are hard to find - tend to be standalone systems. It is conceivable that the developers of an embedded KBS, which is therefore "hidden" from the users, might wish it to be hidden from publicity as well! We shall return to this point about reports of working KBSs in chapter 2.

1.3 Other Fruits of AI Research

1.3.1 Natural language understanding

The problem of human-computer communication (particularly in the direction from the human to the computer) has existed ever since the computer was invented. Indeed, it seems more or less standard practice for any new computer language to claim that it "uses English-like commands"; we believe this was said of COBOL in its day!

Ideally, the human should be able to interact with the computer exactly as with another human. As a philosophy, this is virtually identical to the Turing test mentioned in section 1.1, although ideally we would not wish to restrict the interaction to being via a terminal; this gives some indication of how hard such an ideal might be to attain. A more reasonable suggestion is that the computer should be able to use a restricted version of the human's language, and this seems to have been a general goal of most people in the computer industry. However, up to now, the human has always had to adapt (to a greater or lesser extent) to the needs of the computer, despite the claims referred to in the preceding paragraph. This gives the familiar "four generations" of languages as shown in Figure 1.4.

Generations of Languages	
1st	**Machine code** **(e.g. strings of binary or hexadecimal** **characters)**
2nd	**Assembler** **(e.g. single letter commands)**
3rd	**"High level" languages** **(e.g. FORTRAN, COBOL, BASIC, Pascal, C)**
4th	**4GLs** **(e.g. Focus, Ramis, Mantis, Powerhouse)**
"5th"	**AI/Declarative languages** **(e.g. Prolog, LISP)**

Figure 1.4: Five generations of languages

None of these generations really apply directly to AI languages. However, the role of AI and especially Prolog in the Japanese Fifth Generation computer project has led some people to describe AI languages as fifth generation languages. We are not entirely happy with this. It is reasonable if one considers that the main distinguishing feature between the different generations is the extent to which the programmer needs to tell the computer <u>how</u> to perform a particular task as opposed to merely <u>what</u> is to be done, but not if one takes the alternative view that each generation should represent a further step towards natural language. Certainly, AI languages such as LISP provided a useful vehicle for machine representation of sentences in English or similar natural languages, and much progress towards natural language interfaces has been made. Some of this has appeared in the commercial arena in the functionality of fourth generation languages and report-writing tools. However, LISP or Prolog code does not appear any more English-like to us than that of

4GLs - definitely less so in the case of LISP! We would really regard AI languages as more like third generation languages, tailored specifically to representing lists or statements in predicate logic in just the way that FORTRAN was originally tailored towards representing algebraic formulae.

There is still considerable debate about the extent to which computers will ever fully understand sentences in English. Depending on your perspective, English may be seen as either hopelessly imprecise or as permitting the subtlest nuances and shades of meaning. It is true to say that current systems are capable of a degree of natural language processing, but not really of any understanding. Progress is faster in areas where the natural language is constrained, and especially where it has a substantial proportion of technical terms; thus intelligent front-ends to another computer package, such as a database or an operating system, are feasible with current technology.

It is also true that most NLU work has concentrated on the printed word. This is understandable, because the printed word is static and hence easy to replicate for test purposes, and because it avoids the additional problems of having to cope with handwriting or, worse still, speech and voice recognition (see section 1.3.4). Thus considerable advances have been made in areas such as machine translation of technical documentation, and automatic abstracting of research reports. Such activities take place routinely in several large corporations, but often still require some human post-translation editing. Most systems cover translation between French and English (in both directions), with either German or Spanish replacing one or other of these being the next most common. Systems including non-European languages are extremely rare, except for Arabic and Japanese; among the most successful machine translation systems for the latter are those produced by Fujitsu (in Japan). However, most of these operate effectively in batch mode on large mainframes, although "one sentence at a time" translation is now possible. Most existing systems were developed for the corporations concerned, but the sale of machine translation packages is now on the verge of becoming commercially viable.

If we consider interactive work, it seems reasonable to argue that speech recognition will in the long term be at least as important as recognition of the printed word. After all, many managers are either unable or unwilling to type accurately, and electronic mail systems do not yet seem to be replacing the telephone, even if they complement it in useful ways. Unfortunately, speech is not always grammatical, containing errors, interjections, corrections and so on. This means that much of the work on recognising the printed word does not transfer easily to the spoken word, and so there is a long way to go yet.

1.3.2 Pattern recognition

Natural language could be thought of as one form of pattern recognition, but here we mean the far more general activity of visual recognition of patterns, sometimes called "machine vision". This is extremely important for robotics, and many practical applications now exist. The most common task performed is automated inspection, and the most common users the automobile and electronics industries. It is, however, arguable how much of the credit for these successful implementations belongs to AI, and how much to more conventional signal processing ideas. We shall not pursue this debate here! Despite the successes in robotics for manufacturing, pattern recognition is at present some way away from having direct effects on other business/management problems. It does however seem plausible that successful machine vision would have a considerable effect on security systems such as those for electronic banking which currently work in terms of coded PINs (Personal Identification Numbers). This area is one in which two developments offer a lot of potential, namely parallel processing and neural networks; current machine vision has been severely handicapped by the amount of processing power required on a sequential processor.

1.3.3 Intelligent computer-assisted learning (ICAL)

We have already said - twice - that we aren't happy with the adjective "intelligent", but it is in common use in this area to distinguish it from "ordinary" CAL. The essential difference is that whereas ordinary CAL is an automated version of a programmed learning text, albeit with the potential for a much better human interface, ICAL is intended to be adaptive. The alternative phrase "intelligent tutoring systems" perhaps conveys a little more of the flavour of ICAL systems, even if it also gives a misleading impression of their current abilities. A good ICAL system should be able to modify its teaching strategy to suit the individual who is using the system. This implies three things about the system:

•It must be able to model the pattern of the student's responses (and therefore presumed knowledge) in some way.

•It must be able to reason about the knowledge it has regarding the subject it is trying to "teach". (The "knowledge" in a conventional CAL system is stored in such a way as to make this impossible.)
•It must allow for flexibility in the interaction between the student and the system.

One particular advantage of ICAL which has been suggested is that a system which is actually capable of performing a certain task, as well as just "teaching" about it, should as a result have the potential to be a better teacher of it, based on the idea that students learn by example. Thus a good ICAL system would need to include an expert system or KBS. This would not be easy to achieve - for example, it might be that the system's knowledge needs to be represented in different ways for the two purposes of teaching the task and performing it - but it is certainly more feasible for ICAL than conventional CAL. This would be consistent with the view taken by proponents of the systems approach that "every good regulator of a system must be a model of that system"; by implication, having a good model of how to perform the task is essential in order to begin modelling the student's knowledge of the task. Not surprisingly, it is often difficult to distinguish between an ICAL system and the "tutor" role which we have identified as one of those possible for a KBS.

1.3.4 Speech recognition

Speech recognition adds another dimension to the problems of natural language understanding. Problems include the effects of background noise, changes in pronunciation according to whether words are spoken in isolation or in a sentence, and variations of accent between individuals. Perhaps the biggest problem of all is that everyday speech is not grammatical, as attempts to transcribe an interview or conversation often reveal. Conversations often include repetitions, corrections and incomplete sentences. Voice recognition goes even further, namely to try to identify the speaker (perhaps for security purposes). Most work given either of the two labels is in fact concerned with speech recognition, and this is what we shall deal with in the remainder of this section.

There are two ways in which the problems of speech recognition may be partially eased:

•by restricting the vocabulary of words which may be used;

•by restricting the number of users.

Current commercially available systems can only cope with very restricted versions of each of these two cases. For example, the vocabulary may be limited to the digits 0 - 9 and the words "yes" and "no" for a so-called *speaker-independent* system, one which will in theory deal with any user. The other possibility is a *speaker-dependent* system, covering a somewhat less limited range of words for a single user, who must "train" the system to recognise the words as they are pronounced.

Small speaker-independent systems such as the above example, along with non-AI developments such as speech synthesis and digitised recorded speech, form the rapidly developing area of "voicemail" systems for business use, of which Digital's DECVoice is an example. Another use of this technology for speaker-independent systems which has appeared recently is in automated telephone systems such as "quiz-lines", where multiple-choice answers to the questions limit the range of possible spoken responses.

As for the future, a press release in 1989 from the European Commission's Esprit programme stated that:
"By the year 2000 it is expected that the technology will be available for international telephone calls to be automatically/simultaneously translated."

Many predictions about machine translation and speech recognition have proved over-optimistic in the past; it will be interesting to see how accurate this one proves to be.

1.3.5 Models of human cognition

This is in some ways the most basic, and also the most contentious, area of AI. It was one of the original driving forces behind the creation of AI, and has led to a lot of the research which has been carried out since then. Whether this research actually has shed any light on human cognition, as opposed to ways of using a computer to simulate tasks apparently involving thinking, is a moot point. Later in this book we shall be looking at some of the structures used to represent knowledge explicitly; there are some researchers who believe that these resemble the structures humans actually use implicitly (i.e. in our heads), some who believe they do not, and some who believe the comparison is irrelevant. Further discussion of this is beyond the scope of this text; one well-presented view of this topic is presented by Margaret Boden (BOD87), but of course other authors' views will differ from hers!

1.4 An Applications Point of View

It is possible to view KBSs from many different angles. Ours will be that from the viewpoint of applications in industry, commerce and government, with a slight bias towards managerial rather than scientific domains. Normally our interest will be that of the user organisation, rather than that of KBS hardware or software vendors. We must stress that this is no more or less valid than any other viewpoint - for example, that of AI research. However, we should remind you that there are several viewpoints, and that what is important from one of them may be less important or even totally unimportant from a different one. In our view, many of the current arguments within AI and KBS stem from unrecognised differences of viewpoint. We shall look more closely at the consequences of different viewpoints on building KBSs in section 2.1.

Our chosen viewpoint means that the most important considerations are:

-    relevance to commercial needs;

-    robustness and maintainability of the finished system;

-    relationship of KBSs to other potential solution techniques, especially other types of computer system.

Although the detailed features of KBSs are certainly relevant - we shall be dealing with them at length in later chapters - we feel that, from the business viewpoint, the similarities between the various types of computer system are often more important than their differences. Thus we shall in many cases be re-interpreting "well-known" lessons as they apply to KBS development, rather than looking at it as something in isolation. However, there are differences, and we shall begin to consider them in the next section.

To give an idea of what we mean by the other types of computer system, we present below a list of some of the types which we can distinguish. It is intended purely for illustration; the categories are not intended to be either exhaustive or mutually exclusive:

• Data processing systems -   transaction processing

management information systems

database systems

- Decision support systems

- "Technical" systems - simulation

  computer-aided design

- Real-time systems

- Desk-top publishing systems

- Word processing systems

We shall be particularly interested in looking at the similarities between KBSs and data processing, decision support and "technical" systems. Note also that when we refer to "conventional computer systems" without giving any more detail, we are thinking of data processing or possibly real-time systems. (For some reason, decision support systems still seem to be thought of as unconventional. This point is not entirely flippant, and we shall return to it in chapter 4.)

Another consequence of our viewpoint is that we shall spend relatively little time in this book on some of the "nuts and bolts" of AI such as the details of predicate calculus or propositional logic. Suitable sources for this kind of material, for those of you who are interested, include Ford (which uses Prolog throughout) (FORD87), and chapters 6 & 7 of Graham and Jones (GRA88).

1.5 Differences between KBSs and Conventional Computer Systems

Perhaps the most important difference is that most organisations of medium size and above have quite a lot of experience of developing and using conventional computer systems, but relatively few have significant experience of KBSs. Fewer still have experience of large KBSs.

Despite this, or perhaps even because of it, a common reaction from many data processing professionals when they encounter a KBS for the first time is: "This is no different from what I do already." To some extent this is certainly true - at the level of program modules, there is little to distinguish a KBS from a conventional computer system written in the same language. However, both the nature of the systems and the way in which they fit into the operations of the organisation are likely to differ substantially.

Among the differences which can be identified are the following:

• The technology used in typical data processing (DP) applications is well established; there is little doubt as to whether it is actually <u>possible</u> to build a DP system for that application. This is not the case with the present state of development of the KBS field.

• Involvement of high-level managers or non-computing technical specialists in the actual <u>building</u> of a DP system (as opposed to its commissioning) is rare. The nature of a KBS makes the close involvement of one or more domain experts almost inevitable.

• As the tasks for which a KBS is suitable are often inherently more complex than those which a DP system can perform, the user interface normally has to be correspondingly more sophisticated.

• It is extremely difficult, and sometimes impossible, to specify the performance objectives of a KBS in the way that is often advocated for DP systems. This has implications both for estimating the resources required to develop the system, and for the extent to which prototyping is likely to be required as part of the system development process.

• The fact that KBSs typically contain judgements and rules of thumb, which are <u>not</u> correct 100% of the time may cause problems in the way in which people react to the system and its uses - apart from the practical problems it poses for system testing.

All these points will be covered at greater length in succeeding chapters.

One obvious final difference is in terms of the ease of replacing a non-computer system with a computer-based one. In a traditional data processing application, the manual procedures are often explicitly set out, e.g. in the form of procedures manuals(!). There is thus little uncertainty as to what the task itself entails, and the computer system could be based on a straightforward step-by-step "translation" of the old manual system. (N.B. We are saying it <u>could</u> be, not that it <u>should</u> be!)

However, where a KBS is suitable, it is most unlikely that the required knowledge or expertise will have been written down, or made explicit in any other usable form.

A simple example of a "chunk" of expertise

Often what distinguishes knowledge or expertise from information is the way in which it is written down or made available. A typical user guide to a piece of computer software is arranged in terms of the functions of the various commands; similarly, a hardware manual is likely to be arranged according to what the switches on the printer or the keys on the keyboard do. Yet often we actually need to retrieve that information, i.e. <u>use</u> the expertise, in a way which is based on the context in which the system is being used. The question to be answered is : "I want to do this - how do I do it?" or "This is happening/not happening - what do I do?".

So, for example, although the manual tells you the circumstances in which the keyboard on your terminal has no effect (if you know where to look!), in order to have any usable expertise you need to be able to access it in the form of "rules" like the following:

```
IF the user is a novice
AND the user is complaining that nothing appears on
the screen when the keys are pressed
THEN the "No Scroll" key is probably pressed down.
```

Some of the better manuals these days do indeed have "fault finding" sections written with this type of emphasis, but they are much harder to write than a conventional manual because of the fuzziness of the context in which difficulties arise compared to the technical specification of what the system is supposed to do.

It is perhaps significant that the sort of knowledge needed here is often knowledge about <u>how</u> to perform a task rather than <u>what</u> task needs to be performed. This of course parallels the different generations of languages mentioned in section 1.3.1. It is probably no coincidence that it is only since the widespread appearance of expert systems that the importance of trying to write down, or otherwise "record", information on how to perform a task has been realised.

1.6 Summary

In this chapter we have given a brief introduction to artificial intelligence, and to the place of knowledge-based systems within it. We have indicated some of the key features of the way in which KBSs operate, and some of the differences between KBSs and conventional computer systems.

We have also identified ourselves with looking at KBSs from an applications point of view. The three most important considerations from this viewpoint were identified as: relevance to commercial needs; robustness and maintainability of the finished system; and the relationship of KBSs to other potential solution techniques, especially other types of computer system. In our view, all three aspects are best addressed by using an appropriate methodology to build the KBSs. The remainder of the book deals with the justification for and the details of this methodology.

References

(ADD85) T.R. Addis, *"Designing Knowledge-Based Systems"*, Kogan Page, London, 1985.
(BOD87) Margaret A.Boden, *"Artificial Intelligence and Natural Man"* (2nd. edition), MIT Press, London, 1987.
(FORD87) Nigel Ford, *"How Machines Think"*, Wiley, Chichester, 1987.
(GRA88) Ian Graham and Peter Llewellyn Jones, *"Expert Systems: Knowledge, Uncertainty and Decision"*, Chapman and Hall, London, 1988.

Chapter 2: Knowledge-based Systems - a Solution in Search of a Problem?

2.0 Introduction

In the previous chapter we gave several examples of knowledge-based systems which have been developed, but also pointed out that there is much more to artificial intelligence than simply knowledge-based systems. In this chapter we consider some of the reasons why KBSs have generated so much more interest than most other AI applications, and start to look at the general lessons which others have been drawing from 10 years or more of KBS work. More specific lessons are discussed later in the book, particularly in chapter 6. One point which should emerge clearly is that in our view some of the authors on the subject are at cross purposes. Since they are talking about essentially different concepts, it is not surprising that misunderstandings and confusion arise.

2.1 What Sort of Problems May Be Addressed Using KBSs?

Most writers on operational KBSs stress the importance of selecting an appropriate problem before attempting a KBS approach, but few offer a precise set of criteria for measuring the "suitability factor" of any given problem. Examples include Prerau (PRER85), Waterman (WAT86), and Zack (ZACK87). Of these, we would suggest that Prerau's paper (PRER85) gives the most useful guide to assessing the suitability of a problem for a KBS approach. The difficulty of establishing measurable criteria has meant that much of the understanding of what makes a problem amenable to a KBS approach has been obtained empirically, and often relies on the "gut feel" of the knowledge engineer, i.e. the person given the task of building the KBS. An even more significant difficulty from the point of view of this book is the implication in much of the literature that:

> FIRST you decide you want to attempt a KBS approach, THEN you look around for a problem to address.

THIS IS PUTTING THE CART BEFORE THE HORSE!

We might ask, at this stage, is this part of the literature then of any value at all? At first sight, the answer would appear to be 'no'; after all, this seems to be committing one of the classic errors in trying to apply any problem-solving technique, namely selecting the solution first and only then looking for a problem which fits it. While this is undoubtedly true in certain circumstances, it does hinge on a crucial assumption: that there IS a real commercial problem to be solved. In our view, many articles and books about KBSs are written in a situation where there is no real problem to be solved. The work is still valuable - at least, the good bits are - but it is not surprising, therefore, that the concepts in these writings don't always transfer well to situations where the major objective is to solve (or at least alleviate) a real problem.

2.1.1 Three perspectives on building KBSs

We suggest that in thinking about work on building KBSs, it is useful to distinguish three different perspectives, which differ according to the underlying purpose for which the work was done. These three perspectives are:

•Exploratory
•Solution-driven
•Problem-driven

PERSPECTIVE	ORIENTATION	SOLUTIONS CONSIDERED	RANGE OF KBS TECHNIQUES CONSIDERED	TIMESCALE
EXPLORATORY	Research	KBS only	Broad	Long
SOLUTION-DRIVEN	Practice (Learning?)	KBS only	Narrow	Short
PROBLEM-DRIVEN	Practice	KBS or non-KBS	Broad	Variable

Figure 2.1: Three perspectives on building KBSs

Exploratory KBSs

The term exploratory applies where the main purpose of the work is to build a KBS, with no real concern as to how the resulting system will be used, if at all. The principal focus is therefore on concepts. This of course is what people typically think of as a "research" system. The development of the system may shed light on such aspects as the process of developing a KBS, tools for building KBSs, languages for writing KBSs, structures for knowledge representation and so on. It is almost inevitable that in any field which grows out of an academic research area, as KBS did from AI, the early work will be exploratory. For example, the key question in the development of DENDRAL, the first expert system, was whether it was possible to build the system at all. For similar reasons, some exploratory work will continue to be required for as long as the field concerned continues to develop. However, once a research field has reached the stage of practical application, the perspective of exploratory work can be misleading, because of the concentration on internal aspects (of the KBS, in our case) rather than external aspects.

Solution-driven KBSs

We use the term solution-driven to describe the situation where an organisation or individual decides to invest in a product and only then thinks about what precisely to do with it. The focus is therefore on the product itself. This should of course be familiar to all of us as a significant element in the market for Christmas and birthday presents, but the appearance of solution-driven approaches in industry and commerce is somewhat rarer. This is in contrast to the exploratory work on techniques or technologies already mentioned above, which is often widespread in industry as well as in academia. In recent years the influence of solution-driven approaches on building KBSs has been more noticeable than in almost any other field, most often taking the form of "let's buy an expert system shell for our PC and see what we can do with it". There are both psychological and commercial reasons for this. Firstly, the amount of publicity about expert systems and AI - mainly resulting from the exploratory work - makes people think that they should find out something about it. It is often difficult for someone who is not a research worker in the same field to get much out of an article describing exploratory work, as these tend to concentrate on concepts whereas the novice finds outputs easier to contemplate. Secondly, the exploratory expert systems work spawned a large number of companies marketing expert systems products. Initially, these companies sold only to the research sector, but many of them were only too well aware of the existence of a commercial market which was potentially much larger. With the general lack of public understanding of expert systems, it was easier to sell the products on the lines of "here's our new shell, isn't it exciting" rather than trying to sell them to fill a perceived need which (presumably) few people had yet perceived. Shells to run on PCs inevitably had an advantage over other expert systems or AI products in this process, because they were (and still are) cheap, intended for inexperienced users, and aimed at hardware which by about the end of 1985 the purchasing organisation was very likely to have available already.

Problem-driven KBSs

Rather than the term problem-driven, we could equally well have used "business-driven". The over-riding goal from this perspective is to tackle a business problem. The focus is therefore on the problem; the methods and techniques used to tackle it are of secondary importance. In our view, it is the only approach which is viable for a department or individual which intends to be a user of a particular solution technology rather than a trail-blazing developer of it. The question "when is it appropriate to use this solution technology" must then be augmented by two further questions:

•In what circumstances is this solution technology superior to other solution technologies? In other words, is it **necessary** to build a KBS rather than any other type of system?
•How do we judge when the "return" (however one chooses to define it) from applying this technology exceeds the initial "investment"? In other words, is it **desirable** to build the KBS at all?

Thus this perspective differs from the other two in that it has to admit the existence of other techniques for tackling problems, and take a comparative stance towards these competing technologies.

2.1.2 Existing KBS work related to these perspectives

We must stress that none of these three perspectives on KBS development is superior to the others. All have a place, at least in the short- and medium-term while the field continues to develop; however, different perspectives are appropriate in different circumstances, and different uses are likely to be made of work done from the three perspectives. The overall perspective of this book is on a problem-driven approach to building KBSs, but we will need to draw on work from the other two perspectives as well.

Exploratory KBSs

To summarise some key conclusions from the work on KBSs so far, the majority of reported work takes an exploratory perspective, although since 1988 the balance has begun to shift towards the other two perspectives. Even now, exploratory work is probably in the majority, however. This means that some issues which are vital from a problem-driven perspective are often skipped over or ignored completely. Examples include:

•No comparison of the KBS approach with other approaches to performing the same task.
•No discussion of potential implementation difficulties (often the end-user of the system is never identified).
•Use of hardware/software which would be uneconomic for a system in everyday use.

On the other hand, KBS technology is not so developed that exploratory work is no longer required. This is particularly true of topics such as the way in which knowledge is represented in the system, the construction of genuinely useful explanation facilities and the integration of KBSs with other more conventional computer systems.

Solution-driven KBSs

Turning to work from the solution-driven perspective, undoubtedly its greatest influence has been its contribution to the popularisation of AI, KBSs and particularly expert systems. At least one of the major U.K. shell vendors has been marketing its product to large organisations on the basis of "buy this shell, set up a small group of people to exploit it and you <u>will</u> find applications in your organisation". This is a commendable approach in marketing terms, because it has a built-in fall-back position based on the exploratory perspective too; even if the expert systems group does not succeed in building any expert systems for operational use, its members (and hence the organisation) will have learned something about expert systems. Such a demonstration of being at the leading edge of technology may have been all the organisation was really seeking in the first place. In many cases however, this approach <u>has</u> produced systems usable in practice; large organisations typically have many areas of activity which are "governed" by complex manuals or rule-books. Often these rule-books represent a pre-KBS attempt to transfer expertise from the organisation's specialists in a particular area to a much larger group of less skilled - or at least less specialised - staff. An "electronic rule-book" often scores over the original simply because of its vastly superior user interface, and this type of application is very well suited to the IF...THEN... rules typical of first generation PC shells.

The solution-driven perspective has three principal limitations. The first is that it can convey a very narrow view of the potential for using KBSs in the organisation, i.e. that KBSs are all small, stand-alone systems running on a PC and constructed using IF...THEN... rules. The second is that even if this narrowness of view does not occur, the constraints of the product may make further development difficult. For example, if it becomes clear in the course of a study that the knowledge representation structures provided by the tool being used are inadequate, then the work already done may have to be repeated more or less from scratch, with a correspondingly increased expenditure of time and money. The third limitation of this perspective is that it can lead to a concentration on developing KBSs in the wrong areas of the organisation's activity. If the main objective is to find an application that suits the shell, it should not be surprising if this is not the application with the greatest payoff, the greatest visibility or the greatest strategic importance to the organisation. Indeed, the characteristics of "easy" applications often compound this problem; they frequently involve relatively low-level expertise, and a well-defined small group of potential users. This "cherry-picking" approach can lead to a situation where one or two reasonably successful applications have been built for a small, fairly self-contained unit within the organisation, but there are no more obvious applications in that unit. This often means there is also no clear way of extending the work into the rest of the organisation, and the prospects for further KBS work are then not very bright.

Problem-driven KBSs

The main difficulty with work on KBSs from the problem-driven perspective is that there is very little of it. In fact, much of the work which purports to be from a problem-driven perspective we would actually classify as solution-driven, because it takes for granted that some system should be constructed and that the system should be a KBS, and therefore does not consider the two questions we set out above. In addition, some of the most notable commercial successes amongst KBSs clearly began as exploratory work. It is not always easy in such cases to distinguish general lessons from accounts of their development. There is, however, a great deal of work written from a problem-driven perspective which is relevant to building KBSs; it just doesn't have a KBS label! Many of the difficulties inherent in a problem-driven approach to building KBSs have been considered by people working in fields such as conventional software engineering and operational research for many years. To some extent, the existence of KBSs can then be seen as simply adding another possible solution technology to those which already exist, although there are new aspects specific to the nature of KBSs which we shall be considering at length in the later chapters of this book.

2.2 What Factors Determine an Application's Suitability for a KBS Approach?

Let us slip out of the problem-driven perspective for the moment, and into an exploratory one. This lets us consider whether it is <u>possible</u> to build a KBS, without for the moment worrying about whether it is either necessary or desirable to do so. The factors summarised below are an interpretation of the criteria judged to be important, based on our own experiences and the work of the authors mentioned at the beginning of section 2.1. The importance of factor (ix) below was particularly borne out by the experience of the early part of the *Intellipse* project, which will be described in more detail in chapter 7.

FOCUS OF THE FACTORS	FACTORS
THE PROBLEM ITSELF	Narrowness of the domain Complexity of the problem Nature of the problem
THE HUMAN EXPERTS	Nature of the experts Training
THE EXECUTION OF THE TASK	Speed of solution Sensitivity of the problem Conventional solutions
KNOWLEDGE ACQUISITION	Written material

Table 2.1: Suitability factors

(i) *Narrowness of the domain*: The problem should be well-bounded, and the boundaries, within which data relevant to the solution can be found, well-defined. Problems which rely significantly on general knowledge about the domain are very unsuitable for a KBS approach.

(ii) *Complexity of the problem*: The problem should not involve a great deal of common sense reasoning. This point is also related to that of general knowledge. It should be possible to structure or factor the problem solution to some extent, and to partially represent the solution, for example, in the form of a hierarchical structure diagram.

(iii) *Nature of the problem*: The problem should be primarily cognitive in nature. Problems requiring visual or other sensory skills are not appropriate.

(iv) *Nature of the experts*: Except in a very small number of cases, at least one expert in the domain is necessary. The expert needs to be able to articulate his/her knowledge and be available and willing to co-operate in the project.

(v) *Training*: Established "professional" domains, like medicine, in which expert performance is attained after long periods of systematic formal training, are more likely to be suitable for a KBS than are domains such as artistic design, in which new entrants to the field often rapidly achieve performance rivalling that of the established experts. Existing training techniques in a more formalised domain ought to reflect the problem-solving strategies built up in the domain over many years, either explicitly or implicitly. Knowledge acquisition may therefore be correspondingly easier, although this is not always the case.

(vi) *Speed of solution*: Does the problem take seconds, minutes, hours or days to solve? Problems which must be solved in real-time, involving large quantities of data, may involve insurmountable performance difficulties for a KBS approach, at present. The advice of Hayes-Roth to "seek problems which experts can solve in a 3 minutes to 3 hours timespan" is probably the best in terms of timescales.

(vii) *Sensitivity of the problem*: Domains such as medicine, the law or personal finance can involve sensitive ethical and legal issues. The use of a KBS in these domains, therefore, may not be appropriate, even though it may be possible to construct them.

(viii) *Conventional solutions*: It is unwise to attempt to build a KBS until conventional, algorithmic solutions have been considered. The complexities of KBS design and construction are such that conventional solutions, if available, are likely to be less expensive to develop, and easier to maintain.

(ix) *Written material*: The existence of manuals, procedures, case studies and other documentation in the domain will greatly assist the development of a KBS - especially in the early stages of knowledge acquisition.

N.B. Readers who are "on the ball" will have noticed that points (vi), (vii) and (viii) in the above list take us back into the problem-driven perspective; as we have said, there are no hard and fast divisions!

2.3 Operational KBSs

Thousands of systems bearing the names IKBS, KBS or ES have now been reported in the literature. Only a small percentage of these can be classed as operational systems, although there are signs that this percentage is increasing. We should stress that obtaining precise information on operational KBSs is often difficult. This is partly because of commercial secrecy, partly because some systems may not be classed as KBSs by their owners or developers, and lastly because there is no accepted definition of the term *operational*. Some people seem to regard any system which works as being operational - this indeed being true, from an exploratory perspective. We, on the other hand, feel that unless a system has at least undergone a full trial with the intended end-users, then it has little claim to be called operational. Even then there is still the crucial distinction between those KBSs which have been tried in practice and those which are actually in normal use, but at this stage of KBS development we think that it is worth giving a "special mention" to systems which have reached the stage of a trial, simply because relatively few KBSs have even made it that far. There are other subtleties in the KBS marketplace, in addition. For example, shell or tool vendors often produce or distribute "packaged solutions" constructed using their product, such as the Pension Choice system mentioned in section 1.2. That system certainly is in practical use, but some of the others in this category, although they are undeniably finished products and available on sale, have never actually been used by anyone other than their developers and testers.

A look at some of the surveys and reviews which have been published over the past three or four years will illustrate the changes which have been occurring in the systems being reported.

Waterman (WAT86) identified 180 systems in the *catalog of expert systems* included in his textbook published in 1986. This was not intended to be a complete list, but to illustrate the five stages of development of expert systems which he had identified. These were:

•Demonstration prototype
•Research prototype
•Field prototype
•Production model
•Commercial system

The distinction between Waterman's final two categories matches the point we made earlier about the distinction between systems which have been in full use on a test basis, and fully operational systems. Waterman's definition of the commercial system category was "The system is a production model being used on a regular commercial basis". Only eight of the systems in Waterman's list were classified as "commercial systems" and of these only two were said to be in everyday use. Also in 1986, Buchanan (BUCH86) listed over sixty "working" ESs covering twelve application domains. The corresponding edition of the *CRI Directory of Expert Systems* (CRI86) listed six hundred ESs, but many of these - probably the majority - were not operational in any usual sense of the word. The 1986 Ovum Report on *Commercial Expert Systems in Europe* (OVUM86) identified some fifty examples of "expert systems in Europe known or reported to be in routine operational use" and some two hundred "commercial applications", i.e. systems developed outside the purely academic arena. (The figure of 200 included the 50 in the operational category.) Here again we see the distinction between systems which are in full operational use and systems which could be (but aren't being) used, or have been used in tests. This distinction has led some authors to use the term "fielded" for systems which are in regular routine use, but we do not feel this is necessarily any clearer than the term "operational" in its definition.

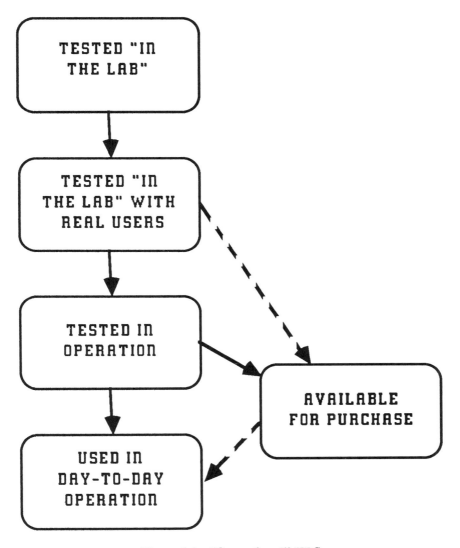

Figure 2.2 : "Operational" KBSs

Continuing with the position as it was a few years ago, in an article in *Computing* in 1987 (DURH87), Brian Johnstone, manager of Intelligent Systems at *Istel*, a leading UK software house, was quoted as saying that:

> "The users of expert systems form a very elite club with extremely limited membership! Most expert systems activity is in the academic or prototyping environment. The number of

41

expert systems in regular everyday use is still probably less than 100 worldwide." (Page 22.)

There was thus a considerable measure of agreement between the various surveys in the 1986-1987 period. To some extent, the order of magnitude figures we have seen here continue to be true even now, depending upon where you look for your KBSs to be reported. For example, a recent survey by Mingers and Adlam (MING89) of articles appearing in the published literature in the period 1984-1988 concluded that, of over 1000 articles surveyed in the computing and operational research literature, only 10 of the expert systems described were "really in use". If anything, this appears to show an even smaller proportion of real practical applications of KBSs than the surveys we have just mentioned! It should be noted, however, that the authors concerned were not certain how representative their sample was, for instance because of the difficulty of obtaining some conference proceedings.

However, at about the same time as the 1986 and 1987 reviews were being published, the increasing recognition of the importance of KBSs in commerce and industry was leading to a visible change in some of the published literature. One way in which this was being shown was by the emergence of two annual conferences which were oriented towards operational ESs. One of these was the International Expert Systems Conference in London, UK, first held in 1985. The other was the International Workshop on Expert Systems and their Applications in Avignon, France; although first held in 1981, the emphasis for the 1987 and subsequent conferences shifted very clearly towards operational ESs. Indeed, in 1987 a short (and, according to the authors, "deliberately unrepresentative") survey of expert systems in UK business carried out by d'Agapeyeff and Hawkins for the Alvey Directorate (D'AGA87) found that "...the count of operational applications should, on a national basis, rise sharply within a year".

By 1989, the position had shifted to such an extent that books and reviews concentrating solely on systems which were described as being not merely operational, but also showing demonstrable commercial benefits, were beginning to appear. Examples of this include "The Rise of the Expert Company" by Ed Feigenbaum, Pamela McCorduck and Penny Nii (FEIG88), an unashamedly "evangelising" text aimed at senior managers, and "24 Studies of British organisations that have Expert Systems in Successful Operation", a Financial Times briefing by Bruce Andrews (AND89). The book by Feigenbaum *et al* lists some 150 "Expert systems in use", and at a seminar in July 1989 Feigenbaum estimated that there were around 3000 KBSs in day-to-day use.

	Waterman	Buchanan	Ovum	Johnstone	Mingers and Adlam
Fully operational	8	60	50	<100	10
Able to operate/ Tested in operation	?	-	200	-	-
TOTAL	180	-	-	-	1000

Table 2.2:
Surveys of "operational" systems

43

As you can see, there is some divergence of opinion between those who feel that fully operational KBS applications are now becoming commonplace, and those who feel that real practical KBSs are a very small minority of the total of reported KBSs. We feel the real position lies somewhere in between (you guessed we'd say that, I'm sure!), in that many of the fully operational KBSs which do exist are not properly "reported".

In some cases, especially in domains related to finance, fully operational KBSs do exist which are not publicised for reasons of commercial confidentiality. This is not, however, as common as some authors would like to have their readers believe. The real reason for the above divergence of opinion stems in part from the ever-present differences of perspective. The Mingers and Adlam survey concentrated on the academic literature. Where work is being done from an exploratory perspective, it shouldn't be too surprising if the results never become a fully operational system, and the most likely people to publish articles in the academic literature are of course academics - publishing papers is part of an academic's job. By contrast, some successful KBSs may never be reported in the academic literature, not for reasons of secrecy, but because they are developed entirely by commercial organisations, working from a problem-driven perspective, and no-one thought of academic journal publication! However, such systems are often described in what we would call "magazine-type" publications and articles, or as part of company or product advertising. We would suggest that an examination of these shows most clearly the increase in fully operational systems, although claims made in advertising material should of course be taken with the proverbial pinch of salt! As a final example of this complication, some of the reports which do appear still leave some doubt as to whether they are describing an operational trial or a fully operational system, even when written in an apparently open, non-secretive style.

For example, consider an article which appeared during 1989 in the "advertising" magazine produced by a well-known software house. It describes a KBS for use in auditing a certain type of invoice. The article makes it clear that the system has been built, and that it detected a $700 error in a test run on a small sample of invoices. It also implies that the system will be going into operational use, but nowhere does it actually say that it will be. Thus this could be seen either as a description of an operational system, or of a small-scale trial, depending on your viewpoint, and how you choose to "read between the lines". This point should not be seen as a criticism of the software house concerned, or of this type of publication in general; many articles, and even books, by authors with no product to sell, are just as vague. Nevertheless, it does illustrate the problem of judging what really is an operational system. For a longer discussion of the problems of knowing what to believe about the KBS literature, the reader should consult the very shrewd analysis by Stevenson (written in 1987 although the book in which it appears was published in 1989) (STEV89) of the hype surrounding KBSs in the UK financial services sector.

The "Star pupil"

The best publicised, and almost certainly the most commercially successful, operational KBS is the *XCON* system, originally called *R1*, used by Digital Equipment Corporation (DEC). In 1980 McDermott (MCD80) described R1 as follows:

> "R1's domain of expertise is configuring Digital Equipment Corporation's VAX-11/780 systems. Its input is a customer's order and its output is a set of diagrams displaying the spatial relationships among the components on the order; these diagrams are used by the technician who physically assembles the system." (Page 269.)

At that time, according to McDermott, R1 had a database of 420 components and a knowledge-base of 772 rules. In 1986 (VAN86), van de Brug *et al* reported that XCON had grown to a database of 10,000 components and a knowledge base of 4,000 rules. Dennis O'Connor, the DEC executive responsible for the original R1 project, was quoted in 1987 (DURH87) as claiming that R1/XCON had saved his company $40 million in that year. Much of this is accounted for by the belief that it would have been impossible for DEC to have continued its policy of tailoring systems to customer requirements without the existence of XCON.

2.4 The Key Features of KBS Construction

2.4.1 Knowledge engineering

Among the main elements in constructing a KBS are the elicitation and representation of the expertise of a human expert, and the translation of this knowledge into a machine-executable form. This process is usually referred to in the literature as *knowledge engineering*, and the person developing the KBS is correspondingly referred to as the *knowledge engineer*. Much has been written on the subject of knowledge engineering, particularly in relation to the knowledge elicitation or acquisition phase (HART86), (HAYES83), (WAT86).

45

Typically, knowledge engineering involves very close interaction between the knowledge engineer(s) and the domain expert(s); a type of interaction which has no direct parallel in the development of other types of computer system. As most authors agree that the process is helped by there being a good rapport between the two parties, it is a trifle alarming to see terms like "extracting the knowledge from the expert" used in discussions of knowledge elicitation!

Another significant insight can be gained by looking at one of the most commonly seen descriptions of the process of building an expert system, that given in both Hayes-Roth *et al* (HAYES83) and Waterman (WAT86). This identifies five stages in the evolution of an expert system:

> "Identification — Determining problem characteristics
> Conceptualisation — Finding concepts to represent the knowledge
> Formalisation — Designing structures to organise knowledge
> Implementation — Formulating rules that embody knowledge
> Testing — Validating the rules that embody knowledge."
> (Page 24.)

The exploratory perspective is clearly visible here, since no explicit mention is made of any problem-driven aspects after the first stage. The emphasis is clearly on "embodying" the knowledge, rather than using it.

It is also most important to note that the term knowledge engineering is used with both a wider and a narrower meaning. Some authors use it to mean the whole process of building a KBS, from the original investigation of the problem through to implementation. Others restrict it to the parts of this process which involve transferring the knowledge from the human expert into machine-executable form. Of course, if you're taking an exploratory perspective, there isn't much difference between the two meanings, because the knowledge transfer is the main objective, and this is where potential for confusion arises.

We are happiest to use the term knowledge engineering with its wider meaning, i.e. for the whole process. Even here we have one slight reservation, namely that calling the process knowledge engineering implies that you knew all along that building a KBS was what was required - a solution-driven perspective! As for the narrower meaning, we feel that using the alternative term *cognitive task analysis* (CTA) gives a better description of the process of knowledge transfer going on during - and as a part of - KBS construction. This term is used to signify that CTA is a phase of development of KBSs which can be regarded as complementary to the stages of conventional analysis, design and implementation in commercial DPSD. The overall process may well best be called knowledge engineering for KBSs and software engineering for conventional systems. These ideas will be discussed in chapter 4 where the differentiation between KBS development and DPSD is made more explicit and again in chapter 9 where our proposed methodology is set out. The description of knowledge engineering given here is our summary of the process as it has been described by other authors. The later discussion will compare this description with findings based on our experience and on lessons from related fields such as conventional software engineering and "soft" systems.

2.4.2 Cognitive task analysis

Perhaps the simplest view of an expert's knowledge or expertise is that it consists of facts, rules, heuristics and an inference strategy. The following simplified example concerning the operation of a circuit consisting of a battery, bulb and connecting wire, explains each of these categories.

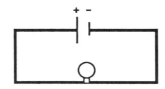

Figure 2.3: Simple electrical circuit

Examples of some FACTS: Metals conduct electricity.
Copper is a metal.

Example of a RULE: IF the connector is copper,
AND the battery is OK,
THEN a current will flow through the circuit.

Example of a HEURISTIC: IF the bulb does not light,
THEN the battery might be flat (Probability 0.7),
OR the bulb might be faulty (Probability 0.2),
OR the connector might not be a conductor (Probability 0.1).
ACTION -*CHECK THE BATTERY FIRST!*

INFERENCE STRATEGY: a set of heuristics used by an expert to navigate efficiently from a problem description to an acceptable problem solution, without necessarily having to identify and test all candidate solutions.

Despite the example, the difference between rules and heuristics may not be entirely clear to you, especially as heuristics are often referred to as "rules of thumb". Basically, rules are <u>always</u> true/valid (ignoring philosophical issues such as "what is truth?", that is), and it is usually possible to produce rigorous arguments to justify them. Heuristics are the expert's best judgement, and <u>may not be valid</u> in all cases; justification must therefore be by examples rather than rigorous argument.

The functional difference for the KBS between rules and heuristics can be shown by considering a KBS which is designed to choose from a set of possible outcomes, e.g. a diagnostic system. When a rule is applied to a set of outcomes (we'll be more precise about the terminology in chapter 3), then any outcome which is inconsistent with the rule <u>cannot</u> be a solution. When a heuristic is applied, any outcome which does not match the heuristic <u>may</u> be a solution but is unlikely to be one.

The objective of cognitive task analysis is to identify and codify the facts, rules, heuristics and inference strategy which the expert employs to solve problems in the application domain. (Note that something more sophisticated than a rule-based representation may be needed; this is discussed in chapter 3.) The process of CTA has three basic components:

Acquisition - acquiring the basic knowledge from the human expert.
Representation - organising and structuring the knowledge.
Execution - codifying the knowledge into a machine-executable format.

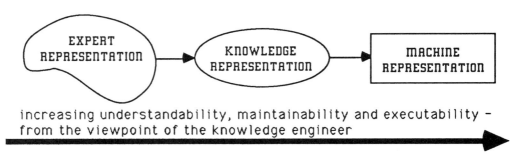

Figure 2.4: Cognitive Task Analysis

Figure 2.4 summarises the process of cognitive task analysis. CTA can be very complex, owing to the intrinsic difficulty of acquiring and representing the knowledge of a human expert. The acquisition stage, in particular, is often identified as a bottleneck in KBS development; this is often known as the "Feigenbaum bottleneck", as Ed Feigenbaum was probably the first to identify it as such.

CTA involves several major difficulties. These include the human's inability to express the knowledge possessed, the differences between everyday ways of expressing knowledge and suitable ways for explicitly representing it, and the unavoidable complexity of any process for testing the knowledge acquired.

The next three sub-sections give an overview of the key issues involved in the acquisition, representation and execution stages respectively. Acquisition is discussed here at rather greater length than the other two stages, since it is the stage which is least affected by hardware and software considerations of the three. Representation and execution are discussed further in chapter 3.

Acquisition

Many techniques have been devised for knowledge acquisition. Some have been borrowed from conventional systems analysis and subsequently modified to suit the needs of KBS analysis. The techniques range from the formal to the informal; from those which are "driven" by the knowledge engineer to those which are "driven" by the expert; and from those which are fully visible to the expert to those which are hidden. It is also important to note that some of the techniques for knowledge acquisition also encompass parts of the representation and even execution stages. In this sub-section we shall discuss generic techniques for knowledge acquisition; specific software tools to support one or more of these techniques will be covered in chapter 3 and chapter 6.

There are several different techniques by which the knowledge engineer, working with the human expert(s), can make explicit the inferencing process and data which the expert uses to solve a problem. Unlike many aspects of AI/ KBSs, most writers on the subject of knowledge acquisition tend to agree on which are the most commonly used knowledge acquisition techniques. They are:

•structured interviews
•protocol analysis
•repertory grid analysis

•rule induction by machine
•case study observation
•introspection.

We shall now give a brief summary of each of these techniques.

Structured interviews
Interviews, or in their most basic form simply "talking to the expert", are the most natural thing to do for most would-be knowledge engineers. Informal interviews offer the chance to produce a rough "map of the territory" which the expert's domain covers, and also to help to build up a good working relationship between knowledge engineer(s) and expert(s). However, as all interviews are time-consuming, completely informal interviews are not likely to be a very effective use of the time available. At the earlier stages of knowledge acquisition, semi-structured or focused interviews are recommended, whereby the knowledge engineer works to a list of topics to be covered in a particular interview session, but does not specify the precise questions to be asked of the expert. For example, if the domain of the KBS is deciding whether or not to grant loan applications, a topic might be "find out if all the information about an applicant is always obtained before starting to make a decision". Once the process of knowledge acquisition is more advanced, structured interviews may be introduced. This usually consists of working through specific questions which the knowledge engineer has produced, such as "is an applicant earning less than the minimum annual income figure *automatically* rejected at this point?". This structured interview can take the form of simulated consultations, aimed at clarifying or fleshing out specific parts of the knowledge base. However much (or little!) structure an interview may have, it is always advisable to tape-record it for future reference, as long as the expert is willing.

Protocol analysis
One of the problems with any interview-based strategy for knowledge acquisition is that the interviewer has to steer the process. This can be difficult, particularly in the early stages when the gap in understanding of the domain between the expert and the knowledge engineer is the greatest. Protocol analysis hands the task of guiding the "interview" over to the expert, by requiring that the expert thinks aloud while working through a series of either simulated or (preferably) real case examples. This method is also known as analysis of *verbal* or *verbatim* protocols, since the aim is to produce a verbatim transcript of the expert's explanation which can be used in the succeeding stages of the process. Again, tape-recording is likely to be necessary for the subsequent analysis; indeed, the role of the knowledge engineer during the solving of the

examples is so passive that it could be argued that their presence is not required at all. Protocol analysis can be extremely useful in eliciting the broad structure of the knowledge an expert possesses and the way in which it is applied, but is likely to need to be supplemented by another method in order to flesh out the detail.

Repertory grids

Although having little knowledge of the domain compared to the expert, it is still possible for the knowledge engineer to control the "interviews" by using some kind of domain-independent scientific interviewing technique. The one most commonly used in building KBSs is that of repertory grids, also referred to as Kelly grids or personal construct theory. It is also in common use in "soft" systems and operational research, which we shall return to in chapter 5. The technique is based on a theory of human cognition which was developed by the psychologist Kelly; it uses the building-block of a *construct*- a distinction between two terms (*poles*) which can be regarded as opposites when talking about elements in the domain of interest. For example, Cheap as opposed to Expensive, and Single-user as opposed to Multi-user are two constructs relevant to computer hardware. Note that there may or may not be intermediate positions between the extremes. The repertory grid is a two-way classification of the elements relevant to the domain against the constructs; in all cases the judgements involved are subjective, hence the adjective *personal*. The most common method of building up a repertory grid for an individual is to decide on the list of elements first, and then to present them in threes, asking the individual (in our case, the expert) to indicate how one of them differs from the other two. For example, the triplet of computer hardware elements {Amstrad PC, IBM PC, Apple Macintosh} might elicit the Cheap...Expensive construct from some people, or a construct relating to operating systems or ease of use from others.

Rule induction by machine

Unlike the other techniques, this one must be carried out by computer, and therefore *de facto* requires that a knowledge representation schema has already been chosen. Further consideration of this technique will therefore be deferred until the representation sections of chapter 3.

Case study observation

Here the knowledge engineer acts as an observer while the human expert actually performs the cognitive task which it is desired to capture in a KBS. Normally, the knowledge engineer does not interrupt at all, although this is more feasible with some tasks than with others! As such, the suitability of this technique is more dependent on the domain itself than is the case for any of the other techniques. Once again, a tape-recording is likely to be essential, and some studies have gone as far as using video recordings. In tasks involving interaction with computers, it may also be possible to produce a log of transactions for comparison with what the expert says he or she did.

Introspection
Often mentioned, a trifle unfairly, as the technique of last resort, this is where the knowledge engineer actually interrupts the expert during the consideration of an example, to ask "tell me what you are thinking now" or "how would I do that?". This is in contrast to protocol analysis, where the knowledge engineer should only interrupt in order to remind the expert to keep talking!

Probably the most detailed summary of the various knowledge acquisition techniques is the book edited by Kidd (KIDD87). This covers all the techniques mentioned above, and more; each chapter in the book has been contributed by a well-known expert on the technique concerned. The book by Hart (HART86) and the relevant chapter of the one by Graham and Jones (GRA88) are less detailed, but very readable.

The choice of which technique(s) to use can be influenced by many factors, the most important of which are listed below:
- the availability and motivation of the expert;
- the ability of the expert to articulate verbally, or otherwise, his or her expertise;
- the degree of complexity of the problem domain;
- the nature of the expertise involved;
- the overall scale of the project;
- the availability of manuals and other written material;
- the experience of the knowledge engineers;
- the availability of tools or computer-based environments for supporting acquisition;
- the expert's reaction to the use of audio or video tape recorders;
- the amount of development resources available.

The material which first emerges from the acquisition process may be in the form of transcripts of taped interviews, video recordings, hand-written notes, rough diagrams and so on. The volume of material produced may well be considerable. In the case of one of the Alvey Programme's demonstrator systems, a system to help interpret welfare benefits legislation produced for the UK Department of Social Security, it was necessary to store the manuals and documents concerned on computer so that it was feasible to access them at all! The next step requires the organisation of this raw knowledge, by using a particular representation schema.

Representation

While the choice of acquisition technique is largely dictated by factors which leave little room for manoeuvre by the knowledge engineers, the choice of representation schema is more open. Five basic data structures are generally used for knowledge representation: *production rules, frames, semantic networks, objects* and *declarative logic.* Each of these mechanisms is very versatile and the ultimate choice will depend on the type of procedural control required and the degree of familiarity of the knowledge engineers with the different techniques. The representation schema can also be influenced by the features offered by the implementation tools being considered. Most of the KBS shells are designed to support one particular form of knowledge representation schema and/or inference mechanism, and even the special-purpose languages and mid-range tools often have a strong built-in bias. In addition, if rapid prototyping is to be used to expand and refine the system's knowledge-base, it may well be important to use a representation schema which the expert feels happy with.

Execution

Once the knowledge representation schema has been chosen, the raw cognitive model must be systematically translated into the new format. This is almost certain to involve back-tracking to the acquisition stage, to fill in omissions or clarify dubious points. It may also necessitate a re-think about the representation schema, if the one chosen appears to be proving unsatisfactory. With the current state of the art of cognitive task analysis, it is almost inevitable that this will happen on occasion, since not enough is known about representing different kinds of expert knowledge. In addition, the knowledge engineer is always less knowledgeable about the domain than the expert, and hence the possibility of needing to correct errors or inadequacies must be allowed for in this phase.

The actual translation can take one of two forms:

•an entirely paper-based exercise
•direct entry of the raw cognitive model into the shell or toolkit being used

Where paper-based translation is used at this stage, the coding into machine form usually takes place during the phase of the project corresponding to that of implementation in conventional software engineering. It is, however, more common for the knowledge to be entered into the machine at this stage, especially if a prototyping approach is being followed. We shall discuss the merits of these two approaches later, in chapter 4.

2.4.3 Explanation facilities and the prospective user

Very often the impetus for building a KBS is the desire to remove the organisational bottleneck which arises when only a limited number of experts are available to perform an activity lying on some critical path in an organisation. The intention may be to enable non-experts to perform tasks previously only carried out by the expert. In this case, it will be necessary to define precisely the competence of the expected non-expert user, so that an operational KBS is built which does not rely for its success on a level of expertise in the user which the latter does not possess. For example, any questions which the system poses to the user must not require judgement which the user is not able to exercise. This point was discussed in Edwards and Bader (EDW88).

In order to assist the user, it is often desirable for highly user-interactive KBSs, especially in domains such as medicine or finance, to make explicit to the user the reasoning behind any advice offered, or the purpose for which a question is being asked. For this type of KBS, elaborate explanation facilities may need to be built into the system. Indeed, one of the main characteristics of early KBSs, as d'Agapayeff (D'AGA85) pointed out, was their ability to "...provide explanations of their reasoning on demand". However, the explanation facilities provided with most KBS tools simply reproduce the particular rules (or their equivalent) used in the last part of the consultation, in the knowledge representation format which the tool uses. This type of explanation facility is extremely useful for the knowledge engineer (and perhaps also the human expert) when developing the system. However, its relevance to the end-user of the KBS is limited, especially where the style of the KBS is that of an expert consultant or tutor. The position can be still worsened when some of the rules in the KBS are used for procedural control. In the extreme, this can lead to situations where, for example, the justification given for asking a question amounts to "I am asking the question because I want to know the answer"!

Nevertheless, the ability of an expert system to explain its reasoning is still regarded by some as a key feature of the technology, and indeed one of the defining properties of an expert system. Waterman (WAT86) emphasised this in his book on ESs referred to earlier:

> "Most current expert systems have what is called an *explanation facility*. This is knowledge for explaining how the system has arrived at its answers. Most of these explanations involve displaying the inference chains and explaining the rationale behind each rule used in the chain. The ability to examine their reasoning process and explain their operation is one of the most innovative and important qualities of expert systems." (page 28.)

The amount and type of explanation facilities in a KBS will ultimately depend on the type of application domain, the style of the KBS, and the nature of the intended user. It may well be necessary to include different types of explanation facility for different purposes.

It should be obvious that appropriate explanation facilities cannot be produced without involving the prospective users of the system in this part of the design process. However, the literature contains many descriptions of the development of KBSs in which this doesn't appear to have happened! Since this would be a sure-fire recipe for disaster, such descriptions should be regarded as evidence of at least one of the following, rather than as good practice:

•The KBS is being used by the experts themselves, rather than by non-experts.
•The development work was done from an exploratory perspective.
•The KBS is not in full operational use.

Consideration of explanation facilities is only part of the whole issue of the human-computer interface (HCI). Wider aspects are dealt with in chapter 3.

2.5 Summary

In this chapter we have presented a general overview of the field of knowledge-based systems, to complement the examples given in sections 1.2 and 1.3. Our main purpose here was to give you an idea of the general nature of the field, so that you can start to relate it to your own experience of other types of system. We now go on to present more detail about KBSs and the tools for building them, and then to make our own comparisons with other types of system and different "solution technologies".

References

(AND89) Bruce Andrews, *"Successful Expert Systems"*, Financial Times Business Information, London, 1989.

(BUCH86) B.G.Buchanan, "Expert Systems: Working Systems and the Research Literature", *Expert Systems*, Vol. 3, No. 1, pp 32-51, January 1986.

(CRI86) *"The CRI Directory of Expert Systems"*, Learned Information, UK, 1986.

(D'AGA85) A.d'Agapayeff, "A Short Survey of Expert Systems in UK Business", *R & D Management*, Vol. 15, No. 2, pp 89-99, 1985.

(D'AGA87) A.d'Agapayeff, *"Report to the Alvey Directorate on the Second Survey of Expert Systems in UK Business"*, IEE on behalf of The Alvey Directorate, London, 1987.

(DURH87) T.Durham, "Moving Experts Forward One Step at a Time", *Computing*, pp.20-21, September 17, 1987.

(EDW88) John S.Edwards and Jon L.Bader, "Expert Systems and University Admissions", *Journal of the Operational Research Society*, Vol. 39, No. 1, pp.33-40, 1988.

(FEIG88) Edward Feigenbaum, Pamela McCorduck, and H.Penny Nii, *"The Rise of the Expert Company"*, Macmillan, London, 1988.

(GRA88) Ian Graham and Peter Llewellyn Jones, *"Expert Systems: Knowledge, Uncertainty and Decision"*, Chapman and Hall, London, 1988.

(HART86) A.Hart, *"Knowledge Acquisition for Expert Systems"*, Kogan Page, London, 1986.

(HAYES83) F.Hayes-Roth, D.A.Waterman and D.B.Lenat(eds.), *"Building Expert Systems"*, Addison-Wesley, USA, 1983.

(KIDD87) A.L.Kidd(ed.), *"Knowledge Acquisition for Expert Systems: A Practical Handbook"*, Plenum, New York, 1987.

(MCD80) J.McDermott, "R1: An Expert in the Computer Systems Domain", *Proceedings of the 1st Annual National Conference of the American Association for Artificial Intelligence*, pp.269-271, Stanford, USA, 1980,.

(MING89) John Mingers and Jane Adlam, "Where are the "real" expert systems?", *OR Insight* Vol.2, No.3, pp.6-9, July-September 1989.

(OVUM86) *"The Ovum Report - Commercial Expert Systems in Europe"*, Ovum Ltd., London, 1986.

(PRER85) D.S.Prerau, "Selection of an Appropriate Domain for an Expert System", *The AI Magazine*, Vol. 6, No. 2, pp.26-30, Summer 1985.

(STEV89) Hamish Stevenson, "Expert systems in the UK financial services sector: a symbolic analysis of the hype", pp.276-303 in *"Knowledge-based Management Support Systems"* (eds. G.I.Doukidis, F.Land & G.Miller), Ellis Horwood, Chichester, 1989.

(VAN86) A.van de Brug, J.Bachant and J.McDermott, "The Taming of R1", *IEEE Expert*, pp.33-39, Fall 1986.

(WAT86) D.A.Waterman, *"A Guide to Expert Systems"*, Addison-Wesley, USA, 1986.

(ZACK87) B.A.Zack, "Selecting an Application for Knowledge-Based System Development", *Proceedings of the Third International Expert Systems Conference*, pp.257-269, Learned Information (Europe) Ltd., Oxford, 1987.

Chapter 3 : KBS/AI Concepts and Tools

3.0 Introduction

We don't often give "instructions" in this book; most of the time we simply hope that you will find our opinions and suggestions useful. However, this is one point where a command is justified: *If you have never seen a demonstration of a system constructed using a PC-based expert system "shell", arrange to see one as soon as possible!*

Expert system shells are certainly not the answer to all your organisation's problems, and possibly not the answer to any of them. However, we believe that you need to have at least a little idea of the area of the market about which there has been the most noise in recent years, and there's no substitute for "hands-on" experience. If the demonstrators you choose will not let you get your hands on the system, choose another vendor who will. Having given you this command, we leave you to draw your own conclusions as to the potential value of what you are seeing. As far as we are concerned, the question to ask is of course not "does it look impressive?" (it would be a poor demo if it didn't), but one or more of the following:

- does it do anything which we can't do at present?
- does it do anything which we don't do at present?
- what about it looked similar to applications we have built/seen?
- what about it looked different from applications we have built/seen?

The best role at this stage for the expert systems shell demo is as a taster for what the various tools and environments in the KBS world might have to offer. We have already pointed out in chapter 2 that the solution-driven perspective on building KBSs which sometimes goes hand-in-hand with acquiring an expert system shell is not always desirable.

In the remainder of this chapter we shall describe some of the software and hardware available for building KBSs. We'll also introduce some more of the concepts and terminology of KBSs which you need to know, to add detail to the overview which we gave in the previous chapter. As product development continues to be extremely rapid, it is inevitable that any description of this kind will be out of date in the time it takes to go from the keyboard to the printer. We believe, however, that it is a reasonable description of the "state of the art" at the time of writing.

3.1 KBS Concepts

Figure 3.1 shows the typical structure of a standalone KBS, together with the three types of people most involved with building and using it. The same concepts apply to integrated or embedded KBSs, although they may not be as visible to the end-user, and the knowledge engineer may find tasks affected by the non-knowledge-based parts of the system. In this chapter we shall generally treat the KBS as a standalone system for simplicity, though the wider considerations will also be mentioned where necessary.

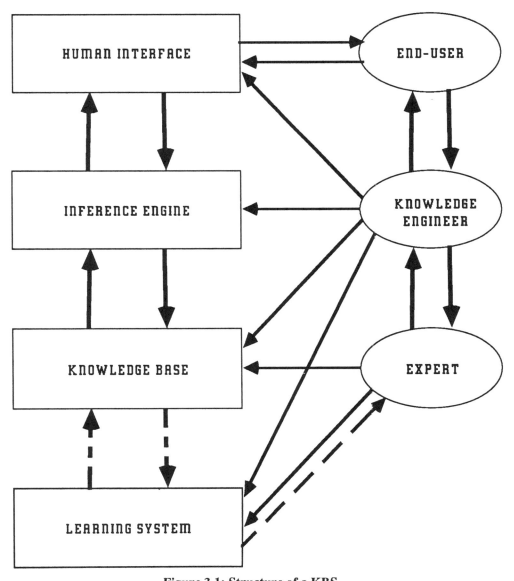

Figure 3.1: Structure of a KBS

3.1.1 The knowledge base

There are many possible ways of structuring the knowledge base to represent the expert knowledge about the domain. The best known of these are:

•Rules
•Frames
•Semantic nets
•Objects
•Declarative knowledge

Rules

We have already given examples of rules in chapters 1 and 2. This is because rule-based knowledge representations appeal to our sense of familiarity in two ways. Firstly, there is the similarity with the way in which instructions are given in manuals, handbooks, codes of practice, etc.; this particularly suits the "expert consultant" style of KBS. Secondly, the rules are similar to constructs in conventional third generation computer languages such as FORTRAN or BASIC. It is worth pointing out, however, that not everybody makes the distinction between rules and heuristics which we did in section 2.4; instead they lump them all together as "rules". We'll see later in this chapter that the situation is even more confused when looking at some of the rule-based software packages available.

The rules in the knowledge base are also sometimes referred to as *production rules* or *productions*, in order to stress the point that the purpose of representing the knowledge in a KBS is to be able to apply it. Thus with a typical rule structured on the lines of:

IF <condition is true>
THEN <take action or draw conclusion>

the truth of the condition statement is not tested until the system is run. When it is run, if the condition is true (often described as "the rule fires"), then a change in the state of the KBS is produced - hence the term production rule. This change might be, for example, a decision about the truth of the conclusion statement (an inference rule), or to transfer control within the KBS (a control rule).

One of the weaknesses of a rule-based representation is that a rule is essentially a one-way relationship between the condition part and the conclusion part.

More elements may be added to this relationship by having several clauses in the condition part, joined by operators such as AND and OR, and by having more than one conclusion or action. However, this does not help in using rules to represent more complex relationships between the truth of any two statements; in such cases, a rule-based representation is often at best unwieldy and at worst impossible.

Example

Suppose we have two conditions A and B, tested for in different ways, which always appear to occur together or not at all. This is easy to represent as the two rules:

IF A THEN B
IF B THEN A

However, while these are fine as static statements, any attempt to use these rules as the basis for inferences of any kind is in danger of leading to circular reasoning. To overcome this, we would need to treat (A and B) as a single condition in our system's knowledge base, which might give rise to problems of maintaining the knowledge base if new cases arise in which A and B do not occur together.

Frames

A frame is a concept originally proposed by Marvin Minsky (MIN75), which is able to represent the attributes of a particular object or concept in a more richly descriptive way than is possible using rules. The frame typically consists of a number of *slots*, each of which may contain a value (or may be left blank). The number and type of slots will be chosen according to the particular knowledge being represented.

An everyday example of a frame-like representation of information is the type of indicator board often used at airports, rail stations etc. One column ("frame") from the train indicator board at British Rail's Birmingham New Street rail station is shown in Figure 3.2.

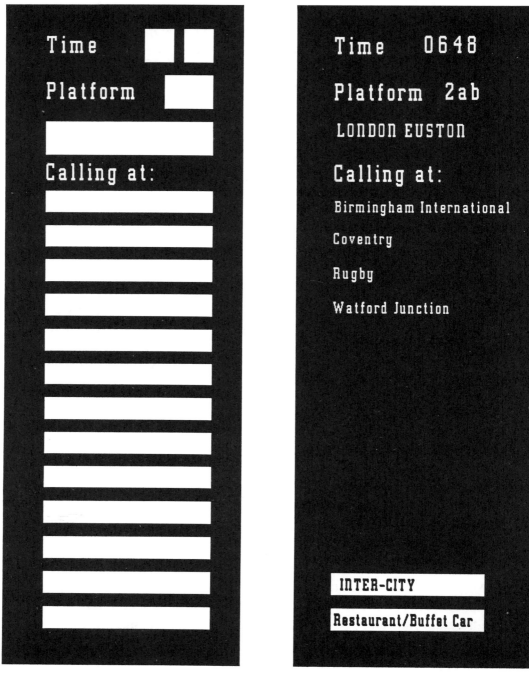

Figure 3.2: A frame-like representation from everyday life

In this frame, there are several different types of slot, showing:

•The train's ultimate destination station

•The scheduled time of departure
•The platform number
•Intermediate stations at which the train stops
•Special information such as catering facilities

Representing this information as rules would be possible, but unwieldy. Just think how many rules would be required of the form:

IF This train is the 0648 to London Euston
THEN Rugby is an intermediate station stop.

Our example has many of the features of frames in knowledge representation:

(i) Different slots contain different types of value. For example, the scheduled departure time must be a time on the 24-hour clock, whereas the ultimate destination must be a station name. Neither value would be acceptable in the other slot.

(ii) Some slots *must* have a value in them, i.e. the ultimate destination, the scheduled time of departure and the platform number. The other slots may be blank (there might be no intermediate stops).

(iii) The number of values in the slots may vary, as is the case for the number of intermediate station stops. As in our example, there may be a maximum number of values imposed by "hardware" constraints.

(iv) A slot may contain a reference to another frame. If there are too many intermediate station stops to fit in one column, an arrow pointing to the next column/frame appears in one of the intermediate station stop slots in the first column/frame.

There are also features of frames which this simple example does not illustrate. These include the provision of a default value for a particular slot in all frames of a certain type, and the use of more complex methods for "inheriting" values and properties between frames, plus the simpler point that the actual name of the slot does not appear on the indicator board, whereas in most KBSs it would be displayed.

Objects

An alternative approach to representing knowledge about a domain is to define various types of object which are relevant to that domain, together with their associated properties. Thus, using the same domain as the previous example, we might define a class of object called "train departure" or even simply "train". This object would have properties such as ultimate destination station, departure time, platform number, and so on. The difference from frames is that with an object-oriented programming environment (often abbreviated to OOP), the objects can be regarded as if they were able to act as independent entities. Control of the system is achieved by sending instructions known as messages to the objects, and by objects sending and receiving messages between themselves. So, for example, an object can have associated with it the ability to draw itself on the VDU screen. Other parts of the KBS can draw this object simply by sending it a message telling it to draw itself, without needing to know how the particular draw procedure works. This is a great advantage when prototyping.

Semantic nets

Another way of representing more complex relationships is to use graphs. A semantic net is a particular type of graph in which descriptions (hence the term *semantic*) are applied not only to the nodes (points) in the graph, but also to the lines joining them. Thus the nodes represent concepts or objects, which have various properties associated with them, and the lines represent the relationships between the concepts. The objects are, not surprisingly, very similar to those we have just described, but the approach to specifying relationships between them and to system control is very different. A reasonable analogy is that the semantic net is intended to describe static relationships, whereas the object-oriented paradigm concentrates on (dynamic) changes. Figure 3.3 shows a simple example of a semantic net.

The semantic net approach obviously has some similarities to entity-relationship approaches to data modelling in conventional computer systems design.

Again the idea of inheritance - and especially *controlled* inheritance - comes in, as with frames and objects. In this case relationships such as *is_a* and *has_part* serve to define a hierarchy for the various concepts.

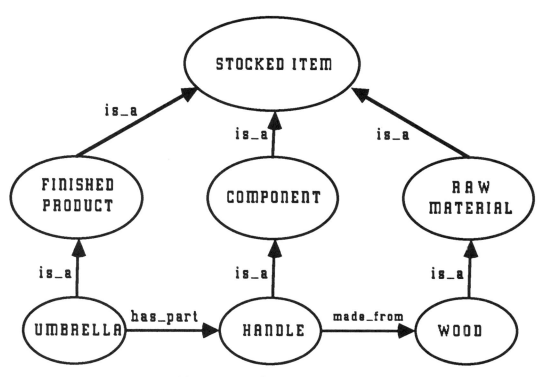

Figure 3.3: A simple semantic net

Declarative logic

Declarative logic is similar to the use of production rules; some authors see a difference between the two categories, whereas others regard the former as merely a subset of the latter. The principal difference appears to us to be a more explicit attempt to separate the items making up the knowledge base of the KBS from those which actually control the operation of the system. It is most commonly seen in the form of systems written in the language Prolog. This is perhaps where the difference of opinion arises, since Prolog contains sophisticated pattern-matching facilities which examine both the condition and conclusion parts of IF...THEN... statements simultaneously. This is an issue more related to the inference engine (see the next section) than the knowledge base itself. We feel that, in abstract terms, declarative logic does come into the same category as production rules, but that Prolog (as a tool/product) does offer facilities which differ from those of rule-based expert system shells.

Multiple representations

It is also possible to use two or more forms of knowledge representation simultaneously in the same KBS. For example, one of the slots in a frame may contain a rule. Similarly, a rule may be used to control the inheritance of properties between objects in a semantic net.

3.1.2 The inference engine

The inference engine controls the execution of the system as far as using the knowledge in the base is concerned. The somewhat peculiar term appears to have been chosen to evoke memories of Victorian computing pioneer Charles Babbage's "Difference Engine" and "Analytic Engine"; this is probably at least as sensible as naming the conventional programming language Ada after Babbage's co-worker Ada, Countess Lovelace!

The two most basic ways in which an inference engine can operate are termed *backward chaining* and *forward chaining*. As usual, we shall illustrate these by reference to a rule-based system for clarity. At any point during a run of the KBS (often termed a *consultation* by analogy with the expert consultant role), the inference engine must calculate which rule should be tried next. It may be helpful to think of there being an *agenda*, i.e. a list of things to be done, in descending order of priority. Essentially the inference engine performs only two different tasks:

•Changing the order of items on the agenda
•Actioning the item at the top of the agenda

It is possible that several items may be being actioned simultaneously, since any given task may require the completion of several sub-tasks for its own successful completion. For example, testing the truth of the condition part of a rule may require values to be assigned to some variables, perhaps by asking a question of the user, or by invoking other rules. Typically, questions to be asked of the user, and messages to be output to the user, go straight to the top of the agenda. The principal difference between forward and backward chaining concerns the order in which the various rules stand on the agenda at any time, and thus particularly which rule is examined next when the top agenda item is "find the next rule which fires".

Backward chaining

A backward chaining system always has a top-level goal being actioned at any time. This is typically an overall conclusion or recommendation, the truth of which is being examined. Thus a backward chaining fault-diagnosis KBS would work through the possible causes of the fault in turn, seeking to see if each cause is consistent with the "evidence", and either stopping when it finds one which is, or finding all causes consistent with the information given. The key question is always "are the conditions which prove this goal satisfied?". The inference engine of a rule-based backward chaining KBS would thus proceed by examining the conclusion parts of rules. Rules whose conclusion parts correspond to the current top-level goal go to the top of the agenda; each is then examined in turn to see whether the condition part is true. This may be established by looking at the current state of the knowledge base, asking a question of the user, or examining other rules whose conclusion corresponds to the relevant condition. This may involve going through several levels of rule, which is where the chaining part of the name comes from. The backward part arises because this type of inferencing always works backwards from a likely-looking conclusion to find (and test) the conditions which must apply for that conclusion to be true.

Forward chaining

In a forward chaining KBS, there is usually no equivalent to the "current top-level goal" of a backward chaining system. Instead, the system will continue a particular consultation until either all possible inferences have been made from the available information, or one of a set of suitably high-level conclusions has been found to be true. A forward chaining fault-diagnosis system would begin by obtaining information about the symptoms of the fault, and make inferences based on this information without any "pre-conceived ideas" as to which possible cause should be considered first. Again it might stop either as soon as it finds one cause to be justified by the evidence, or continue to find all causes which are justified by the evidence. The key question here is always "what can be concluded from the conditions which are satisfied?". A forward chaining inference engine proceeds by searching for a rule where the condition part is true, given the current state of the knowledge base, and which has not already "fired", i.e. has not *already* been used to change the state of the knowledge base. If it finds one, this rule then fires, i.e. its conclusion part is now labelled as true in the knowledge base. The process then starts again with the knowledge base in its new state. Thus in this type of inferencing, the system is always working forwards from those conditions which are true to see what further conclusions may be inferred.

As our examples of fault diagnosis illustrated, it is perfectly possible to construct a KBS for a similar task with either a backward chaining or a forward chaining system. In fact, most real-life systems are likely to incorporate some combination of the two. Backward chaining is often to be favoured where any or all of the following apply:

•Only a small proportion of the rules are likely to fire during any one consultation.
•The task of the KBS is to assign each case to a particular one of a relatively small number of mutually exclusive categories.
•Possible outcomes are different in kind. For example, "accept loan application" and "reject loan application" in a credit evaluation system have very different consequences; the KBS might well treat one of these as effectively the default decision.

Forward chaining has advantages when:

•The information available is in a standard form (perhaps literally *on* a standard form).
•Many of the potential outcomes may be simultaneously true.
•Some of the inference chains are much shorter than others.

Tree search approaches

The two descriptions above relate principally to rule-based systems. Inferencing approaches with declarative logic are broadly similar, but where other representations are used, inferencing may well be more difficult, because of the lack of standardization of the terms used. For example, we may define a slot in a frame or a relationship in a semantic net to be (literally) anything we choose. This flexibility costs us the logically rigorous inference processes which can be used with rules.

In many cases, including the rule-based systems, it is possible to describe the knowledge-base using some kind of tree-like structure. Inference then translates into a problem of searching the tree, which is an area in which much work has been done over the years by mathematicians. The most basic approaches to search problems are depth-first search (which tries one "branch" through as many levels as possible) and breadth-first search (which tries at most one further level on each branch in turn before moving to a different one). These have some similarities with backward- and forward-chaining respectively. Improved search methods normally rely on some kind of "hill-climbing" technique, which will need to be tailored to the relationships between the items making up the tree for that particular knowledge-base.

3.1.3 The human interface

The considerations relevant to the human interface of a KBS are exactly the same in kind as those relevant to any other type of system. However, two factors are worth stressing. One is that the nature of the interaction between a user and a KBS is different from that with many conventional systems, in such a way that it makes a good user interface even more important. The other is that the human interface of many conventional systems is often barely acceptable.

There is very little literature about the techniques that can be used to ensure that an interface is devised which will maximise the usability and effectiveness of an operational KBS. Most of the available advice consists of guidelines which are either too general, or at the other extreme too specific, to be transferred easily to a new KBS development. This aspect of KBS design is still the subject of basic research (BERRY87), (EIKE86). The following is a summary of the factors which we feel may significantly influence the choice of interface:

- the degree of expertise of the prospective KBS user(s);
- the amount and nature of direct user interaction required;
- the amount of textual explanations required;
- the importance of static or animated graphics;
- the degree of menu-type interaction necessary;
- the amount of concurrent help facilities required during operation;
- the appropriateness of windows, icons and mouse-style operation (Wimps);
- the importance of making explicit the inference process and data being used.

The information necessary to evaluate these factors is related to the type and style of KBS, the nature of the expert task and the degree of competence of the prospective users.

3.1.4 The learning system

The primary purpose of the learning system is to keep the knowledge base up-to-date. It may also be used for constructing the knowledge base in the first place, but our main concern in this section is with the structure of the KBS rather than how it is built; we shall cover that in detail later. The most important point to note about the learning system is that it might not be part of the computer system at all. (Hence in Figure 3.1 it is shown connected to the rest of the KBS by arrows with broken lines.) Machine learning is a somewhat controversial topic, and has not yet reached as high a level of acceptance as have KBSs generally. Nevertheless, whether it is part of the KBS on the computer, or a human system for updating the KBS, some kind of learning system is necessary. Without a learning system, the performance of the KBS will inevitably degrade with time - very rapidly, in some domains, for example those dependent on frequently-changing legislation, those advising on choice between products/services, or those advising on medical treatment. With such a mechanism, it may well be that the system's performance actually improves over time, as would be expected of a human performing a knowledge-based task.

The major practical success in machine learning so far is the technique of *rule induction*. Whereas in other cases, the knowledge about the domain must be structured by the knowledge engineer(s) and the expert(s) working together, rule induction is based on the age-old approach of learning by example. It is important to realise that, contrary to the impression given by some articles on the topic, this does not necessarily remove the need for human assistance in building the KBS. At least one expert is still required in order to define the attributes which are relevant to the decision being made. A set of examples, known as the "training set", is then collected, giving the values of all these attributes, together with the "correct" decision. Again an expert's judgement may be required to supply this; it is often impossible to obtain independent or objective confirmation of the correctness of a decision. (See our discussion of evaluation in chapter 8.) Indeed, even the knowledge engineer may still be required, to help the expert to produce appropriate attributes and examples. The rules for the knowledge base are then induced on the basis of the training set.

Other methods of machine learning have been proposed, and are the subject of much current research. These include *genetic algorithms*, where several versions of an algorithm or rule-set compete for "survival". New versions are produced by controlled changes to those versions which are more successful in tests, while the less successful versions are eliminated. A partly random change is sometimes introduced to avoid the equivalent of too much "in-breeding"!

Neural networks form perhaps the hottest current topic in AI research, and are just beginning to reach the stage of practical application. This involves not only a different approach to machine learning, but also to the structure of the machine itself. Further discussion of these methods are beyond the scope of this book. Forsyth's book (FORS89) gives a very readable summary of recent developments and future hopes/expectations.

3.2 Tools Used to Build KBSs: an Overview

Implementing a KBS, as with any other type of computer system, involves decisions about hardware and software. While conventional tools can be used, there is a great deal of software specifically intended to assist in the building of KBSs, and also some specialised hardware.

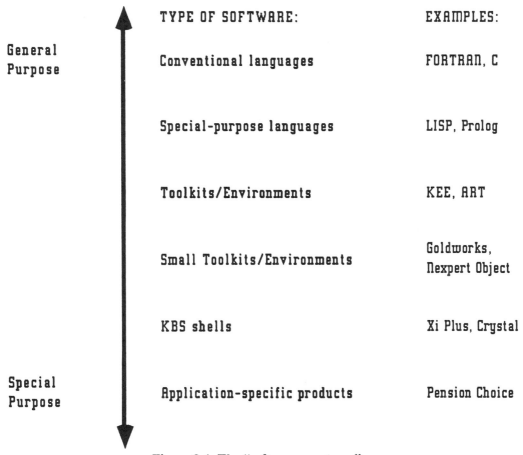

Figure 3.4: The "software spectrum"

The various types of software which can be used are shown in Figure 3.4, going from conventional third generation languages at the general-purpose end of the spectrum, through to shells and even application-specific packages at the special-purpose end. We have identified six categories here, although it is possible to identify more or fewer. The broad differences between the various software choices are as follows: KBS/expert system shells and AI/KBS toolkits or environments are specifically designed to support the knowledge representation schemata and procedural control commonly used for KBSs. As a result they can be very fast and convenient to use, once their extensive range of facilities has been mastered. However, they do not offer the execution speed and flexibility for interface design which is possible using conventional programming languages like C and FORTRAN. It is also the case that building a KBS in a language , whether special-purpose AI or conventional third generation, can be very expensive in development time and it is unlikely that the resulting code could be utilised easily in another application domain. On the other hand, the knowledge representation schemata and inference engines already provided in shells or toolkits may restrict the options open to the KBS builders, even though they speed up development. Table 3.1 shows the distribution of software used in building KBSs, according to a survey we carried out of 405 KBSs which had been reported as reaching at least field trial stage by the end of 1988. The sixth category, application-specific packages, only comes into these figures once for each such package, as our survey did not cover sales of such packages.

Conventional languages	11%
Special-purpose languages	23%
Toolkits/environments	10%
Small toolkits/environments	1%
KBS Shells	56%

(Note that percentages may not sum to 100% because of rounding effects.)

Table 3.1: Distribution of types of software for KBS development

Figure 3.5 shows the various types of hardware, first divided into three categories, each of which is then further sub-divided, to make eight categories in all. By and large, the main effect of the hardware is to limit the choice of software available; the other effect is that the general style of the user interface is normally determined by the hardware, although it is possible to get around

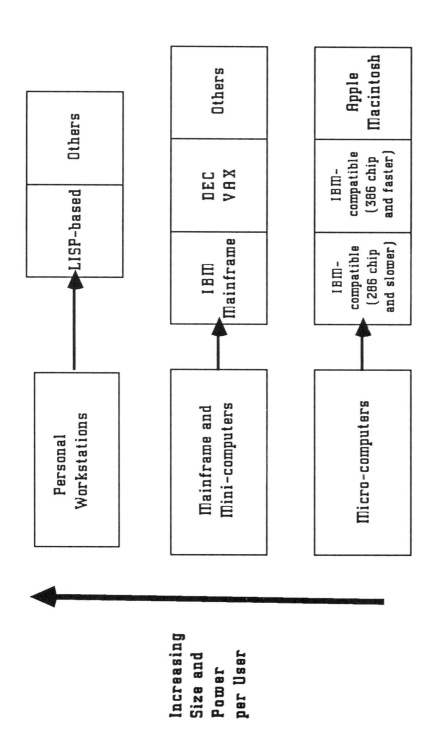

Figure 3.5: Types of hardware

this to some extent with appropriate programming effort and/or special add-ons. The distribution of hardware used in building the KBSs in our survey referred to above is as shown in Table 3.2. Note that in many cases in our survey the hardware was not clearly identified; these have been excluded from the figures.

Personal workstations	**17% of which**	**LISP workstations**	**15%**
		Other workstations	**2%**
Mainframe / mini-computers	**33% of which**	**IBM mainframes**	**9%**
		DEC VAX	**13%**
		Others*	**11%**
Micro-computers	**50% of which**	**"Ordinary" IBM and compatibles**	**48%**
		386-based IBM and compatibles	**2%**
		Apple Macintosh	**1%**

* More than half of this category (6%) consists of mainframe systems in Japan which have a specialised "back-end" LISP processor, the Fujitsu FACOM-α, attached. This appears to be the only commercially available product of its kind.

(Note that percentages may not sum to 100% because of rounding effects.)

Table 3.2: Distribution of types of hardware for KBSs

If we look back to the headings in section 3.1, we therefore see that the combination of hardware and software choices will affect all the first three components of the KBS, sometimes directly and sometimes indirectly. The effect on the fourth component, the learning system, is somewhat different, in that until very recently all of the software available for machine learning was of a single type. This in itself severely limits the possibilities for the rest of the KBS. The leading commercial products for rule induction are all of this single type; this includes ExpertEase, SuperExpert and Rulemaster, all of which are based on the ID3 algorithm devised by Quinlan. In effect, ID3 produces a decision tree which is consistent with the examples in the training set. Normally, it will be possible to produce several such trees from a given training set, and the algorithm selects the tree which is the simplest in information-theoretic terms. When using this approach to rule induction, it is vital that the training set fully represents all the different possibilities, in order to induce a rule which discriminates properly between cases. Thus it is often desirable to form the training set from hypothetical examples defined by the human expert, rather than from real data, which is often "noisy" and also tends, naturally enough, to contain mainly the most common cases. (It may well be the uncommon cases which it is most important for the KBS to handle correctly.) Again we see that rule induction still requires a human expert.

Choosing the right tool to build a KBS is a complex task, requiring careful consideration of a large number of interdependent factors. Figure 3.6 illustrates some characteristics of the different tools available and shows the two most frequently used tools.

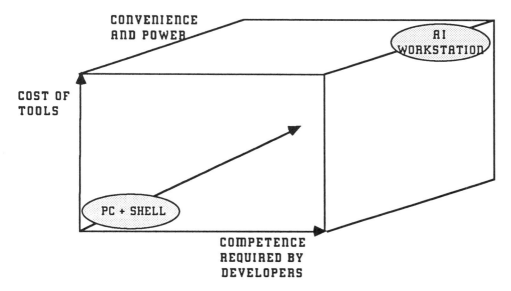

Figure 3.6: Comparing the tools

The following is a list of important factors which should be considered in relation to KBS tool selection. It illustrates the *logical* factors which can influence tool selection. Pragmatic commercial considerations may also be relevant. For example, a mainframe-based system will probably have to be on the mainframe which the organisation already has - it is unlikely that many organisations would purchase a new mainframe solely to implement a KBS! The experience of the knowledge engineers and the likely ease of obtaining professional coding assistance for them may also be important. Such considerations are not discussed here, but will be dealt with in later chapters under the topic of determining the commercial need which the KBS is addressing.

SCOPE:	Prototype or operational system?
SIZE:	Small (< 100 rules), medium (< 500 rules), large? Volume of external data involved.
TYPE:	Stand-alone, integrated or embedded?
STYLE:	Assistant, critic...?
PROBLEM:	Classification, prediction...?
USER:	Expert, novice, general public...?
USER INTERFACE:	Graphics, Wimps, animation...?
EXTERNAL INTERFACE:	Does the KBS need to link to a PC, MIS, DBMS, other...?
KNOWLEDGE REPRESENTATION:	Frames, objects, semantic nets, rules...?
CONTROL:	Type of inferencing mechanism required?
ALGORITHMS:	How many conventional programs required?
DISTRIBUTION:	Single PC only; distributed PCs + floppy disks; LANs; mainframe...?
PERFORMANCE:	Batch, on-line, real-time...?
RESOURCES:	Development budget and time constraints?
DEVELOPERS:	Training required to use development tools?

Bear these considerations in mind, as in the remainder of this chapter we look in more detail at some of the pros and cons of the various software and hardware choices with respect to the various phases of KBS development.

3.3 Knowledge Acquisition

This is the phase where the choice of hardware and software should have the least effect, at least during the initial stages of knowledge acquisition. Ideally, the first pass at cognitive task analysis should be done with a clean slate, and without any pre-conceived ideas as to how the knowledge will eventually be represented in machine form, let alone the machine on which this will be done.

It may not be possible to forget hardware and software completely, however. One of the important tasks in the early stages of knowledge acquisition is to put the expert in an appropriate frame of mind. A co-operative, lucid expert is essential. In order to achieve this, it may well be necessary to give the expert an introduction to KBSs, to ensure that it is known precisely what the process of knowledge acquisition is supposed to be achieving. This will almost certainly involve a demonstration of some kind of KBS - it would be a poor introduction if it did not. There is thus the danger of introducing some bias in favour of the technology used in the demonstration. This may apply to the expert, the knowledge engineer (who presumably already has some reason for choosing this technology) or indeed both.

The one exception to everything we have said so far in this section is if it has been decided that a rule induction approach should be adopted. In this case, it makes sense to structure the whole process of knowledge acquisition around the package to be used and its terminology, provided that the expert can express their thinking in those terms. If not, then there will still be just as much of a job at this stage for the human knowledge engineer. The latest rule induction tools are somewhat less restrictive; many are designed to produce rules in a suitable format for one of the PC shells, for example VP-Expert includes a rule induction module, while Xi Rule can be used to induce rules for Xi Plus. These rules may then be modified in the usual way. In addition, some products can now deal (probabilistically) with contradictory examples in the training set, which the products referred to in the previous section cannot.

An attempt to get the "best of both worlds" in knowledge acquisition, and perhaps the most novel use of rule induction, is that practised by expert system developers at BP International. They use a rule induction package in their initial meeting with the expert. The expert is invited to have a short ("10 minutes") hands-on session with the package, with the objective of gaining his/her interest and confidence. This is a key part of BP International's initial "feasibility study" for a KBS. It is worth noting that the "expert system" produced in this session is usually thrown away, or at best used as background material to assist the knowledge engineer(s). Knowledge acquisition then proceeds in whatever way is appropriate for the domain and the expert concerned.

Later passes in the knowledge acquisition process, and refinement of the knowledge base, are dealt with in the sections entitled "system execution".

3.4 Knowledge Representation

By contrast with knowledge acquisition, here the differences resulting from different software are considerable. Hardware has little influence, except in so far as it limits the choice of software available. KBS Shells, toolkits/environments and special-purpose languages all offer built-in knowledge representation schemata of various kinds, whereas conventional languages do not.

Another highly relevant point, although at first it may not seem to come under the heading of knowledge representation, is the question of supporting other operations such as calculations and database access, as well as inferencing. In general, these tasks may be achieved either by having appropriate facilities in the software being used, or the ability to link quickly and rapidly to other packages which do offer those facilities. Few practical KBS applications can be constructed solely using inferencing, so these capabilities are highly necessary. In fact, the use of KBS tools for calculations is a good example of one of the difficulties arising from work done in the exploratory perspective. Since the main research focus was on systems to perform inferencing, numerical calculation was not really considered; as a result, the performance of some of the early expert system shells on even the simplest arithmetic was exceptionally slow, and the actual functionality was not much more than that of an entry-level 4-function pocket calculator. This was one aspect which was rapidly improved once the problem-driven perspective began to make a contribution.

We shall now consider the differences in more detail, using the structure in Figure 3.4.

Application-specific products

With such a product, there are normally no choices about knowledge representation to be made. All the key decisions have been made for you by the developer of the product. Indeed, depending upon the particular product, the purchaser may well be unaware of the precise knowledge representation schema used.

KBS shells

In the vast majority of these products, only one built-in knowledge representation schema is provided, and it is normally impossible to add any other one. In the most basic PC-based shells, the knowledge base must take the form of a combination of facts and IF…THEN… rules, as we have already used in some of our simple explanatory examples. The inference mechanism is also fixed to be simple backward chaining, although it is possible in most products to use rules to impose a limited amount of control. Early versions of the Crystal and Xi shells worked in this manner.

The corresponding basic mainframe and mini-computer based products, such as SAVOIR, tended to have exactly the same "facts, rules and backward chaining" structure.

Some of the more successful "first generation" products on both PCs and mainframes also had this "facts, rules and backward chaining" structure, but in addition allowed explicit treatment of uncertainty in both the facts and the rules. This was accomplished by using what are called *certainty factors* or *confidence factors*, corresponding very roughly to probabilities. Two slightly different "schools" developed, one descended from the early geological expert system PROSPECTOR, and the other from MYCIN and EMYCIN. An example of the first type of shell is SAGE, originally available on mainframes and later on PCs, while TI's Personal Consultant series of shells takes the second approach.

Another development from the most basic shells is the inclusion of limited forward chaining facilities. This is probably the most common structure in the PC shell market at present. Examples of this include Xi Plus and Insight 2+. In Xi Plus, a forward chaining capability is included in two ways. The first is the inclusion of special forward chaining rules, which are distinguished from the backward chaining rules both by a different name - demons - and by a different format, which is WHEN…THEN… instead of IF…THEN…. The demons are intended mainly for displaying reports and other similar actions associated with control rather than inferencing. The second is that forward chaining may take place on the normal IF…THEN… rules as well; the nature and amount of this type of forward chaining are both under the control of the system builder. The choices are:

•No forward chaining at all
•Forward chaining only on user-supplied data
•Forward chaining only on inferences made
•Forward chaining on both user-supplied data and inferences made
In the latter two cases, there is a further choice as to how far the forward chaining goes, i.e. whether the system makes inferences on inferences; the options here are:
•Single forward chaining, i.e. only one level of inference is made before forward chaining stops
•Full forward chaining, i.e. all possible inferences are made

A further development which is highly relevant to knowledge representation, although it may not appear so at first, is the ability to link to spreadsheet or database packages, to enable parts of the task which are not knowledge-based to be represented in a more appropriate way. Most PC shells now offer import and export facilities for the market-leading spreadsheet and database packages. This is less common with mini- and mainframe products, perhaps because the market for other applications is much more fragmented than for PCs.

Some of the shells available now, for example the higher-level versions of Leonardo and Personal Consultant, include the opportunity to use a frame-like knowledge representation, but these have not as yet achieved a substantial market share. Whether these should continue to be classed as shells is, of course, a moot point.

Mid-range KBS products

One of the principal distinctions between these and the shells (until the developments mentioned above) was that the mid-range products offered a choice of knowledge representation schema. In general this consists of a combination (to a varying extent) of rules, frames, and an object-oriented representation. Thus, for example, Goldworks offers rules, frames and object-oriented programming, M.1 offers frames and rules, and Nexpert Object offers rules and objects. The inferencing mechanisms of the mid-range products may also be superior, for example more sophisticated combinations of forward- and backward-chaining than in the shells.

Toolkits/environments

The toolkits have built much of their strength on permitting the KBS builder to use a variety of knowledge representation schemata and inferencing mechanisms, without being constrained to use only those facilities already provided. At the other end of the scale, the close relationship between the workstation hardware and the language LISP made it important to provide some "building blocks" for knowledge representation to avoid working in "raw" LISP. Many of the environments were specifically designed to enable object-oriented work to be carried out, this being most obvious in the name of the Xerox Corporation's LOOPS, which stands for Lisp Object-Oriented Programming System.

Access to other types of package is often constrained not so much by the toolkits themselves as by the relative lack of (for example) database packages to run on an AI workstation. This can have the drawback that the knowledge-base has to be structured to cope with items which are not really "knowledge".

Special-purpose languages

LISP and Prolog offer the KBS builder a considerable amount of flexibility, but are not always quite as general as some of their proponents would have us believe. LISP is based around a structure consisting of lists of elements, together with what is effectively a pattern matcher which can operate on these lists. This is excellent in terms of placing no restrictions on the way in which knowledge is represented, but does leave the KBS builder with the task of constructing an actual inference engine from the pattern matcher. This is easier for some types of KBS than for others, and the simple rule-based system does not seem to be the easiest! Prolog by contrast is based around a structure of statements in propositional logic, and what amounts to a built-in backward-chaining inference engine. It has the advantage over the shells that it can be made to do this "backward chaining" type of inference on much more sophisticated data structures than production rules, but can lead to difficulties when more open-ended, forward-chaining inferencing is required.

Links with other packages were originally extremely difficult to provide, but more recent versions of the special-purpose languages overcome this problem. The main restriction therefore concerns what other applications there are which run effectively on the same hardware as the KBS. A common way round the poor numerical capabilities of the early versions of Prolog is to write the Prolog compiler/interpreter in a language such as C, which may then also be used for the numerical routines.

Conventional languages

If you want to build your knowledge-base in a conventional language such as

FORTRAN or COBOL or C, you will need to write your own knowledge representation schema from scratch. This does have the benefits of complete flexibility, especially compared with products which offer only one very limited form of knowledge representation, but the extra time and effort involved may be considerable. Inferencing is also completely flexible, but possibly even more time-consuming, as few conventional languages offer the pattern-matching facilities of the special-purpose languages. A clearer benefit is the ease with which non-KBS facilities such as calculations, database access, screen handling and so on may be incorporated in the system; the precise advantages offered vary according to the particular conventional language being chosen, but interfacing with another system written in the same language is always likely to make the task relatively straightforward.

3.5 System Execution - for the Knowledge Engineer

3.5.1 Software issues

In order to construct the knowledge-base easily, the knowledge engineer needs facilities for the rapid entry and easy modification of knowledge elements; ideally, this means a high-quality, special-purpose editor. Also needed are tools which help in designing the user interface and other aspects of the KBS such as controlling a consultation.

It is also useful to be able to carry out automatic checks on the structure of the knowledge base, such as searching for conditions which there is no way of testing. In addition, explanation facilities of various kinds are often more useful to the knowledge engineer than to the user.

Application-specific products

With this type of software, the bulk of the knowledge engineering has been done by the product's vendor, so all that remains is to customize the package to your organisation, if the package permits it. Normally this consists solely of entering data, or of selecting which modules of the system are to be used. The purchasing organisation may therefore not require a knowledge engineer as such.

KBS shells

The range of facilities offered by the various shells to help the knowledge engineer is considerable. After all, one of the reasons for developing shells in the first place - at least according to those marketing them - was the hope that they would become so easy to use for system building that no knowledge engineer would be required! (The expert would produce the system.) While some experts do undoubtedly succeed in doing this, they are definitely in the minority, especially when it comes to producing systems for use by others. Nevertheless, the resulting products are certainly easy to use, especially for the inexperienced user. We have, however, found that those whose major experience is in FORTRAN or BASIC programming sometimes find the non-procedural aspects of building a rule-base in a PC shell off-putting. They feel that they are not entirely in control of the way the system operates, and indeed the existence of the inference engine means that this is true. People whose PC experience is of the spreadsheet/database type do not seem to have this problem.

Rather than attempt to outline all the shells, and which facilities they offer (an impossible task!), we shall describe the combined "best practice" of those on the market.

This includes:
> fast execution,
> full-screen editing within the shell itself,
> multiple windowing,
> ability to make global changes,
> ability to control the sequence in which items appear in the knowledge-base,
> good screen handling facilities,
> ability to keep a log of consultations.

> For rule-based systems:
> > checking for conditions which there is no way of testing,
> > for conclusions which are never used by the KBS,
> > for circular reasoning,
> > for identifiers which are never assigned a value.

> For systems dealing with uncertainty:
> > graphical representation of how one factor affects another,
> > use of different types of scale for uncertainty.

KBS shells all have built-in explanation facilities of various kinds. These are usually described as being for the benefit of the user, but as was discussed in section 2.4, they are often more useful to the knowledge engineer, especially in understanding how the inference and control mechanisms of the KBS are operating. For example, during a sample run of the system, it may be very helpful for the knowledge engineer to be able to ask the KBS how it reached a particular conclusion and to a lesser extent why it is asking for a particular input. Explanation facilities may also help the expert to understand the knowledge-base, depending on how clear the knowledge representation schema is in the first place!

Mid-range KBS products

Generally like the shells, only better! It is a debatable point, however, as to how much of the improvement over an ordinary shell is actually due to the more powerful PC hardware which most of the mid-range products require to operate at all!

Toolkits/environments

Although toolkits have great flexibility, they are not always superior to the shells and mid-range products when it comes to system execution, partly because more training/experience is required to use them effectively. They do however have many specific advantages, which include:
> Ability to edit graphs.
> Multiple windowing.
> Recall and editing of recent command sequences.
> Standard utilities and libraries.
> Explanation facilities including variable-depth tracing.
> Interrupt and restore facilities during test runs.

Many of the mid-range products offer these features to some limited extent, but where graphically-based knowledge representation schemata are used, for example semantic nets or object-oriented work, then ideally one should be able to edit either the graph or the structure from which is it made up, whichever is most appropriate. By and large this distinguishes the toolkits from the mid-range products, although no doubt this gap will continue to close in the future.

Special-purpose languages

In general the languages themselves have few advantages when it comes to system execution, it being up to the knowledge engineer to make sure that the required facilities are built in. However, LISP and Prolog each has a very specific advantage here, in certain circumstances - and here we spill over from software into hardware as well. Running LISP on a LISP workstation enables the knowledge engineer to take advantage of the power of the machine as no other software can, not only in terms of speed but because the whole system is effectively constructed around LISP. Prolog on the other hand, used in interpreted mode, offers immediate checking of statements for syntax errors as each is entered. (Note that some people regard this as a disadvantage!)

Explanation facilities are more likely to be of the "trace" type, enabling a somewhat limited approach to "how" queries. This may not be too much of a disadvantage to the knowledge engineer, but will make it very difficult for the expert to examine the computer version of the knowledge-base directly .

Conventional languages

Very efficient compilers for fast execution, especially on minis/mainframes. Otherwise, few benefits in themselves. Whoever writes the knowledge engineer's part of the KBS would be well advised to include as many of the desirable features listed under other sub-headings here as possible!

3.5.2 Hardware issues

Hardware issues include the question of delivery to multiple users, perhaps in geographically diverse locations, maybe requiring portability or the capability to function in adverse operating conditions. Together with this there is the related issue of providing run-time only versions at reduced cost, perhaps on cheaper or more readily available hardware as well. Speed of execution is also something which is far more dependent on the hardware than on the software.

PCs

For development, the PC always has an advantage in price terms. Purchase or licence costs are almost always far cheaper for one copy of the software (whichever type it is) on a PC than for a workstation or mini/mainframe. However, the limitations of memory size may cause particular problems during KBS development. These may be overcome to some extent by buying extra memory boards, but this would remove some of the cost advantage, as would any need to buy additional input or output devices such as a mouse or a colour screen to make full use of the software's facilities. Although colour screens are available for just about every kind of hardware, they are much more common on IBM-compatible PCs than on other types of hardware, and this may be another advantage from the point of view of the knowledge engineer.

A further advantage is in the portability of the KBS. Knowledge engineering sessions with the expert(s) are likely to be more successful, and system demonstrations to users or sponsors more impressive, if done on the expert's/user's territory. The widespread presence of PCs in business organisations and the possibility of the knowledge engineer bringing their own portable PC along both help to facilitate this. Note that in some cases it may be better for tests involving users or experts to take place in a "laboratory" environment, however.

Using a PC for development also makes the provision of run-time versions relatively straightforward, since there is no need for translation between packages or between operating systems.

Workstations

The sheer speed of a workstation is a considerable advantage when developing a system, especially when editing the knowledge-base, and indeed the power and control is its main advantage for the knowledge engineer. The principal disadvantages of a workstation are the price that has to be paid for the software, and that it is not always easy to move the system for demonstrations or tests.

The graphics capability of the workstation is very good, but it is more common to see workstations with monochrome screens rather than colour, and not all of the software is capable of using a colour monitor. The PC sometimes has an advantage here.

Extra work may be needed to translate the system into a run-time version, particularly if delivery is to be to multiple users. In such cases, provision of workstations and associated software for each user is likely to be prohibitively expensive, and going from the development KBS to the delivered KBS may well involve translation into a different package or language running under a different operating system on different hardware.

Minis/mainframes

Developing on a terminal-based system has clear advantages in terms of overall power and memory available, but as one user of a multi-user system the knowledge engineer may not be able to obtain as big a share of these as desired - especially at the most convenient times of the day! Delivery of the finished KBS presents no problems at all, being only a question of controlling access (this assumes that development is on the same machine which will be used for delivery - if not, then the comments made about workstations again apply).

Mainframe versions of the various types of software also tend to be more restricted in input and output methods, and the need for use of a mouse or a colour graphics terminal may pose operational problems (for example in speed of transmission) beyond those arising simply from the cost of the extra equipment.

3.6 System Execution - for the End-User

A crucial difference between this and the previous section is that there would be a fair amount of agreement between different knowledge engineers as to the desirability of the various characteristics - though not by any means in how much it would be worth paying for them! When we turn our attention to end-users, the answer is no longer true. More sophisticated facilities are not always an improvement, and in some cases may be a positive liability. In some cases, it is a matter of personal preference, and there is little point in making recommendations on those matters here.

It is not really appropriate to break this section down in sub-sections according to the types of hardware and software, because good knowledge engineers can overcome most of the limitations of their "tools". There are however some contrasts which are worth pointing out under the appropriate headings; in many cases these are not unique to KBSs.

Amongst the key considerations here are the following:

•Robustness
•Familiarity
•Explanations
•User-friendliness
•Security
•Compatibility
•Hardware failure.

Robustness

The end-users should feel that it is not possible to "break" the system accidentally. As well as applying to "normal" inputs, this should also apply to the action of special commands or key combinations.

Familiarity

The degree of similarity to other systems is likely to be very important for the end-user's initial acceptance of the KBS. Unusually in the case of KBSs, this is particularly relevant to the hardware to be used. PCs, and terminals to mainframes or minis, are both quite common. Workstations are much less common, and will thus present problems to all but a few users, especially as their keyboards are often more complex than those of PCs or terminals. If working with a clean slate, the variable speed of response of a time-sharing terminal based system may be off-putting to a new user.

Explanation facilities

"Why" type explanation facilities are likely to be useful during the initial training of an end-user, but their usefulness will decrease as familiarity with the KBS grows. There is little point in having "how" type explanation facilities for the end-user unless the end-user has some choice as to what to do with the output from the system. Thus where the KBS is operating in the assistant, critic or second opinion styles, with a reasonably well-informed user, such explanations are an advantage. However, if the KBS is operating in the expert consultant style, a "how" explanation is only useful in two cases:
- to explain the final conclusion(s)
(and in this case it might well be better to write separate reports rather than relying on the system's built-in facilities);
- when the end-user has the discretion to ignore the recommendation of the KBS (and presumably refer to some higher human authority).

User-friendliness

It is a general phenomenon in computing that the kind of menus and help windows which are very helpful to the end-user of a new system may become rather irritating when the end-user becomes more experienced. It is therefore a great help if some optional "short-cuts" are provided. In the case of a KBS, this is particularly relevant to the issue of volunteering information, or more generally enabling the end-user to have some control over the execution of the KBS. These facilities are certainly useful, but not all shells or application-specific packages allow them. A further possibility is that such facilities are only available in the developer's version of a shell but not the run-time version.

On the other hand, it may be essential in some applications, such as the granting of credit, that all factors are <u>seen</u> to have been considered. Giving the user autonomy as to the way in which the KBS is used might in such a case fall foul of the company's auditors!

A further feature useful to users at all levels of experience is the ability to store an uncompleted session with the KBS with the minimum of effort for completion at a later date. This might also enable two different types of end-user to deal with different aspects of a particular problem.

Security (1)

The knowledge in a KBS may well be valuable, either to competitors or because the KBS is a saleable product. Opinions differ on how to prevent unauthorised access. Some people feel that a single-user PC or workstation fitted with a key-operated lock is the best option. Others feel that the password protection, often at several levels, offered by a terminal-based mini- or mainframe computer is superior. It is also possible to include a password facility in a single-user KBS, and thus get the best of both worlds.

Security (2)

Appropriate back-up copies of the knowledge-base should exist and be properly stored, but except in the case of a completely bought-in application this is really the concern of the knowledge engineer rather than the end-user. How important the backing-up of data is for KBSs compared to some other types of computer system is at present an open issue. The first question is, is there any data to back up? There may not be, unless the KBS has a mechanism for logging consultations. Assuming it has one, then clearly back-ups are useful to ensure the recall of past consultations, especially incomplete ones. It may be particularly important to be able to follow the operation of a KBS working in the automaton role. A key influence on the need to maintain records of past consultations will be what is decided if and when the legal status of advice given by a KBS is determined in the law courts.

Compatibility

Ease of linking to other company systems may well be crucial if the KBS relies on external data which is frequently changing. It is important to remember that these other system are not static themselves, and so the more straightforward such procedures are, the longer the useful life of the KBS is likely to be.

Hardware failure

A hardware failure during operation can have effects of two kinds. The first is the interruption of service; is it possible to do without the KBS? If so, for how long? For an important KBS running on a PC, provision of a complete back-up hardware and software configuration might not be unreasonable. The second aspect concerns any consultation that was in progress when the system went down, and how much information is lost. This will be correspondingly more important the longer each consultation takes.

3.7 Maintenance

The need to maintain the KBS after it has been put into operation stems from three sources:

•Correction of "bugs" and inadequacies in the delivered system.
•Improvement of the functionality of the KBS.
•Compensation for "knowledge drift" over time.

Almost all improvements will need to make use of the learning system, except for aspects which are not related to the knowledge-base, for example improving minor elements of the user interface.

As in the preceding section, most of the factors which are relevant here are not specific to particular hardware or software, and can be compensated for by a skilled knowledge engineer.

Logging KBS consultations

Straightforward "bugs", i.e. clear failures of the KBS to perform as intended, should be relatively easy to recognise and thus report. There is no difference in this respect between a KBS and any other type of computer system. On the other hand, inadequacies (cases where the KBS makes a poor or puzzling recommendation) may be harder to recognise, especially with an unskilled end-user. It is helpful if the KBS is able to keep a log of consultations; this has already been pointed out as an advantage in development.

Can the users update the knowledge-base themselves?

This must in practice be linked to the question "should the end-users update the knowledge-base themselves?". Clearly, where several people use different copies of the same KBS for the same task, this would not be sensible. On the other hand, it offers the possibility of compensating for "knowledge drift" and also of allowing some degree of customisation to the needs of a particular person. This is a particularly important question in cases where the delivered KBS could be a "run only" version of the development system, where adding this option may involve a considerable cost increase.

If end-users are to perform some updating of the knowledge-base themselves, it is vital that they are only allowed to update what is within their competence. Thus it might be reasonable to allow even a very inexpert end-user to change a well-defined "chunk" of knowledge - effectively giving a new value to a parameter. However, only a fairly expert end-user should be permitted to make changes which alter the conclusions which the KBS draws from a given set of data.

Interaction between the learning system and the one in practical operation

If the learning system is not automated, then this revolves round the knowledge engineer, who must ensure that the KBS is modified as and when necessary, with appropriate procedures both for recognising when changes are needed and for delivering updated versions of the KBS to end-users. If there is an automated learning system within the KBS, there is still a considerable management problem associated with it. The knowledge-base must be amended sufficiently often that it does not become out-of-date, but a system which is changed so often that the end-users have absolutely no idea what to expect by way of a pattern of operation is likely to produce a very negative reaction.

3.8 Summary

In this chapter we have looked at the structure of a knowledge-based system, using as our model a stand-alone KBS. We have also looked at the various types of hardware and software which might be used for building a KBS, at the general issues involved, and at some of the more specific pros and cons of the various possible hardware and software choices. Similar considerations will apply to embedded or integrated KBSs, but issues relating to the links between the KBS and the related conventional computer systems will be correspondingly more important.

References

(BERRY87) D.C.Berry and D.E.Broadbent, "Expert Systems and the Man-Machine Interface-Part Two: The User Interface", *Expert Systems*, Vol. 4, No. 1, pp.18-27, February 1987.

(EIKE86) D.R.Eike, S.A.Fleger and E.R.Phillips, "User Interface Design Guidelines for Expert Troubleshooting Systems", *Proceedings of the Human Factors Society 30th Annual Meeting,* Dayton, Ohio, pp.1024-1028, 1986.

(FORS89) Richard Forsyth (Ed.), *"Machine Learning: principles and techniques",* Chapman and Hall, 1989.

(MIN75) M.L.Minsky, "A Framework for Representing Knowledge", pp.211-277 in *The Psychology of Computer Vision*, (Ed. P.H.Winston), McGraw-Hill, 1975.

Chapter 4: Conventional Software Engineering

4.0 Introduction

As indicated in chapter one, our perspective in this book is an applications-driven one. The history of computing owes many of its advances to an applications-driven viewpoint, but probably rather more to a theory- or technology-driven viewpoint...and also some to the business-driven viewpoint of vendors of information technology products. At times different, competing, developments have arisen from two different perspectives more or less simultaneously. Whether competing or not, it is undoubtedly true that there are at least two different views of conventional software engineering, usually referred to as "formal methods" and "structured" or "semi-formal" methods respectively. It is certainly tempting to associate formal methods with a "theoretical" viewpoint, since its most visible proponents tend to be academics in computer science departments, and structured methods with an "applications" viewpoint, since its most visible supporters are practitioners in DP departments. However, it is misleading to see this purely as an academics *v.* practitioners or theory *v.* practice division, since both schools of thought contain both their theoreticians and their practitioners.

Whatever is the case regarding the backgrounds of software engineering developments, it certainly is true that a 1988 survey of large DP departments in the UK showed that:

- Over 60% were using one of the semi-formal or structured methods such as SSADM, LSDM, *MODUS* etc..

- Around 5% were using formal methods.

- Around 30% were using no systematic methods at all.

When we look at smaller systems, especially the "departmental PC" revolution, many systems appear to be created by little more than iterative hacking, as in the classic (?) prototyping model. There is more structure in this mess than there appears to be and, in some parts of the computing world at least, the management of prototyping is accomplished successfully. The best example of this is the case of decision support systems (DSSs), where many of the theoreticians in the field see iterative, evolutionary development as paramount in order for the DSS to achieve its objective(s).

Perhaps the most significant point about conventional software engineering is that the term "software engineering" was deliberately coined in order to give an impression of reliability similar to that evoked - at least for some people- by other engineering disciplines. The credit is usually given to Professor Tony Hoare, who suggested the term at a 1968 conference under the auspices of NATO. This was in response to a profession (perhaps a craft would be a more accurate term) which had earned a reputation for delivering projects incomplete, after time and over budget. Twenty years on, the formal methods school to which Hoare has always belonged is probably not the one which most DP professionals would associate with the term software engineering (although the answers given by academics might be different), and the complaints levelled against those who build computer systems have not changed substantially. In this chapter, we shall discuss some aspects of "conventional" computer systems design. First however, we need to look at the relevance of these approaches to KBSs.

4.1 Why Are Structured Development Methods Relevant to KBSs?

The discussion of operational KBSs in section 2.3 showed that relatively few KBSs are in operational use. The great majority of KBSs built so far have been of an experimental or prototypical nature. In addition, those KBSs which are in fully operational use are mainly small, stand-alone systems which do not interact with other computer systems.

It follows that most writers on KBS development are from an academic or R&D environment, taking what we have called an exploratory perspective, and few of them have considered the need for KBSs intended for operational use to be built to the standards expected in conventional DP systems. Their research background also means they are frequently unfamiliar with conventional DP practices.

If we look at the objectives of using structured engineering methods in commercial data processing systems design (DPSD), we find a general consensus that structured methods are expected to provide the following advantages:

94

- *Control* - the ability to plan, schedule and run a DPSD project according to a fixed budget, and to meet precise delivery targets.
- *Accuracy* - the ability to build a system which will function in detail in an agreed manner.
- *Robustness* - the ability to build a system which will continue to function, even when users do not interact with it in precisely the expected manner.
- *Reliability* - the ability to continue to function on a 24 hour basis, where required, or to be able to be shutdown and re-started in a predictable way.
- *Maintainability* - the ability to add functionality to the system after it is operational, and to fix problems easily where they arise.

This is not a complete list of desirable attributes to be expected from the use of a structured methodology, but is intended to give an idea of what should be expected from an engineering approach. One particular additional attribute which some regard as vitally important in safety-critical systems is *Certification* - the ability to guarantee that the system will perform as desired by the client(s). Others regard this as unattainable; discussion of this topic is beyond the scope of this book.

In our view, all of the attributes mentioned, including certification, may be just as relevant to KBSs as they are to DP systems, although not necessarily to the same degree.

Others have identified similar requirements for KBSs. Although not referring specifically to KBSs, Partridge (PART86a) identified the need to build *practical AI software.*

> "...if we intend to push on with our AI programs into the harsher world of applications software, we will require all of the usual desiderata of practical software:
> (1) perceptual clarity;
> (2) robustness;
> (3) reliability;
> (4) maintainability." (Page 130.)

Similarly, Ford (FORD86) commented on the lack of a methodology for practical AI software.

"AI has yet to evolve a methodology suited to the production of practical software, largely because most AI software has been of an experimental nature, and thus not developed in a disciplined way to satisfy the needs of users, managers, and others one phase downstream in the lifecycle, but also because it has been unable to draw from the methodological foundations provided by SE." (Page 263.)

Our view is that in terms of the attributes listed above, operational KBSs should be regarded as simply a particular type of computer system. This is especially true if future KBSs are to be integrated more fully with existing DP systems. It therefore follows that KBSs should meet the same operational standards already expected in the commercial and industrial environment. Furthermore, since structured methods of software engineering are the most widely established means, at present, of attaining the desired operational standards in conventional DP systems, then it is reasonable to propose that similar engineering methods should be employed in the development of KBSs. This proposition suggests that the following key question be addressed:

To what extent are existing conventional structured methods appropriate to the development of an operational KBS?

This initial question points to two further areas of investigation:

What are the essential differences between DP and KB systems, particularly in relation to the methods used for their construction?

And, if there *are* significant differences:

How does the conventional life-cycle development model need to be adapted to meet the particular needs of KBS construction, and the general requirements of KBSs built to commercial and industrial operational standards?

4.2 The Conventional Systems Development Life-cycle (SDLC) and Formal Methods

4.2.1 The conventional SDLC

There are many versions of the conventional SDLC, and a detailed discussion of their various merits would occupy the whole of the remainder of this book, if not more. However, there are considerable similarities between all of them, particularly the division into a series of separate phases, with identifiable "change-over" points between the phases.

Our description here is chosen as a compromise between one of the many "standard" descriptions (the one which we first learned) and the SDLC used by our collaborators on the *Intellipse* project, BIS Applied Systems.

In this description, the SDLC comprises 6 phases:

- Feasibility and requirements definition
- Analysis
- Design
- Implementation
- Testing
- Maintenance

Feasibility and requirements definition

The system developers, working in consultation with those commissioning the system and its intended users (who may be two different groups of people), establish the general tasks which the system is intended to perform, and constraints (budgetary, time, etc.) on its production. This may involve some study of existing manual or computer systems. The outcome of this phase should include:

- terms of reference
- an analysis of the functional system
- a summary of the requirement for the information system (IS) (N.B. These are "output" requirements in the users' terms)
- an outline description of the proposed IS
- estimates of costs, benefits and timescales

Analysis

The requirements definition established in the preceding phase is used as the basis for constructing a more detailed description (usually called a specification) of the functionality of the system. This is achieved by modelling the relevant areas of business activity. Analysis concentrates on the movement, storage and retrieval of data, and on the processes to be carried out on the data so that the required output from the activity is achieved. Tools for this include flow charts, data flow diagrams, structured English, etc. Figure 4.1 shows a simple example of a data flow diagram, relating to sales of books.

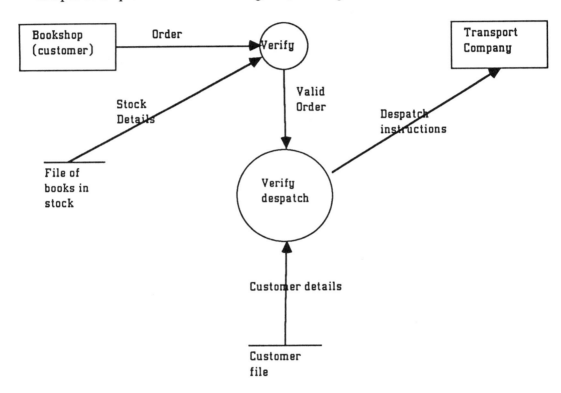

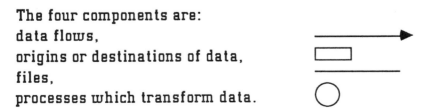

The four components are:
data flows,
origins or destinations of data,
files,
processes which transform data.

Figure 4.1: Example of a data flow diagram

Design

The specification produced in the analysis phase is used to construct the complete system, including all the details of programs, files, records etc. Design concentrates on logical and physical file structures and the processes which access them. One commonly used technique is entity-relationship analysis, or one of the many variants of it, e.g. in our book example, entities might include AUTHOR, BOOK, PUBLISHER, INVOICE and WAREHOUSE, with relationships such as BOOK WRITTEN-BY AUTHOR.

Implementation

The detailed design is turned into executable code, using whatever computer language is appropriate. Provisional versions of documentation, manuals and training material will also need to be produced at this phase, though like the code itself they may require amendment as a result of the testing process.

Testing

This process takes place at several levels. This includes testing of the individual modules or units making up the system, testing the system as a whole, testing the system under normal and unusual conditions, hands-on testing by the intended end-users, etc. The "full system" tests will also be a test of documentation, operating procedures, etc. as well as the computerised part of the system.

Maintenance

This consists of making sure that the system runs in operational use and continues to do so for as long as is required. It includes correcting any errors which have remained undetected so far, improving the implementation of system modules where this is possible, and enhancing the functionality of the system where this is desired by the clients/users. It should be the longest of all the phases in the life-cycle as far as elapsed time is concerned. This does not however mean that it should also be the longest as far as person-hours of work is concerned, too. This can often happen when systems are developed by *ad hoc* methods, and gives the DP manager severe problems with regard to motivating staff.

Whichever of the various structured life-cycle approaches is used, the purpose of structured methods is the same: to reduce the overall cost and effort involved in developing and running a computer system. This is achieved partly by introducing the structure as outlined above in order to cope with the complexity, and partly by shifting resources from maintenance and post-implementation testing to the earlier phases of the process. Standards (to help co-ordinate the work of different people) and explicit milestones (for project management) are two crucial elements in achieving the control necessary.

4.2.2 Formal methods

We have already indicated in section 4.0 that the use of semi-formal or structured methods is much more common than the use of formal methods. We shall therefore devote relatively little space to formal methods here.

Essentially, the objective of using a formal method to specify a computer system is to improve the process of going from the agreed specification of the system to a machine-executable version of that system, by providing better means of checking for errors and by avoiding the introduction of further errors. This is (in part) achieved by producing the specification in a notation which is mathematically valid. Amongst the advantages this gives are that some of the transformations by which the code is produced from the specification may be carried out automatically, and that it may be possible to produce a rigorous proof that a program meets its specification. The advantages of this are clear, especially in safety-critical applications. The disadvantage is that it is not possible to produce such a formal specification in English, or indeed any other natural language. It is therefore necessary to use a specially-designed notation for the specification, of which the best-known is probably Z. Much work has been done on notations and languages for formal system specification, but in terms of practical usage this approach seems at present to be suitable for only a limited range of applications, such as those in the safety-critical area already mentioned, and in defence. Even in these it is not always possible to cover all aspects of the system to be specified.

4.3 Extensions to the SDLC

Most of the criticisms of the conventional SDLC as a method for conventional software engineering centre on two areas:

•The unrealistic nature of the clear-cut division between phases.
•The assumption that the process starts out from a precise and unchanging set of requirements.

These criticisms are often combined in a general dismissal of the classical

SDLC as too idealised, and perhaps too academic, to be of much practical value to data processing departments.

Probably the best overview of the criticisms of the SDLC and some of the proposed remedies for them is given in the tutorial volume edited by Agresti (AGRE86). Many of the proposed "new paradigms for information system development" are based on some form of rapid prototyping. In this and succeeding sections we look at some of the more interesting developments.

One of the most completely described alternatives to the conventional SDLC is Barry Boehm's spiral model (BOEHM88), which expands the SDLC into a number of development cycles in which the system is gradually produced. Boehm describes this model of development as risk-driven, whereas the conventional SDLC is document- or code-driven, so that the greatest attention at any point is given to those aspects of the system which have the greatest design risk. These aspects are then looked at in considerable detail, while low-risk aspects are not considered in detail until a later phase, at which the effort for such choices is available. The spiral model has been used in practice for developing complex software products by the company for which Boehm works. It includes several outputs labelled "prototypes"; we will come back to the spiral model after the next section.

Gladden (GLAD82) was particularly unhappy about the initial requirements being neither complete nor fixed. He proposed the extensive use of mock-ups and demonstrations in order to overcome the problem of obtaining a satisfactory set of requirements. Thus, starting from the system objectives, which he believes are less likely to change than the requirements, hardware and software "mock-ups" would be produced to enable the users to determine their requirements (more) precisely. He even suggests that this might go further to include live scenarios, i.e. actors playing out the human part of the way in which the new computer plus human system would function. This actually goes back beyond the start of most versions of the SDLC, which is not necessarily a bad thing! In chapter 5 we will suggest alternative ways of attempting to achieve the same results.

4.4 Prototyping for Decision Support Systems

We do not have to look very far to find another area of computer systems development (apart from KBSs) in which the use of the conventional SDLC is the exception rather than the rule. The area known as Decision Support Systems (DSSs) is one. DSSs grew up during the 1970s as a result of, amongst other things, the widespread introduction of interactive, as opposed to batch, computing facilities and the coming of the VDU. The arrival of the business micro-computer in the early 1980s provided further impetus for DSS development.

The basic idea of a DSS is to support a human decision-maker by providing a flexible, easy to use and adaptive tool for data analysis and modelling. The emphasis is on support because the DSS is aimed at tasks whose structure is not well enough understood for a decision-making system to be feasible. Thus the users of the system are typically in management positions, whereas for many conventional DP systems clerical personnel form the majority of hands-on users.

A particular feature of a DSS, which some authors would use as one of its defining properties, is that its development is evolutionary. At first sight, this would appear to rule out the use of the conventional SDLC completely as, if the system is evolving, there cannot be a requirements definition to work from; this isn't quite the case, as we shall see later.

This evolutionary process of DSS development, also known as iterative design or prototyping, usually goes along the following lines (for simplicity, here we assume a single end-user):

1. Initial investigation by the end-user and the DSS developer. As well as establishing a working relationship and defining the broad area in which decision support is required, this investigation aims to identify a small sub-system as the first part of the DSS to be built. It should address a part of the decision problem which is of high interest to the end-user, and for which the nature of the computer-based support required is clear.

2. Build the DSS to meet the need identified in (1), with an emphasis on simplicity and usability. For this small system, it is the equivalent of the analysis, design, implementation and testing phases of the conventional SDLC, carried out as rapidly as possible without any formal division into phases and with the involvement of the end-user throughout.

3. The end-user and the developer evaluate the system. Any changes, corrections or enhancements to be made are identified.

4. Carry out these changes/corrections/enhancements, again using the rapid analysis, design, implementation and testing approach outlined in (2). Return to step (3).

The iteration around phases (2),(3), and (4) continues until a reasonably stable system has been achieved. Note that as there is no final "stopping criterion", the process can never be said to be finished. Some regard this as a virtue in terms of flexibility, others as a disaster in terms of an open-ended commitment to the use of resources!

Although it is impossible with an evolutionary approach to have a precise statement of requirements at the outset, it should be possible to make some progress towards such a goal, while still retaining flexibility. A reasonable analogy is with conducting survey interviews. Where the topic on which opinions are being sought is well-structured, a questionnaire ("precise statement of requirements") may be used. Alternatively, for a topic involving more wide-ranging concepts, the interviewer may have a list of topics which need to be covered, and perhaps some standard prompts to help "steer" the interview, but nothing more precise than that.

On the basis of this philosophy, Sprague and Carlson (SPRA82) developed a framework for systems analysis and design for DSSs called the ROMC Approach. This stands for Representations, Operations, Memory Aids and Control Mechanisms. It is *process-independent*, i.e. concentrating on what the system should do in terms of the generic tasks involved, rather than the details of how it should do it, which is in contrast to the flowcharts typical of conventional systems analysis. (It's also in tune with the 4GL philosophy, therefore.)

Representations

These should match the way in which the decision-maker thinks about the problem concerned; if a map is normally used, the computer representation should look like a map. Other possibilities include lists, graphs, reports and statistical analyses.

Operations

What operations are to be done using the system? These might include: gather data, generate reports, choose between alternatives.

Memory aids

What will the DSS do to help the decision-maker remember/focus on the features of the decision at hand? As well as the "obvious" such as databases and workspaces, this heading also includes such devices as triggers, flags and special views.

Control mechanisms

How can the user decision-maker "steer" the human/DSS combination effectively? Apart from human interface considerations such as the use of menus (especially for new users), and short-cuts such as the use of function keys, this might also include the use of standard conventions (to help with rarely-used facilities). Perhaps most important of all, training comes under this heading; a DSS cannot be effective if it is not used.

As with the interviewing example, it is important to note that the ROMC approach leaves much more scope for negotiation about detail - and perhaps even the filling-in of detail by the user - than the equivalent phases of the conventional SDLC.

4.5 Prototyping for Non-DSSs

Since the rise of prototyping for DSSs, there are now several authors who also recommend the use of some kind of rapid prototyping for developing conventional systems. Often this goes hand in hand with the use of 4th generation tools or languages to construct the system. It is important to realise, however, that rapid prototyping may have more than one meaning. The *evolutionary* prototyping which we described in the previous section is not the only possible use of prototyping. The alternative, which in fact pre-dates the evolutionary approach, is usually called *throwaway* prototyping. Here the initial phase is very similar to evolutionary prototyping phases (1) and (2) as in the previous section, but once the prototype has been used to produce a kind of "animated specification", it is thrown away, and the final system is designed from scratch. The prototypes in Boehm's spiral model are mainly of the throwaway type, except for the last one, which is intended to be evolutionary, and this is quite clear. However, some authors do confuse the two uses of prototyping. This is perhaps once again because they are writing from an exploratory perspective; this means that actually building the final system is not a high priority in the work, and the difference between the two types of prototyping is correspondingly smaller.

Misconceptions notwithstanding, most of the authors recommending the use of rapid prototyping for systems similar to conventional DP systems mean throwaway prototyping. Effectively they are aiming to tackle the same weakness in the conventional SDLC, i.e. producing the initial statement of requirements, as Gladden (see section 4.3), but in a very different way. This use of prototyping to identify user-requirements accurately was summed up well by Carey and Mason (CAR83):

> "Prototypes...attempt to present the user with a realistic view of the system as it will eventually appear. With prototypes a distinct attempt is made to produce a 'specification' which users can directly experience. Communication with users, particularly the non-specialist middle management user, is a major motivator behind the recent interest in prototypes." (Page 49.)

The use of prototyping in DPSD for the purpose described by Carey and Mason is closely analogous to techniques used in civil engineering. For example, when a new building is being designed, the developers often build scale models to help finalise the design, and satisfy interested parties that the proposed structure will blend in appropriately with its surroundings. This is particularly interesting given our earlier remarks on how the term software engineering came to be chosen! Note also that the model to be "thrown away" is a scale model, and cannot actually be transformed into the real system by any evolutionary process.

Many of the more recent advocates of rapid prototyping see it as an area of potential application for AI tools and techniques, this being the opposite of our main concern here. For example, Dunning (DUNN85) proposed the use of expert systems for supporting the rapid prototyping of conventional software, using LISP-based tools to animate the specifications and designs of conventional systems. He is clearly interested in throwaway prototyping, since he points out that it is likely that the LISP-based prototype will need to be re-implemented in a conventional language before an operational system is obtained.

Ince (INCE88) suggested that the use of AI languages could greatly facilitate the prototyping of conventional software. He proposed that a set of user requirements could be expressed as *production rules* (see section 3.1.1), and the rules coded into Prolog, allowing the user-specification to be demonstrated very quickly. Ince cited the development by the accountants Arthur Andersen, in Chicago, of a system for accounting for the movement of equipment from one oil lease to another. The requirements for the system were very complex and an expert system shell was used to build up a prototype specification of the system incrementally, which allowed the users to check that the system was behaving correctly in different situations. The ES model of the design was subsequently used to build and test a conventional implementation of the accounting system.

4.6 Contrasting Features of DP and KB System Development

Two authors who have considered the differences between KBS and DP system development are Waterman (WAT86) and Gervarter (GERV83). Table 4.1 illustrates Waterman's view of the differences between knowledge engineering and data processing, while Table 4.2 shows Gervarter's comparison of AI with "conventional computer programming".

Knowledge engineering	Data Processing
Representation and use of knowledge	Representations and use of data
Heuristic	Algorithmic
Inferential process	Repetitive process
Effective manipulation of large knowledge bases	Effective manipulation of large data bases

Table 4.1: Comparison of knowledge engineering and data processing

Artificial Intelligence	Conventional Computer Programming
Primarily symbolic processes	Often primarily numeric
Heuristic search (solution steps implicit)	Algorithmic (solution steps explicit)
Control structure usually separate from domain knowledge	Information and control integrated together
Usually easy to modify, update and enlarge	Difficult to modify
Some incorrect answers often tolerable	Correct answers required
Satisfactory answers usually acceptable	Best possible solution usually sought

(from GERV83)

Table 4.2: Comparison of AI and conventional computer programming

106

Partridge (PART86b) and Ford (FORD86), whom we mentioned in section 4.1, have analysed the differences between AI and software engineering problems regarding their nature and their methods, respectively. Their conclusions may be summarized as follows.

Software engineering problems tend to be static, context-free and to have "answers" or "solutions" which can be assessed as correct or incorrect. They are completely specifiable, and the system's functionality may be defined in abstract terms. Correspondingly, the methods and tools of software engineering are suited to problems that can be characterized as having reliable, static data for which the problem solution space is small.

AI problems tend to be dynamic, context-sensitive and to have "answers" which can be judged as being adequate or inadequate. The problems are not completely specifiable, and definitions of the system's functionality relate to its performance of the task. Thus AI techniques have been developed to deal with a situation corresponding to problems with unreliable and dynamic data, which usually imply a much larger solution space than for software engineering problems.

In our view, however, this comparison is based on the *ideal* of software engineering using formal methods, which differs somewhat from the *reality* of DPSD in the current commercial environment. This point is discussed again later in the chapter.

The authors we have mentioned have mainly focused on *what* the differences are between problems addressed by AI and those approached using conventional techniques, and they are in general agreement about the nature of those differences. The following analysis concentrates on *how* the construction of commercial DP systems differs from current KBS development practices, in relation to the six key phases in the conventional development life-cycle as described in section 4.2. Inevitably, there is some repetition here of points made earlier in the chapter. However, we feel this is essential in order to present a coherent argument. In addition, it should be noted that most versions of the SDLC are at their weakest in the first (feasibility) phase, and provide little or no support for deciding whether it is even worth detailed consideration of building a system at all. This is another vital difference between a KBS and a DP system, since there is much more to be done "before the start" of the life-cycle for a KBS.

Feasibility and requirements definition: how much? *v.* is it possible?

The technology used in building typical DP applications, such as airline booking or credit card management systems, is almost always well established. The balance of debate at the feasibility phase is not concerned with the technical possibility of building the proposed system, but with the time required to build it and the consequent cost. DP projects are often - even now - concerned with computerisation of existing manual systems. It is generally an implicit assumption that there will be no intrinsic difficulty in analysing and understanding the manual system, prior to the formal specification of a computer-based alternative. The feasibility study for a KBS must, as for a DP system, address issues of cost and estimated development time. However, other questions which will need to be addressed are quite distinct:

(i) Problem selection The initial problem analysis will need to consider whether conventional solutions have been adequately considered. As areas in which a KBS may be suitable are currently less well understood than those suitable for conventional DP systems, and probably inherently more complex, this is likely to be orders of magnitude more difficult for KBSs than for conventional systems. The existing "system" may simply be the human expert. An attempt must be made to classify the complexity of the problem. For example, how much common sense reasoning is involved and how long does the expert usually take to solve the problem? The availability and expected co-operation of the experts must be estimated. Building a KBS with an uncooperative and/ or elusive expert will be impossible. An initial technical assessment of the expert's knowledge and expertise will be necessary, in order to establish whether the available knowledge representation formalisms will be able to cope with the problem.

(ii) Human factors The importance of human factors in KBS development has already been discussed in sections 2.4.3, 3.1.3 and 3.6. In particular, the need to define the prospective users of a KBS was identified. Having characterised as accurately as possible, during the feasibility phase, the users of the proposed KBS, it will be easier during the design phase to take account of human factors when specifying the user-interface for the system. The intention of building a KBS may be to allow non-experts to perform at a similar level of competence to that of experts in some specific domain. It is essential therefore that the user-interface within the system is tailored as closely as possible to the prospective users. In a conventional DP project, it is rare to give much consideration to the issue of human factors and user-interfaces. This is because the scope for tailoring the interface in a DP system is constrained by the limited facilities

available on the "dumb terminals" used in most mainframe computer installations. Also, wider human-organisational factors in relation to a new DP system are normally dealt with at a management level, separate from that of the DP department. The lack of involvement of users in the design of computer systems generally has been criticised by several authors (MUM87), (LAND87), (CORD89). They point out that this lack of involvement is often responsible for subsequent problems in the operation of some DP systems. These problems have become particularly acute with the advent of "less conventional" systems such as decision support systems. In this case the hands-on users are typically managers rather than clerical staff, and they are accordingly less likely to be willing to adjust their working practices to fit those the system demands or favours. It is worth noting that a participative design method devised by Enid Mumford for conventional systems, called ETHICS (Effective Technical and Human Implementation of Computer-based Systems) was used in the development of DEC's successful XSEL KBS. This is described in the book "XSEL's Progress" by Mumford and Bruce MacDonald of DEC (MUM89).

(iii) Performance objectives A DP system can have a precisely specified set of output requirements or transactions. It is unlikely that the performance of a KBS can be as easily circumscribed. Indeed, such a specification is likely to be difficult even for a DSS. Although the "combinatorial explosion" associated with many AI systems is often avoided in a KBS, it may not be possible at the commencement of the project to state a semi-formal, closed set of requirements. Some of the requirements may have to be stated in terms of the performance expected from the system. For example, a knowledge-based classification system for analysing rock samples may be specified in terms of the correlation between the system's performance, when used by a 'non-expert', as compared with analysis of the same rocks by an expert. The use of a performance-based requirements statement can also, therefore, serve as a basis for testing a KBS. An example of specifying and testing a KBS for university admissions, using correlation between expert and KBS performance, is discussed in Edwards and Bader (EDW88).

(iv) Prototyping It can be seen from the discussion so far that the nature of KBS construction, particularly the lack of a transaction processing-style statement of requirements, means that it is difficult at the feasibility phase to be as certain about development costs as is possible with a conventional DP project. The history of software project estimation in conventional DP shows that, even with a detailed statement of requirements, accurate forecasting of development effort is frequently an illusory target. Building a small-scale prototype (intended for "throwaway" use) of the proposed KBS can be an effective way of

assessing the feasibility and likely development costs of a full-scale version of the system. A successful prototype can also serve as an *active*, semi-formal specification for an operational system, since users and managers can use the prototype to ensure that the desired functionality and usability of the system have been accurately identified. However, the scope and methods for a prototyping exercise must be clearly defined. A successful small system at the feasibility phase can lead to the continuation of prototyping, in an evolutionary manner, towards an operational system. But the latter approach is unlikely to yield reliable or maintainable software. In conventional DP, it is very unusual to throw away existing code. Therefore the likelihood that a prototype built as part of a feasibility exercise may be subsequently discarded needs to be stated, and budgeted for, at the outset of the feasibility phase in KBS development.

(v) Hard and soft analysis Judgements about the desirability or appropriateness of building a KBS, in relation to the estimated financial or other benefits which may accrue to the organisation, using the system, are not discussed in this section. This type of soft analysis is essential to any proposed computer system project and usually takes place prior to any decision to build a system. This is a difficult task in most situations where a KBS, might be appropriate, and in the next chapter we shall be looking at some ways of accomplishing it. Our discussion in this section is confined to the hard design phase, after the judgement on whether to build a computer system has been made. However, a question that arises when building a KBS, which the KBS developer should address if possible, is: how successful is the expert in solving problems in the application domain? This will be discussed below in the sub-section on testing.

Analysis: data analysis *v.* task analysis

The main part of a conventional DP project (especially as some versions of the life-cycle would have it) begins with an analysis of the existing manual or computerised system, if there is one. The objective is to produce an accurate, semi-formal model of the business activity being studied. This model is concerned with identifying the data required by the activity, the movement, storage and retrieval of that data, and the processes to be carried out on the data, such that the desired outputs from the activity are achieved. Whereas conventional analysis requires the examination of clerical operations and procedures, KBS task analysis is concerned with the problem-solving activity of human experts. The fulcrum for conventional analysis is the *data*; the fulcrum for KBS task analysis is the *expert*.

Formal techniques, such as Codd's relational model, have been developed to support conventional data analysis (CODD70). Relational analysis has its roots in mathematical set theory and its correct application can produce a rigorous formal model. Well established formal techniques for analysing the cognitive activity of an expert, who is solving a problem, do not exist as yet. Also, while conventional data analysis can be done largely by external observation of business procedures, KBS task analysis requires a much more intimate involvement with the expert. We shall reflect further on the use of existing analysis techniques for KBSs in chapter 6.

As well as modelling the expert's knowledge, the analysis phase during KBS construction may need to include a further analysis of prospective users of the KBS, in addition to that carried out during the feasibility phase.

Design: complexity of size *v*. complexity of representation

Many of the complexities which arise in DP design are due to scale. The use of structured methods to develop the system specification can lead to large quantities of documentation, covering every aspect of a project, from analysis through to coding. The volume of documentation, and the need to link individual items of documentation together, mean that documentation management is a major headache. But the problem is one of management rather than understanding.

Large knowledge bases may also present problems of scale. However, in KBS design, complexity mainly arises because of the need to analyse cognitive activity, represent human expertise in a structured form and formalise ill-defined problems, processes and solutions. The problems of knowledge representation are very complex. The data structures employed in a conventional DP system will not be rich enough for the requirements of a KBS. On the other hand, the representation structures commonly used in AI - such as objects, frames or production rules (see section 3.1.1) - are themselves only crude approximations to the knowledge structures apparently employed in human intelligence. In addition, the sophisticated inferencing techniques employed by an expert must be modelled using more restrictive mechanisms, such as forward or backward chaining (see section 3.1.2).

The main tasks during the design phase of a DP system are concerned with defining logical and physical file structures and specifying the logical and physical processes which must access these files. The main output of this phase is a set of detailed specifications for programs which, when executed in conjunction with the data files defined, will generate the output required by the system specification. The design phase for a KBS may also require the generation of program specifications for conventional software components. In addition, it will be necessary to devise an executable knowledge representation schema and inferencing structure, which can adequately model the expert's activity.

Implementation: program debugging *v.* iterative refinement

In the traditional *waterfall* model (BOEHM76), (AGRE86), the development phases are executed sequentially. The implications of design decisions made in the early phases are not reviewed until the code has been executed much later in the development cycle. The waterfall model assumes that, by the time the implementation (coding) phase is reached, the analysis and design phases are complete. The main objective of the latter two phases is to generate a set of program specifications, which are complete with respect to a set of requirements for the system. Any iteration at this stage should simply be between program coding and program de-bugging. According to the model, after the analysis and design phases have been completed the de-bugged programs should meet user requirements without further modification.

Theory and practice in conventional DP systems development have a habit of diverging. The delay between taking a design decision and reviewing its implications often leads to expensive mistakes, since errors made early in the design cycle, but not discovered until later, can be very costly in development time to rectify (BOEHM76). Validation of early design decisions through rapid iteration between design and implementation phases, via the animation of prototype designs, is not encompassed in the traditional waterfall life-cycle. This weakness in the model has led to amended versions being suggested and, in particular, to proposed life-cycle models based on some form of prototyping, as discussed earlier in the chapter.

Even if the linear waterfall development model is sometimes appropriate for conventional systems, KBS construction must include a strategy for incremental development. The waterfall model needs to be revised to accommodate iteration between the various development phases, since in KBS development a significant amount of iteration during analysis, design and coding will be necessary in order to identify, specify and represent the range of problem-types and special cases, which the expert can solve in the application domain. It may be necessary to animate intermediate designs of the system, in order to facilitate validation of the analysis and design by the expert and prospective user. This is why prototyping techniques are particularly relevant to KBS development -

especially during the feasibility phase. The prototyping process can be a very useful method of attaining the desired performance objectives for a KBS. The crucial point is that this iterative process is managed as part of a developmental model which ensures that the requirements of reliability, robustness and maintainability are met.

Testing: acceptance testing *v.* validation of performance

In DP, acceptance testing is designed to establish whether the system meets the set of user requirements agreed by developers and users at the start of the project. The developers are primarily concerned with building a system which meets those requirements. It is the users or owners of the system who must judge the extent to which the specified system will meet the wider, business objectives which prompted the desire to build the system in the first place.

In KBS development, since we are modelling specific human-cognitive activities, developers must be concerned with the performance of the system beyond the purely mechanical replication of certain requirements. Not only must the system be tested to establish whether it successfully models that part of the expert's activity, which it was designed to duplicate or support, but, if practical, an attempt must also be made to validate the performance of the expert in the application domain. For example, where experts with conflicting opinions have been involved in the construction of an operational KBS, the problem owner must arbitrate and decide, on the basis of the desired business objectives, how the KBS should operate. The whole issue of evaluating a KBS, including testing, is considered at much greater length in chapter 8.

Maintenance: bug fixing *v.* knowledge-base upkeep

Maintenance in DP is often a euphemism used to describe the process by which delivered systems are gradually adapted to remove obvious bugs in the software and to add essential functionality which was not envisaged (or at least, not included) at the time the system specification was finalised. Maintenance can absorb a large proportion of the life-time costs of an operational DP system; estimates are usually over 50%, and run as high as 80%.

In KBS development the use of prototyping during the feasibility phase and the animation of intermediate designs may avoid some of the typical problems requiring maintenance. Of course, software bugs may also be present in a KBS and will have to be rectified. However, unlike a conventional system, a KBS is modelling human expertise in a specific domain. Very few fields involving experts remain static; the domain of medical treatment has already been mentioned as a good example. The knowledge-bases and inference mechanisms inside a KBS will have to be continually under review to ensure that the system does not become outmoded because of "knowledge drift". (This was the reason why we included a learning system as part of our standard KBS structure in chapter 3.)

This analysis has identified some key differences between DP and KB systems development. One of the most significant differences is the importance of prototyping throughout the KBS development life-cycle.

4.7 Prototyping in KBS Development

The objectives of prototyping in KBS development, identified in the analysis above, can be summarised as follows:

- To establish the technical feasibility of acquiring and representing the expert's knowledge in machine form, and to illustrate the key functional requirements expected of the system.

- To aid the evaluation and validation of the machine-based rule-bases, using the expert and problem owner as arbiters.

- To help specify the user-interface by animating possible designs.

- To evaluate and validate the inferencing mechanisms chosen for the system.

- To ensure the range of problem types addressed by the expert are covered by the KBS.

4.8 Summary

In this chapter we have reviewed conventional software engineering, particularly semi-formal methods and those based on the conventional SDLC. We have also considered the use of prototyping, both for conventional DP systems and for Decision Support Systems. Our main conclusions are that there are significant differences between KBSs and conventional systems which make the use of prototyping in KBS development extremely desirable, as long as it is properly managed and controlled.

References

(AGRE86) W.W.Agresti, *"New Paradigms For Software Development"*, IEEE Computer Society Press, Washington, USA, 1986.

(BOEHM76) B.W.Boehm, "Software Engineering", *IEEE Transactions on Computers*, Vol. C-25, No. 12, pp.1226-1241, December 1976.

(BOEHM88) B.W.Boehm, "A Spiral Model of Software Development and Enhancement", *Computer*, Vol.21, pp.61-72, May 1988.

(CAR83) T.T.Carey and R.E.A.Mason, "Information System Prototyping: Techniques, Tools, and Methodologies", *INFOR-The Canadian Journal of Operational Research and Information Processing*, Vol. 21, No. 3, pp.177-191, 1983.

(CODD70) E.F.Codd, "A Relational Model of Data for Large Shared Data Banks", *Communications of the ACM*, Vol. 13, No. 6, pp.377-387, June 1970.

(CORD89) C.R.Corder, *Taming Your Company Computer*, McGraw Hill, London, 1989.

(DUNN85) B.B.Dunning, "Expert System Support for Rapid Prototyping of Conventional Software", *Proceedings of Autotestcon 1985, IEEE International Automatic Testing Conference*, New York, USA, pp.2-6, October 1985.

(EDW88) John S.Edwards and Jon L.Bader, "Expert Systems and University Admissions", *Journal of the Operational Research Society*, Vol. 39, No. 1, pp.33-40, January 1988.

(FORD86) L.Ford, "Artificial Intelligence and Software Engineering: A Tutorial Introduction to Their Relationship", *Artificial Intelligence Review*, Vol. 1, No. 1, pp.255-273, 1986.

(GERV83) W.B.Gervarter, *An Overview of Artificial Intelligence and Robotics, Vol.1 - Artificial Intelligence*, NASA Technical Memo NAS 1.15:85836, June 1983.

(GLAD82) G.R.Gladden, "Stop the Life-Cycle, I Want To Get Off", *ACM Sigsoft, Software Engineering Notes*, Vol. 7, No. 2, pp.35-39, April 1982.

(INCE88) D.Ince, "Prototyping Gets a Formal Boost from Alvey Work", *Computing*, pp.20-21, January 28, 1988.

(LAND87) F.Land, "Social Aspects of Information Systems", in *"Management Information Systems: the Technological Challenge"*, Ed. N.Piercy, Croom-Helm, London, 1987.

(MUM87) E.Mumford, "User Participation in a Changing Environment - Why We Need It," *Proceedings of seminar on Participation in Systems Design*, London Business School, April 1987, pp.3-16, Publ. Unicom Seminars Ltd., Middlesex, UK.

(MUM89) E.Mumford and W.B.MacDonald, *"XSEL's Progress: the continuing journey of an expert system"*, Wiley, Chichester, 1989.

115

(PART86a) D.Partridge, *"Artificial Intelligence - Applications in the Future of Software Engineering"*, Ellis Horwood , Chichester, 1986.

(PART86b) D.Partridge, "Engineering Artificial Intelligence Software", *Artificial Intelligence Review*, Vol.1, No. 1, pp.27-41, 1986.

(SPRA82) R.H.Sprague, Jr. and E.D.Carlson, *"Building Effective Decision Support Systems"*, Prentice-Hall, Eaglewood Cliffs, N.J., 1982.

(WAT86) D.A.Waterman, *"A Guide to Expert Systems"*, Addison-Wesley, USA, 1986.

Chapter 5: ORSA Methodology

5.0 Introduction

In the previous chapter, various differences between KBS and conventional DP systems development were identified. Two of them were:

•The need to consider non-KBS, as well as KBS, "solutions".
•The impossibility of setting out from a precise statement of requirements for the system, leading to the need for the KBS development team to consider wider issues than just computing issues.

Indeed, when looking at situations in which building a KBS might be considered, compared with say those in which building a transaction processing system might be considered, it is much harder to establish whether it is sensible to seek a computer "solution" at all.

All of these differences require that the system development be closely linked to the business objectives of the organization (and similar comments apply also to public sector or not-for-profit organizations these days). This chapter therefore concentrates on relating the business objectives and the solutions available. The proposed approach is based on the ideas of "soft" *operational research and systems analysis* (ORSA). The objectives of the chapter are:

(a) To explain why the business objectives are paramount in any solution methodology.

(b) To explain why and how an ORSA approach is of use in transforming the objectives of the organisational system into the requirements for the solution system.

5.1 Why Worry about the Business Objectives?

This may seem like a stupid question to ask, but in fact it is a very important one, particularly if we extend it to read "why worry about the business objectives here". A typical computer project of any kind involves several stages and many people. These people occupy various roles - client, manager, end user, system developer, technical specialist, coder. Some of these roles may overlap. Unless care is taken, there is no reason why the result of any system development should fit the business objectives. This results from the inevitable process of

117

filtering information down this chain of people. The process itself is inevitable because in many system development the client/end-user and the coder almost literally do not speak the same language. This should not be considered as being the fault of either, since it is a consequence of both of them doing the job for which they are being paid.

There is one particular point which distinguishes the literature on KBSs from that on conventional systems development. Most versions of the conventional SDLC explicitly or implicitly mention a number of different "system building" roles, such as business analyst, systems analyst or programmer, even if there is no completely standard definition of them. By contrast, descriptions of KBS development most often refer simply to the "knowledge engineer", implying that this Jack or Jill of all trades does all the work, even though this is rarely likely to be the case for any but the simplest of systems. It is noticeable that this failing of writers on KBS development doesn't occur where the authors are clearly drawing at least in part on conventional SDLC work, for example the work on KADS (see section 6.3.1).

The question of business objectives is particularly important given that many methodologies for the development of conventional DP systems take the system requirement as the crucial document (i.e. the one on "tablets of stone"), and aim solely to produce something which meets that requirement, without specifically linking the development of the systems to the organisational objectives at all. In these circumstances, the requirements document can easily become more of a barrier to communication than a means of facilitating it. Indeed, many of the variants of the SDLC discussed in the previous chapter start from the requirements document rather than from business objectives.

Specific problems arise in four areas: matching responsibilities to roles; sub-optimising; communication problems; and the danger of supplying a technology-driven solution.

Matching responsibilities to roles

Managing the actual process of developing the system is far from straightforward, because of the shift from a management emphasis at one end of the hierarchy to a technical emphasis at the other. This requires an overlap of skills at each of the links in the human chain which does not always exist. As a result, the division of responsibilities within systems development may fail to correspond to the divisions between the roles of the team members. One factor which has often been responsible for this is the long history of DP departments recruiting staff on the basis of their (actual or potential) technical ability, and filling vacancies for higher-level staff by promotion from this group. It has been said, not without a grain of truth, that those promoted under such a system are often those whose technical skills are weakest.

Sub-optimising

What is advantageous for a particular part of a system, whether a computer system or a human activity system, is not always of most benefit to the whole. An apparently optimal design or implementation of one component of a system may have consequences for other parts of the system which make the overall performance worse. These problems increase with both the size of the system and the number of people in the development team. Indeed, for a sufficiently large system, it is probable that considerations of overall structure and communication will override any issues relating to optimising one module. For a KBS, where the connections involved within parts of a large system are probably more complex, and certainly less clear, than for a conventional system, the danger of sub-optimising is that much more acute.

Communication problems

When several different people, with different roles, are all involved in the development of a system, there is no reason why any of them should necessarily appreciate the business need, except for those responsible for the initial feasibility study. With a DP system, even the hands-on users may not appreciate the business need, although this is less likely for a KBS. Equally, analysts may not fully appreciate the business need if they talk mainly to users rather than managers. Those coding the systems may talk only to their own "bosses" (the analysts, say) and have little contact with any of the client group (managers or users) at all. Measures must therefore be taken to avoid the "Chinese whispers" syndrome which might result. The participative design methods mentioned in chapter 4 are one way of helping to achieve this, and a carefully-planned testing programme which involves everyone connected with the system, working together, is another useful weapon. Advocates of evolutionary prototyping feel that it enforces better participation and communication than "classical" system development methods, because of its iterative nature. In particular, those managing the project must set up ways of achieving this kind of communication with groups of people in the different roles, where those in the same role do not necessarily all agree even with each other.

The danger of supplying a technology-driven solution

In any computing project, there is a danger of supplying technology-driven solutions rather than business-driven ones; this is a problem in all areas of computing, but particularly so in knowledge-based systems at the moment. We need say no more about this problem in this section; it is implicit in the description of exploratory, solution-driven and problem-driven perspectives set out in section 2.1 and used throughout this book.

5.2 What is Operational Research?

If the title of section 5.1 may have seemed a trifle silly, this one seems to the author to be positively dangerous, knowing (a) some of the opinions he has heard data processing people express about operational research, and (b) that a dozen OR workers would probably produce more than a dozen different answers to the question!

As usual, we'll avoid putting up a definition to be shot at, but instead take a look at what OR is, or at least what <u>good</u> OR should be, and what OR should not be.

OR should be:

problem-orientated
interdisciplinary
rooted in a scientific approach
flexible

OR should not be:

a branch of pure mathematics
rigid
a collection of unrelated techniques
inhuman/mechanistic

We are aware that some of you may well have had experiences of OR which do not entirely square with this view! All we can say is that, as with any other profession, not all OR workers are as good as the best OR workers. Perhaps more relevantly, many OR workers themselves are wary of the OR label, and a survey by the UK OR Society in 1986 suggested that about half the OR work done in the UK was not actually carried out by people/groups who used that title. There are reasons to suppose that this might include some of the "best" OR work.

There are two important reasons for discussing OR here. The first, which we shall deal with at length in the succeeding sections, is that we feel that the process of OR has much in it that is relevant to the process of building KBSs. The second concerns the nature and the history of OR, which we feel also offers some lessons for the possible development of the field of KBSs. An important feature of OR is that it is not only problem-orientated, but also associated with a battery of techniques. These techniques, however, do not constitute the whole of what OR brings to a practical problem, or even the majority of it. As such, there is a clear parallel with the field of knowledge-based systems. A look at some of the introductory books or courses in KBSs, especially those at the AI end of the spectrum, will reveal a concentration on the techniques - LISP, Prolog, ways of representing knowledge, different types of inferencing structures. This is not a perspective which sheds much light on the situations to which KBSs might be applied in practice. Similarly, introductory textbooks in OR, especially at the mathematical end of the spectrum, are crammed with linear programming, critical path and PERT networks, stock control formulae and so on.

Although the techniques differ, the problem the two fields face is a common one; how to make use of techniques without being carried away by them. OR has, we believe, some lessons to offer because it is an older "solution technology", and because (unlike KBS, which has its roots in AI research), it was originally born of practice rather than theory. Mind you, many of the lessons come from mistakes made - we don't claim OR is perfect! So here comes a short history lesson.

The activity which later became known as operational research began in 1937 in connection with the development of radar in the UK. Although at that time the principles of radar worked well enough in the laboratory, there were all kinds of difficulties associated with using the equipment for a specific practical purpose, namely the detection of enemy aircraft and the initiation of an appropriate response from fighter aircraft and anti-aircraft weapons. Some of these were technical problems with the equipment, resulting from the move out of the controlled environment of the laboratory, but many could be termed management problems. For example, who would operate the radar sets, how would they be used, how many would be deployed, and what action would be taken if/when an enemy aircraft was detected? The multi-disciplinary team set up to tackle these problems after the first relatively unsuccessful trials eventually became known as the operational research section, either because they were doing research into operations in the field, or perhaps because their office was in Operational Headquarters. Later trials of radar were far more successful, and by 1939 the group's reputation was made.

Lesson One: OR arose because what worked well in the research laboratory didn't work so well in practice, and particularly because the use of experimental techniques to solve problems raised new issues which had not previously been considered.

Because of the success of the radar project, OR teams were used extensively in both the UK and the US armed forces during World War II, with the multi-disciplinary teams of scientists tackling all sorts of diverse problems such as the number of ships which should be in a convoy, how best to depth-charge enemy submarines, and planning the maintenance of fighter aircraft. In a sense, this was a "golden age" of OR, with flexible approaches being used on problems of great strategic significance. The OR sections were also free to "poke their noses in" wherever they felt they could make a contribution. Nevertheless, whatever the manner in which a particular problem arose, it was always the problem which was driving the operational research, with the clear over-riding objective of helping the war effort. This was helped in no small measure by the support for OR which existed at high levels in the military and political leadership.

Lesson Two: When attempting to bring a new development into practice in an organisation, make sure you have a "champion" or two in the organisation's higher management levels.

This style of OR continued, in the UK at least, into the national economic and social reconstruction in the late 1940s. Many of the organisations which resulted from the new Labour government's nationalisation programme were far larger than any pre-war organisations, and thus posed new problems. Equally, some of the scientists who had come into wartime OR were looking for something as challenging to tackle in peace-time.

In the US, the situation was rather different, being more of a return to the status quo than a major reconstruction. Few of the military OR workers moved into industry therefore, but many either moved into, or set up links with, universities. Thus it was that in the 15 years from 1945, in the US, most of the standard mathematical techniques of OR began to appear, although some of the stock control formulae had been known about since World War I. Similarly, academic programmes in OR began to appear in American universities, the UK lagging some 10 years behind. Perhaps a key point was the appearance of the first OR textbook, written by Churchman, Ackoff and Arnoff, in 1956. Although the authors had a broad view of OR, and saw that the methods and approach were far more important than any particular techniques, inevitably a large portion of the book <u>was</u> devoted to the specific techniques which had been developed. For many people who until then had known little about OR, the idea of OR being done by scientists became confused as a result with that of the specific training of "OR scientists" in specific techniques. Many later academic programmes thus had a very heavy technical bias. (Doesn't this already remind you of the expert systems field?)

This wasn't too bad in the 1950s and early 1960s, because of the gradual spread of computers into business and administration which was taking place. This presented many opportunities for applying mathematically-based techniques which had previously been impracticable owing to the sheer amount of calculation involved. Thus the techniques achieved some notable successes, but as a result some would say that OR lost its way. Certainly the distinction between UK operational research, still with a solid practical base, and USA operations research, with an increasing emphasis on mathematical models, had become considerable. This has continued to such an extent that what is called OR in the UK now corresponds better to what is called management science, or even decision science, in the USA, not to USA OR.

Lesson Three: Don't let the techniques drive the process. Just because you have some techniques available, and even if they can be used, it doesn't mean that they are the best way to tackle something or that they should be used.

As a reaction to these problems, from the early 1970s onwards, a focus on the methodological and process aspects of OR began to appear in the UK, perhaps in a bid to recapture the past glories which seemed somehow to have been lost in the dispirited UK economic climate of the 1970s. The methodology vs. techniques debate became more heated than ever, and raged on for many years, until it was overtaken by events.

Once again, changes in information technology had a considerable influence on OR in the 1980s, with the phenomenal impact of the micro-computer, especially the IBM PC, on business and management. OR people were often involved in implementing micro-based solutions; this was partly because it was an obvious way to deliver a system to a particular client, and perhaps also partly because many "traditional" data processing departments did not at first wish to become involved with PCs, and someone else had to do the job! In the words of John Ranyard, former President of the UK OR Society: "Computing could now be taken direct to the client without the involvement of another department" (RAN88). It appears that the advent of another, different, solution technology which OR people could and did apply went a long way towards defusing the methodology vs. (mathematical) techniques debate. It's probably worth adding that the ripples from this identity crisis are still felt within OR in the UK today, partly because of the problems caused by the international differences in interpretation of the title.

There is, however, wide agreement within the OR profession that in any practical application of OR the problem structuring aspects, as OR people call them, are at least as important as the technical nature of any solution system which may be devised.

Lesson Four: It ain't what you do, it's the way that you do it!

An interesting counterpoint to the development of OR itself, and one which may account for the techniques-based image as well to some extent, is that many OR techniques have become more or less standard practice in other areas of management. It thus is not surprising that some people may perceive OR as a "supplier of techniques" for that reason. However, there is an alternative view which does even less for the image of OR, at least directly. Many of those who use these techniques as a normal part of their jobs, do so without realising that the credit for their invention belongs to operational researchers.

The best example of this is given by the various network analysis techniques for project management, including critical path analysis, PERT, and many other developments from this original pair. Critical path analysis and PERT were both devised in the 1950s by operational researchers. Within about ten years use of these techniques had become standard practice in the construction industry, and remain so today, normally with no mention of OR. During the 1980s, these techniques, often incorporated in packaged software for "project management" have also begun rather belatedly to make an impact in the computer systems development field. Credit to OR for this is again conspicuous by its absence.

Lesson Five: Perhaps the only way a solution technology/technique can really succeed is for it to become second nature to those working in the problem domain. In such a case, it is likely to be perceived as <u>belonging</u> to the problem domain , and presenting it as a separate subject runs the risk of being counter-productive.

Having looked briefly at OR in general, and indicated some parallels with the development of KBSs, we now look in more detail at the specific OR development which is most relevant to KBSs, namely the methodological approach.

5.3 A Soft OR Methodology

The view we present here is based on that of Robins (ROB85). It comprises five, seven, or an indefinite number of stages, depending on how you do the counting; this in itself is indicative of the nature of soft problems!

1A. Go and see your client(s). Find out:
(a) What the client thinks the problem is, i.e. what is the organisational system concerned and what is it doing that is undesirable?
(b) Why is this undesirable?
(c) What decision(s) would the client like to make?
(d) How does the problem hinder the function of the client and their system in the organisation?
(e) What would your client like you to do for them?

1B. Go and see the organisational system concerned. Find out:
(a) how it works/behaves;
(b) if the complained-of behaviour occurs as stated;
(c) how the people in the system view the problem.

(Note that if an unsatisfactory "solution system", either manual or computer, already exists for the proposed tasks, then this step 1B will have to be carried out on two levels - one for the wider organisational system and one for the unsatisfactory "solution".)

1C. Study the position of the client and their system in relation to the rest of the organisation. Find out:
(a) what these relationships are;
(b) what criteria these relationships imply for assessing the performance of your client and the system;
(c) how this project might affect these relationships in the organisation.

2. Review findings so far and decide, for the time being:
(a) if you can accept the client's account of the organisational system's behaviour and the requirements for the solution system;

125

(b) if you can accept the client's criteria for judging the behaviour of both systems;

(c) if you have sufficient understanding of the way the organisational system works to identify and consider the effect of possible changes;

(d) what you think your client needs from you;

(e) why you cannot immediately satisfy your client's need;

(f) if you have done as much as possible to help the client.

3. Plan further activities/investigations directed to improving your answers to 2(a)-(f) in the light of the review.

4. Report and discuss current ideas with your client and reach joint agreement about your current plan for the solution system to be developed.

5. Carry out this plan and return to step 4.

This description of the process of OR has clear similarities with the process of evolutionary prototyping described in chapter 4. However, there is a difference of focus. The OR process is clearly client-focused (the term "client(s)" appears more frequently than any other), whereas the prototyping process is focused on the supporting <u>system</u>.

5.4 Soft Systems Methodology

To the outsider, there may appear to be little difference between some aspects of OR, especially "soft" OR, and soft systems. However, those in the two camps would certainly claim to perceive some differences, especially at the University of Lancaster, which has for many years had separate departments for each. The late Professor Steve Cook suggested that OR and the soft systems approach were seen by some as differing in the sense of being two sides of the same coin, OR being concerned with solving problems or aiding decisions, soft systems with the design or improvement of systems. To do this, OR often has to study and understand the system in which the problem/decision is embedded, and soft systems has to look at problems arising in the operation of the system. Note that Cook did not necessarily accept this distinction as valid, especially if used to form an artificial division between the two fields.

Given the purposes of this book, the most important point to note is that the background from which the soft systems movement emerged has more in common with conventional computing than does the background of OR (which we described in section 5.2), though there is indeed some considerable similarity between the resulting processes.

The soft systems movement arose from the realisation that hard systems engineering approaches assumed a given objective or objectives, but that in many business problems - especially those involving information technology - the objectives were not clear. This is very much the same as the problem we referred to in Section 5.1 regarding the system specification being treated as "engraved on tablets of stone". It follows from this that any approach to solving problems in organisations must pay close attention to deciding what the problem actually is, or more precisely what would constitute an improvement on the current situation. Indeed, there are many in the systems field who would say that if this aspect can be achieved successfully, then designing whatever technical 'solution" is required becomes quite straightforward. A further complication with regard to establishing the objectives is that different people in an organization may have different objectives for the same organizational system. Any approach therefore needs to be capable of being used with a group of people with differing opinions.

One of the best-known names in the soft systems field is that of Peter Checkland. His work in what he terms human activity systems led to the well-known soft systems methodology which bears his name (CHECK81). One of the key features of this is the development of what are known as *root definitions* of the systems in which the problem or opportunity lies.

Checkland's methodology is shown schematically in Figure 5.1. Note that it is not intended to represent a fixed pattern, or a set "recipe" for how to solve problems. Rather, it is intended as a description of good problem-solving practice. In addition, while the diagram shows the most common links, and the most natural starting-point, all other links are possible if the particular problem situation demands it. The seven stages of Checkland's methodology are as follows:

•1. The initial unstructured problem situation

•2. Investigating the problem situation

•3. Developing suitable root definitions of relevant systems

•4. Using conceptual models to produce an "ideal" system

•5. Comparing the "ideal" model with the real system

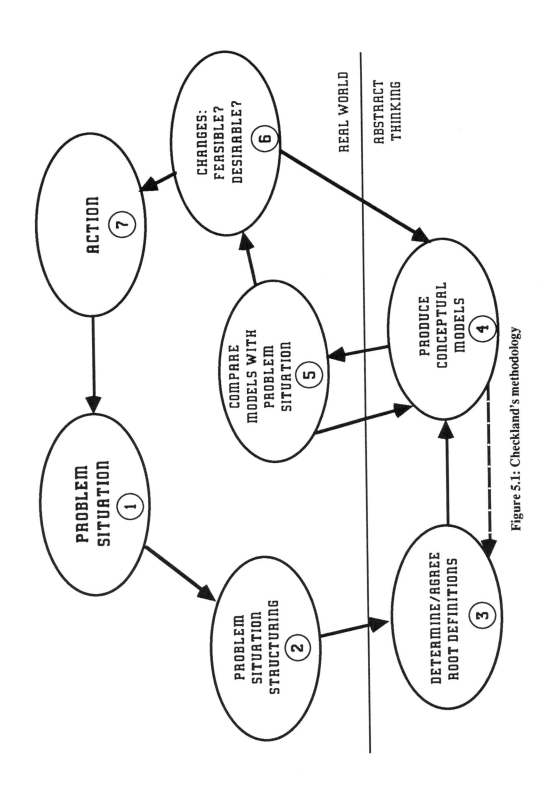

Figure 5.1: Checkland's methodology

•6. Establishing changes which are feasible and desirable

•7. Taking action to "solve" the problem (or at least improve the situation)

The initial unstructured problem situation/Investigating the problem situation

Stages 1 and 2 of SSM are concerned with finding out about the problem situation. Note that the use of this latter phrase is important; the intention is not to find out about "the problem", but to build up as detailed a description as possible of the situation in which someone perceives there to be a problem. This description is usually referred to as the "rich picture", and often literally takes the form of a picture or diagram, which can be gradually built up and/or refined as necessary. (Evolutionary prototyping again!)

Checkland himself suggested that the rich picture should include the elements of both structure (slow to change) and process (continuously changing) within the problem situation, and forming a view of how both are related in this particular case.

An especially difficult aspect of stage 2 is avoiding the imposition of the analyst's own bias on the problem situation (and therefore on the rich picture). This is not to imply that some kind of neutral objectivity is being sought, for two reasons: first, the different biases or viewpoints which different people involved may have are part of the problem situation - a very important part; second, one of the tenets of the soft systems approach is that in problems involving human activity systems, objectivity is not a meaningful concept. (As an aside, this contrast between hard and soft problems/systems is very similar to the contrast between DP systems and KBSs which we discussed in the previous chapter.)

Developing suitable root definitions of relevant systems

Stage 3 has as its aim the production of root definitions of systems that are relevant. It is important to realize that this does not mean "choose several systems that are relevant to the problem and produce one - presumably 'correct' - root definition of each". Far from it, the root definitions should be those which help to give insight into the system concerned. More than likely someone from a hard systems background would perceive them as alternative definitions of the same system, rather than definitions of separate systems, but again the idea of the system is not meaningful; there is no such thing as a, or the, correct root definition.

The root definition is a statement of what the system is, or if you prefer to think of it another way, of what the system is for. Checkland produced the mnemonic CATWOE to help judge whether or not a root definition is well-formulated; note that this does not say anything about how helpful in terms of insight the root definition is.

C	Customers	The beneficiaries, or indeed the victims, of the activity which the system performs.
A	Actors	Those who carry out, or cause to be carried out, the main activity or transformation of the system.
T	Transformation	The heart of the root definition. The process or activity which the system carries out.
W	Weltanschauung	(A German word meaning "world-view".) The outlook or viewpoint which makes this root definition a meaningful one. Often this is stated implicitly rather than explicitly in the root definition.
O	Owners	Ownership of the system. Not always the person who manages or runs it. A reasonable heuristic to decide ownership is to ask "who has the power to 'kill' the system?"
E	Environment	Constraints placed on the system by interaction with other, wider systems. These systems are usually taken as given, i.e. not defined in the root definition.

Using conceptual models to produce an "ideal" system

In stage 4, each of the root definitions produced in stage 3 must be expanded into the minimum necessary set of activities which the system must do in order to accomplish the transformation as defined. The modelling concepts used will include formal (soft) systems concepts, and may also include other systems thinking if appropriate.

Normally the expansion will be accomplished in a series of stages (evolutionary prototyping yet again), to ensure that a consistent level of resolution is maintained throughout. Except where there is, unusually, some explicit reason for wishing to develop a particular part of the conceptual model in greater detail, using the same level of resolution for all parts of the model will facilitate the comparison to be made in the next stage.

Comparing the "ideal" model with the real system

In this stage, the "ideal" conceptual models produced in stage 4 are compared with the actual real world system. It is important to stress again that there is no "correct" system, but that the purpose of the comparison is to gain insights into potential changes which could lead to improvements. This nevertheless does not rule out the possibility that the comparison will reveal some technical errors in the conceptual models which require amendment.

The process of comparison itself is somewhat complicated by the difference in status of the two things being compared. The conceptual models concentrate on what the "ideal" system must, logically, do, whereas when observing the real system it is easiest to see how it operates. The distinction between the "whats" and the "hows" can often lead to problems; Wilson (WILS84) gives a clear explanation of the sometimes awkward distinction between the two. Roughly speaking, any particular "what" may have several different alternative "hows" - different ways of actually achieving the same task. The purpose of the comparison at this stage is to consider whether the existing "how" for a given "what" is the most appropriate (if there is one), or which "how" would be appropriate (if the system is not currently carrying out this "what" task). One of the reasons for the distinction between the abstract thinking and the real world in Checkland's methodology is that without explicit conceptual modelling people often find it difficult to disentangle the underlying "what" from the "how" which they can see in the real system. This leads to a great deal of difficulty in thinking of any way in which the system can operate other than the way it currently does operate; the classic "can't see the wood for the trees" problem.

Establishing changes which are feasible and desirable

The goal of the previous stage is that the comparison should yield changes which may be desirable. The concept of desirability here is linked to a particular root definition and Weltanschauung, and therefore subjective, as usual. For this reason (among others), it is important to establish whether or not the changes are organizationally feasible as well. If you prefer, you may think of this as whether they are politically feasible (with a small "p") in the organization.

Taking action to "solve" the problem (or at least improve the situation)

As you would expect, those changes which have been identified as both feasible and desirable need to be put into action by means of an appropriate implementation plan. The problem situation is then monitored to see if the changes have had the desired effect, or indeed any other effects. This brings the process back to stage 1 again.

5.5 Soft Methodologies in General

It's worth stressing why we believe that a concentration on soft aspects of the organisation's problem is so important in the context of knowledge-based systems. This is because of the very nature of the problems for which a KBS may be helpful. If a KBS is going to be of any use at all, then by definition some kind of transfer of knowledge or expertise must be taking place, or be desired to take place. In the majority of cases, this transfer will cut across at least one of the internal boundaries of the organisation concerned.

Some examples of what we mean:
Bank mortgage lending expertise being put at the fingertips of branch managers, or indeed clerks - the result is a transfer of knowledge from head office department to branches.
Taxation advice system - transfer of expertise from legal department to finance department.
Ernst and Whinney's VATIA system (see section 1.2) - transfer of expertise from VAT Group to those carrying out audits "in the field".

There is, however, one common case where the soft aspects of the problem may seem to be less in evidence, at least at the start of the project. This is where the KBS to be constructed is a stand-alone expert system designed to be used by the domain experts themselves, perhaps to improve the consistency of their decision-making, or to permit closer integration of some numerical technique (in real time, say) with the rest of the decision-making process. If this really is the case, then the expert is in a good position to define the relevant "local" organisational objectives which the system is intended to meet, as the system will be functioning as the expert's assistant.

The reason for our slight scepticism as to whether this really does avoid the soft aspects of the problem revolves around whether a successful KBS will continue to be used solely for its original purpose. If it is successful as an assistant to the expert, there are likely to be pressures for it to be used in other ways, such as training new experts or making decisions when the expert is temporarily unavailable. (You may well argue that from the management point of view, the latter use shouldn't be permitted, but with a successful KBS the temptation will surely be there.) The moment this happens, we are back in the soft arena again, and unless the relevant issues have been considered or (better) are re-considered, the outcome is likely to be anything from unfortunate to disastrous.

One consequence of this soft aspect is that the knowledge engineer or whoever else has the job of constructing the KBSs does not have to be a technical expert. At least, that appears to be the view of the majority of writers on the subject these days, in contrast to the initial period when all knowledge engineers seemed to be expected to have doctorates in AI. We agree with this, but only up to a point. The knowledge engineer certainly does not have to be an expert in artificial intelligence, but in any large KBS development it is unlikely that no technical expertise is required. This is particularly true where we are talking about adding an embedded knowledge-based component to an existing system. There is an implicit assumption in much of the expert systems literature (and for once we specifically mean expert system and not KBS) that the knowledge engineer does everything from interpreting the organisational objectives through to coding the system. It might be a valid description if the system is functioning as the expert's assistant and it is written entirely in one of the PC-based shells without any calls to other programs, but not in our view any more generally than that.

5.6 Summary

In this chapter we have proposed the use of "soft" operational research and systems analysis (ORSA) as a way to investigate the problem or opportunity in hand in an organization and determine what sort of action is required. This action might be building a KBS, or might be something entirely different. In addition, we have drawn some lessons from the history of operational research which seem to apply equally to the field of knowledge-based systems.

References

(CHECK81) P.B.Checkland, *"Systems Thinking, Systems Practice"*, Wiley, Chichester, 1981.

(RAN88) J.C.Ranyard, "A history of OR and computing", *J. Opl Res. Soc.* Vol.39, No.12, pp.1073-1086, 1988.

(ROB85) P.C.Robins, "The Methodology of Operational Research", pp.17-31 in *"Managing with Operational Research"* (Ed. J.B.Kidd), Philip Allan, Deddington, 1985.

(WILS84) B.Wilson, *"Systems: Concepts, Methodologies and Applications"*, Wiley, Chichester, 1984.

Chapter 6: Lessons from Other KBS Work

6.0 Introduction

In this chapter, we will be considering other people's work on methodologies for building KBSs, particularly in so far as it has influenced our own ideas and proposals. Most of the work in the area we are discussing looks at KBSs as a field in isolation - an applied area of AI, if you like to think of it that way - seeking few if any lessons from other areas which build computer systems or solve problems.

Not all other authors have ignored software engineering or soft systems completely, however, and it should be no surprise that those who <u>have</u> seen some potential for integration, such as Partridge and the team working on the KADS project, are those whose work has had the most influence on ours.

6.1 Current KBS Development Methodology: the Textbook View

A reasonable place to look for KBS development methodologies is in the so-called "classic" KBS textbooks. The most common <u>description</u> of KBS development is one we have already discussed in section 2.4.1, produced by Buchanan *et al*, which appears both in Hayes-Roth, Waterman and Lenat (HAYES83), and in Waterman (WAT86). It consists of five stages, which are referred to as tasks or phases, in the building of an expert system:

> "Identification: Determining problem characteristics
> Conceptualisation: Finding concepts to represent knowledge
> Formalisation: Designing structures to organise knowledge
> Implementation: Formulating rules that embody knowledge
> Testing: Validating rules that embody knowledge."
> (Page 24.)

This does not represent a structured methodology but simply a statement of the general stages associated with KBS development. In particular, it does not identify detailed tasks to be performed in KBS construction. This was not the original intention of the description since, at the time the 1983 book was written, the development of KBSs, especially those intended for practical use, was still in its infancy. Waterman's 1986 book expands on the detail of various aspects of expert system development, but neither these terms nor any others are really used to give a structure to the development process. Thus Waterman gives plenty of useful advice and tips, particularly about the internal aspects of KBSs, but nothing that could be classed as a methodology in our terms.

Unfortunately, this set of stages has been taken up by others as being "the" current KBS development methodology, presumably because of its appearance in two of the most well-known textbooks (and elsewhere!). This has led to some strange comparative methodological articles appearing in which this description is given a significance far beyond what appears to us to be the intention of its creators. We shall deliberately not give references to any of these articles! It is also worth noting that this description has always been addressed specifically to expert systems.

Our conclusion overall is that there is no widely-accepted, commercially robust, KBS development methodology at present. Many - perhaps most - KBSs are developed by *ad hoc* methods. This is as would be expected of a new area of activity. Nevertheless, some significant methodological developments have taken place, and we now go on to look at the most important of them.

6.2 AI Methodology compared with DP Methodology

Derek Partridge is one of the few academics to have been working on the similarities, differences, links and divergences between AI and conventional software engineering. He (PART86b) characterised the prevailing AI methodology as RUDE:

Run-Understand-Debug-Edit.

According to Partridge, traditionally, AI programs have not been developed by implementing what he terms a *completely specified problem*, unlike conventional programs. AI program development has usually been characterised by the run-understand-debug-edit cycle (the RUDE cycle), which can become random code hacking, in the worst case, or incremental analysis and redesign in its better manifestations.

The RUDE paradigm is synonymous with the use of iterative prototyping and a simplified version of it is illustrated in Figure 6.1.

Partridge clearly stated the need for improvements in the RUDE paradigm, in order to yield a sufficiently robust, disciplined (and presumably structured) derivative that could be used to construct commercial AI software.

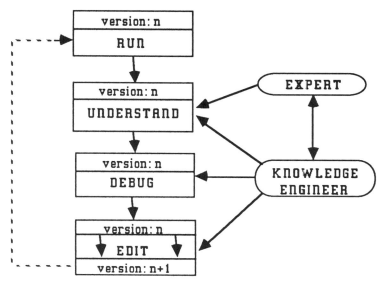

Figure 6.1: The RUDE cycle

He has attempted to combat some of the weaknesses he identified by proposing a "complete life-cycle environment" for AI software based on the RUDE paradigm. The proposed environment is discussed more fully in his book (PART86a) and is based on a model of "controlled code modification" of "AI program abstractions":

> "Code modification should be systematic and based upon the abstract representations that underlie a given inadequate implementation. We have to work with the machine-executable description but we use the underlying specification and less abstract intermediate representations (a possible design sequence) as the basis for guiding implementation development." (Page 122.)

Partridge did not discuss his RUDE life-cycle explicitly in relation to commercial KBS development and his approach is therefore not intended to be a complete methodology. He did, however, succeed in identifying some of the fundamental issues associated with producing practical KBSs.

One issue in Partridge's analysis which is worthy of further discussion here is the notion of "completely specified problems", as referred to earlier, on which he bases his characterisation of conventional software engineering. For

137

example, he said (PART86a):

> "In software engineering there is the opportunity, which should be exploited to the full, of capturing, independent of any particular persons, a complete and rigorous specification of the problem. That is not to say that human wishes can be ignored, on the contrary that must be taken into account. But this contrasts sharply with typical AI problems wherein certain humans are the only known embodiments of adequate implementations." (Page 120.)

We cannot entirely agree with this. It does apply in some cases, for example when a payroll or accounting system is being designed to meet specific requirements, which may have been laid down by law or statute. However, although these are the "bread and butter" DP applications, they do not in our experience form the majority of system development work. In this majority of cases, complete problem specifications in commercial DP are simply a statement, *at a particular time*, of the problem, as it is perceived or understood by developers, users and problem owners. This perception is just as liable to change, re-statement and re-design as many of the problems being approached by AI and KBS developers. Indeed, in the case of decision support systems, which reached the commercial arena before KBSs, it is not only possible but indeed expected that the system's functionality will be extended as time passes, as we pointed out in section 4.4.

The problem of iteration in DPSD was also referred to in chapter 4, and Boehm (BOEHM76) identified its potential dangers for successful DP development. Iteration is sometimes unavoidable, or even desirable, in order to accommodate changes in the perceptions and requirements of those concerned with a particular application. Commercial DP uses the structured conventional life-cycle to control any iteration and, above all, to enable the results of iteration to be *documented* and *maintained*. Thus, the lack of a "completely specified problem" does not necessarily mean that AI or KBS software development cannot benefit from some of the techniques which have evolved for managing conventional system development.

The RUDE paradigm is an exploratory perspective on building KBSs, and is thus perhaps the most appropriate description for those doing research and development into KBS systems. The RUDE cycle also encompasses well the iterative refinement which is necessary for KBS construction. However, an *engineering* methodology for KBSs needs to provide a method for constructing an initial system from which the RUDE cycle can begin, as well as encompassing some form of *control* of the iterative process of development. The use of a KBS development methodology, without these last two features, is likely to lead to problems of documentation, maintenance and testing, all of which must be easily accomplished in an engineering methodology. Thus, in order to engineer a practical KBS, the iterative features of the RUDE paradigm need to be incorporated within a structured and controllable framework.

6.3 Structured KBS Development Methodologies

6.3.1 KADS

One sustained attempt to look at a structured methodology for KBS development has been a series of collaborative projects partly funded by the European Community's ESPRIT programme. The partners in the project were STC Technology Ltd., Scicon Ltd., SCS GmbH, Cap Sogeti Innovation, the University of Amsterdam and the Knowledge-based Systems Centre, originally at the Polytechnic of the South Bank in London. Hayward (HAY86) discussed the overall philosophy behind the project, suggesting that the common approach of "rapid prototyping" for developing expert systems was commercially foolhardy. The project therefore proposed an alternative development method, based on the philosophy of structured development methodology, "as familiar from conventional software development". The aim was to partition the development process, so that a system proceeds through a series of structured descriptions according to a well-defined process.

Hayward went on to describe the methodology as based on a four-phase life-cycle comprising knowledge acquisition, system design and implementation, testing, and operational use. It is clear from that paper and others that the project team saw its work as being very much what we have termed exploratory.

Reports of the project so far have concentrated on two aspects. The first was to build up a sound theoretical basis for the methodology, particularly as far as modelling domain expertise was concerned, and the second was detailed work on the knowledge acquisition stage.

This latter work led to a system known as KADS (originally standing for Knowledge Acquisition and Documentation Structuring, but now also described as Knowledge Analysis and Design System), which was originally implemented in Prolog on *Sun* workstations.

Most of the work on KADS has been reported by Breuker and Wielinga from the University of Amsterdam (BREU87, HAY88, BREU89), and it is worth giving a brief outline here. They see the process of knowledge acquisition as being one of interpretation from the original verbal data into some appropriate representation structure, i.e. a modelling process involving abstraction and transformation. Note that the judgement of what is appropriate is made from the point of view of representing the knowledge, not from the point of view of implementing a KBS. This is consistent with both the separation of phases in what we called CTA in chapters 2 and 3, and the common split between logical and physical design in conventional software engineering (see chapter 4).

Breuker and Wielinga identify five levels of analysis in this interpretation or mapping from verbal data to knowledge, namely:

•Knowledge identification
•Knowledge classification
•Epistemological analysis
•Logical analysis
•Implementational analysis.

As the analysis proceeds, the representational primitives ("building blocks") used change from linguistic (at the knowledge identification level) to those normally seen in the implementation of KBS software such as pattern-matching or truth-testing (at the implementational analysis level).

KADS provides interactive tools to support analysis within this framework, and produces outputs based on a four-layer model of the relevant expertise, the layers being:

•Domain level
•Inference level
•Task level
•Strategic level.

The domain level expertise is the lowest, containing concepts, structures and static relations such as is_a (see section 3.1). Above this comes the inference level, containing meta-classes such as "solution" and "hypothesis"; it describes the inferences which can be made, but not how or when they will be made in any particular application. The task level expertise specifies how the inferences may be controlled to perform a particular task, which is defined in terms of its goals; goals and tasks form the basic objects of this layer. The strategic level expertise relates to monitoring and controlling the whole process of problem-solving using the knowledge-base. Perhaps not surprisingly, coverage of this strategic level in KADS has so far been rudimentary.

The KADS project has looked at the way KBS development could be *structured* but, although it has linked its work with conventional software development models, the KADS system does not yet offer a detailed framework of procedures which can be adopted easily in the commercial DP environment. It has however made considerable strides in providing tools and techniques for knowledge acquisition.

6.3.2 TRESSA

The KBSC referred to in the previous section has now moved from the Polytechnic of the South Bank into the private sector, having been acquired by Touche Ross Management Consultants. They used the work on KADS to help develop an expert system to help those contemplating an expert system application to do a quick feasibility study (an expert system about expert systems!). It is called TRESSA (Touche Ross Expert System Selection Adviser), runs on an IBM-compatible PC, and uses some of the KADS methodology. Further development - assuming it is recommended as feasible by TRESSA - follows on KADS lines. The stages in the KBSC's methodology are given in an "interview" with Frank Hickman in Andrews's book (AND89) as:

•Problem definition
•Knowledge gathering
•Knowledge elicitation
•Interpretation models
•Conceptual model
•Design model
•Implementation

Most of these stages are self-explanatory, given the various descriptions we have already seen. The "knowledge gathering" stage represents the use of published material such as books in order to acquire some knowledge of the domain before involving the human expert in the knowledge elicitation stage. We also again see the split between the representation of the knowledge for the purposes of knowledge elicitation (the interpretation models, followed by the conceptual model) and its representation for machine execution (the design model).

6.3.3 STAGES

Another UK accountancy and management consultancy organization, Ernst and Whinney, has been active in the area of KBS methodology, developing its own development method called STAGES (Structured Techniques for Analysis and Generation of Expert Systems). This was used on, amongst others, the VATIA system mentioned in chapter 1. However, published accounts, such as that in (AND89), say relatively little about the methodology itself, concentrating on the systems which it has been used to build.

Both Touche Ross and Ernst and Whinney are involved in the government and private sector-sponsored GEMINI project. The acronym began its life as Government Expert systems Methodology INItiative, but has now become General Expert systems Method INItiative. The change from "government" to "general" obviously reflects the injection of private sector funding; whether the change from "methodology" to "method" is significant or not remains to be seen.

6.3.4 A conventional DP view of developing KBSs

Robert Keller (KELL87) has taken a rather different approach to what he terms "an AI system development methodology", although he also makes it clear that he regards AI as being synonymous with expert systems as far as practical applications were concerned.

Keller's methodology is firmly rooted in the structured life-cycle approach to conventional software engineering, as would be expected from the author of an earlier book entitled "The Practice of Structure Analysis" (KELL83). This is clearly visible in the style of his AI/expert systems book, since all the stages of his methodology are presented in the form of data flow diagrams (DFDs). Figure 6.2 shows a DFD corresponding to Keller's "Preferred AI Project Life Cycle". Like most authors, he contrasts this with existing AI project approaches.

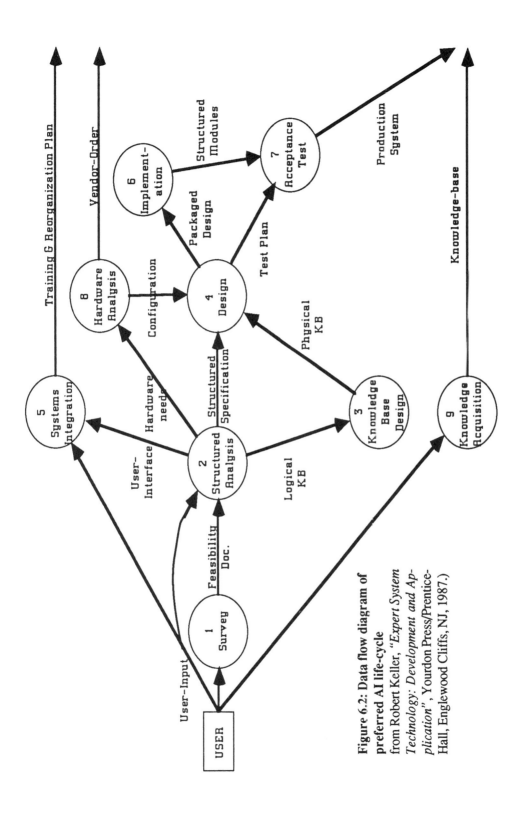

Figure 6.2: Data flow diagram of preferred AI life-cycle from Robert Keller, *"Expert System Technology: Development and Application"*, Yourdon Press/Prentice-Hall, Englewood Cliffs, NJ, 1987.)

The activities in Keller's life cycle are:

- Survey
- Structured Analysis
- Knowledge Base Design
- Design
- Systems Integration
- Implementation
- Acceptance Test
- Hardware Analysis
- Knowledge Acquisition

The attempt to keep as close as possible to the conventional life cycle is readily apparent here, the only differences being the change of name from Database Design to Knowledge Base Design, and the addition of the final activity on the list, Knowledge Acquisition.

Keller states that this latter activity might equally well be called Structured Knowledge Analysis. Both this alternative term and the positioning of the Knowledge Acquisition activity in Figure 6.2 suggest that his view of what is meant by Knowledge Acquisition is somewhat different from the conventional view, as we described in section 2.4.2. This appears to be because Keller regards it as being possible to specify the knowledge structure of an expert system without specifying the inference mechanism(s) which will operate on the knowledge base(s) so produced. An inferencing capability is then obtained by using the built-in inference engine of an expert system shell or of a special-purpose language such as Prolog.

From our own experiences, we are not convinced that this would be a suitable way to tackle anything more sophisticated than a smallish stand-alone system. Nevertheless, Keller's views are noteworthy as being a contribution to KBS methodology from the "high priests" of the structured life cycle who publish through the Yourdon Press!

6.4 A Project Management Perspective

A very different view of what the problems of building KBSs are, and what needs to be done about them, was presented by Cupello and Mishelevich (CUPE88). Their perspective, like ours, is concerned with applications, and their paper is entirely about managing what they call knowledge/expert system projects. It is probably significant that it appeared in a "mainstream" computing journal. Indeed, many of their recommendations are not really specific to KBSs, but would represent good practice for any system development.

They assume that the KBS to be developed is a demonstration prototype in order to help a company investigate KBS technology. In addition, they assume that it is a more complex system than a simple rule-based system built with a shell on a PC. Thus the development software and hardware will consist of a large object-oriented toolkit and either a LISP-based or more general-purpose Unix-based workstation. Their concerns are as much with budgets, organizational politics and human issues such as finding a champion for the project as with any knowledge acquisition or programming aspects. In our terms, what they are proposing is actually an approach to building a prototype from a problem-driven perspective! (Naturally enough, their proposals sometimes slip into more of a solution-driven perspective.)

Their recommendations fall under the following headings:

•People issues (i.e. the composition of the team building the KBS)
•Training
•The user champion
•The executive champion
•The politics of project approval
•Budget and scheduling
•Selection of an appropriate problem

As far as points specific to KBSs are concerned, they recommend that it is extremely important for the team to include outstanding computer programmers/analysts with above average interpersonal skills (perhaps easier said than recruited!). They advocate training in four aspects of KBSs: LISP, the software tool-kit, the hardware to be used and knowledge engineering methodology. They suggest that the training in knowledge engineering methodology should be provided by one of the "...several organizations that advertise consultancy services in the area of building knowledge/expert systems", and discuss how to choose the best such consultant, but say little about what this training does, or should, comprise.

The "political" headings do not contain any recommendations relating specifically to KBSs rather than to any project involving a new technology. The "budget" heading outlines the recommended project as having a budget of between $150000 and $250000, for a maximum duration of twelve months, and involving not more than two full-time people (a programmer and a user champion). Selecting the appropriate problem is done in three stages: inviting propositions from user departments, reducing their number to about half-a-dozen by reference to the criteria set out by Waterman (WAT86) and Prerau (PRER85), which we have discussed in chapter 2, and bringing in a consultant to choose two *(sic)* problems to work on.

The management focus of this is commendable, but we believe that the methods which are suitable for building a prototype are not necessarily suitable for building a robust operational system. It is perhaps significant that the sample schedule shown in the paper includes "system building" as one activity with no identified sub-divisions.

6.5 Summary

In this chapter, we have looked briefly at others' ideas about a robust, structured methodology for KBSs. We have concentrated in particular on the KADS project, and on the ideas of Partridge. Our synthesis of these ideas, and our own, will be presented in chapters 8 and 9. Before that, we shall give a description of the largest project we have been involved with, *Intellipse*, in order to show where and how our ideas developed.

References

(AND89) Bruce Andrews, *"Successful Expert Systems"*, Financial Times Business Information, London, 1989.

(BOEHM76) B.W.Boehm, "Software Engineering", *IEEE Transactions on Computers*, Vol. C-25, No. 12, pp.1226-1241, December 1976.

(BREU87) Joost Breuker and Bob Wielinga, "Use of Models in the Interpretation of Verbal Data", pp.17-44 in *"Knowledge Acquisition for Expert Systems"*, (ed. Alison L.Kidd), Plenum, New York and London, 1987.

(BREU89) Joost Breuker and Bob Wielinga, "Models of Expertise in Knowledge Acquisition", pp.265-295 in *"Topics in Expert System Design"*, (eds. Giovanni Guida and Carlo Tasso), Elsevier/North-Holland, Amsterdam, 1989.

(CUPE88) James M.Cupello and David J.Mishelevich, "Managing Prototype Knowledge/Expert System Projects", *Communications of the ACM*, Vol.31, No.5, pp.534-541 and 550 *(sic)*, May 1988.

(HAYES83) F.Hayes-Roth, D.A.Waterman and D.B.Lenat (eds.), *"Building Expert Systems"*, Addison-Wesley, USA, 1983.

(HAY86) S.A.Hayward, "A Structured Development Methodology for Expert Systems", *Proceedings of KBS '86*, pp.195-203, Online Publications, Pinner, UK, 1986.

(HAY88) S.A.Hayward, B.J.Wielinga and J.A.Breuker, "Structured analysis of knowledge", pp.149-160 in *Knowledge Acquisition Tools for Expert Systems*, (eds. J.H.Boose and B.R.Gaines), Academic Press, London, 1988.

(KELL83) Robert Keller, *"The Practice of Structured Analysis: Exploding Myths"*, Yourdon Press/Prentice-Hall, Englewood Cliffs, NJ, 1983.

(KELL87) Robert Keller, *"Expert System Technology: Development and Application"*, Yourdon Press/Prentice-Hall, Englewood Cliffs, NJ, 1987.

(PART86a) D.Partridge, *"Artificial Intelligence - Applications in the Future of Software Engineering"*, Ellis Horwood, Chichester, 1986.

(PART86b) D.Partridge, "Engineering Artificial Intelligence Software", *Artificial Intelligence Review*, Vol.1, No. 1, pp.27-41, 1986.

(PRER85) D.S.Prerau, "Selection of an Appropriate Domain for an Expert System", *The AI Magazine*, Vol. 6, No. 2, pp.26-30, Summer 1985.

(WAT86) D.A.Waterman, *"A Guide to Expert Systems"*, Addison-Wesley, USA, 1986.

Chapter 7: The *Intellipse* Experience

7.0 Introduction

This chapter describes work carried out by a team including the author as part of a collaborative project funded under the Alvey Directorate's software engineering programme (project number SE057). The project collaborators were Aston University, BIS Applied Systems Ltd (BIS) and the British Steel Corporation (BSC). The original aim of the project was to investigate the potential application of intelligent knowledge-based systems (IKBS) to the design of commercial data processing (DP) systems. The project later began to examine the potential use of conventional software engineering techniques for the design and implementation of knowledge-based systems, and it was this part of the work which led to the writing of this book.

We must stress that this is not to be seen entirely as an example of "how to do it"; the methodology which we are proposing in this book developed partly as a result of our experiences in the *Intellipse* project, and at times the project itself was more an example of "how <u>not</u> to do it". We hope it will be made sufficiently clear when we are describing good practice, and when we are describing bad practice!

The *Intellipse* project was a close collaboration between Aston and BIS, with BSC involved as and when progress demanded. The collaboration was greatly facilitated by the geographical proximity of the university to BIS's office (about 15 minutes walking time), especially as far as the technical side of the project was concerned, where face-to-face meetings - or rather side-by-side meetings in front of a computer screen - were essential. This may seem a very minor point, but such minor points are often crucial to the success of projects. The work to be contributed by each of the collaborators was set out in the project specification as follows:

> "BIS will provide the main input on system design methodology and the building of the designer role IKBS tools.
>
> The academic partner (*Aston*) will provide the main input on creating the English-based query evaluator, which will provide the adviser interface.
>
> The user (*BSC*) will review the specifications, evaluate the

products and make suggestions for modification, as the project develops, to ensure that the tools produced will be of real benefit to subsequent industrial users." (Page 18.)

It became clear from the start that changes would be needed in the designated responsibilities listed above, in order to meet the actual demands of the project objectives, and to utilise effectively the expertise available within each of the collaborating organisations. In practice, Aston and BIS worked together on all aspects of the project. This was an early recognition of one of the crucial differences between DP system and KBS development, namely that the degree of interaction needed between the parties involved is much greater for KBSs. We therefore give this as our first example of "how <u>not</u> to do it".

7.1 The Original Project Specification

The project specification submitted to and approved by the Alvey Directorate stated that:

> "This project aims to produce a set of IKBS based tools which can be used in the system design stage of a commercial data processing development."

The tools were to be based on BIS's paper-based Structured Systems Design (SSD) methodology. This methodology is also referred to as *MODUS*, although this is not strictly correct, as SSD is only a part of BIS's *MODUS* services for computer-based information system management and development. *MODUS* covers the areas of strategic planning, resource management, project management, system development and production management. The components of *MODUS* are procedures, techniques, documentation, automated aids, training and implementation support.

The *MODUS* framework recognises the following phases for the conduct of a project:

- feasibility study,
- systems analysis,
- systems design (computer and clerical),
- programming,
- system testing,
- acceptance testing,
- implementation, and
- post-live review.

149

The reader will note that these are similar to, but not identical with, the software development life-cycle as it was described in section 4.2. SSD is concerned with the *systems design* phase which follows systems analysis and precedes programming. The development phases are regarded by BIS as discrete entities in their own right, and the use of SSD need not be in relation to any of the other *MODUS* phases. The input to the SSD phase is a set of documentation, arising from the analysis of a user's system requirements. This analysis usually covers any existing manual or computer systems relevant to the project, and data and files which will be needed by the proposed system. The output from the SSD phase is a set of program and file specifications from which the software for a computer system could be built.

The proposal went on to describe the proposed mode of operation of the IKBS tools.

> "...the IKBS based tools will have two styles of operation, a designer mode and an adviser mode.
>
> When operating in designer mode, the expert system will provide the lead, by working through the procedural rules of the sub-process..[within SSD].., and extracting from the user, the information necessary to carry out the required tasks.
>
> When operating in adviser mode, it is expected that a designer will approach the IKBS with a problem associated with applying either the procedural techniques or documentation rules and will wish to receive advice, and perhaps be 'walked through' a specific part of the sub-process against his problem.
>
> It is proposed that, to enable the adviser mode of operation to be effective, a front-end query evaluation component should be developed which can be used with each expert system."

Later in the chapter we will describe the architecture of the *Intellipse* tools eventually devised; it will be seen that the *Intellipse* concept differs significantly from the original proposals above. We believe that such a shift will occur more often than not when building a large KBS. Certainly nothing we have seen in conventional software engineering leads us to change this view!

We also believe that we were driven by a problem-driven perspective through-out, as the style of the above proposal demonstrates. However, there were times in the project when we had to adopt an exploratory perspective ("the only aim is to make it work") precisely because we did not know how - or indeed whether - some of the things we were attempting could actually be done.

Note in particular three assumptions implicit in the responsibilities :

•The work most appropriately done from an exploratory perspective was to be done by the academic partner, and the more problem-driven work by the two industrial partners.
•One knowledge-base would serve for both the adviser and designer modes.
•It would be possible to develop the interface and the knowledge-base for the adviser mode simultaneously.

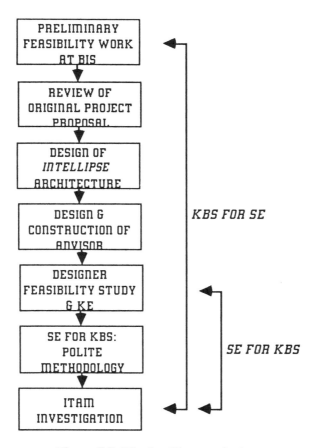

Figure 7.1: The *Intellipse* project

151

7.2 The Main Project Phases

This section gives an historical outline of the work involved in the *Intellipse* project. Figure 7.1 illustrates the main phases of the project. The theme of *knowledge-based systems applied to software engineering (KBS for SE)* was present throughout the project; the complementary *SE for KBS* theme, which provided the impetus for this book, only manifested itself strongly during the latter phases of the work. It is important to remember that the *Intellipse* project represented a learning experience - we didn't "know it all" before we started, and indeed we wouldn't claim to, even now!

The *ITAM* work referred to in Figure 7.1 relates to the last phase of work of the *Intellipse* project and is concerned with an investigation into the feasibility of using KBS tools to support the design and maintenance of a database management system (DBMS) application. This was the first formal application of the POLITE methodology, and will be described in more detail in chapter 9.

7.3 The Key Changes to the Proposal

7.3.1 The rise and fall of the natural language interface

A brief study of existing commercial and research-based natural language front-end (NLFE) systems indicated that four key problems needed to be solved before any work on a NLFE to the proposed IKBS tools could be started:

(i)   The detailed reasons for including a natural language interface had to be identified, and the consequent functional specification for the interface defined.

(ii) The breadth of semantic information to be contained within the IKBS knowledge bases (KBs) had to be specified.

(iii) An analysis of the prospective users of the IKBS tools was necessary, to help identify the functional requirements for the NLFE.

(iv) It was necessary to know the precise data structures to be employed in the KBs before a NLFE design could be attempted.

It was concluded that at that point in the project the design and functional specification of the IKBS tools was too incomplete, and the extent to which natural language capability was required too vague, to enable any serious work on a NLFE to begin. Any attempt to carry on at that stage would have therefore had to be entirely from an exploratory perspective, and hence unlikely to integrate with the problem-driven work.

Indeed, further investigation at a more appropriate point in the project indicated that the natural language capability required by *Intellipse* was of a very limited nature (see section 7.10.2).

7.3.2 Building the IKBS components

It was found necessary that BIS and Aston collaborate more closely on particular areas of the project than was envisaged in the original project proposal, for a number of reasons.

Firstly, the complexity of systems design suggested that an extensive review of the project specification was necessary to determine the overall feasibility. In the course of this, it was found to be desirable for the majority of the knowledge engineering for *Intellipse* - certainly the cognitive task analysis phases - to be done by people who were not experts in SSD. An expert practitioner in SSD takes many of its rules and procedures for granted and it is difficult for the expert, alone, to make explicit the principles and techniques which are important for the inexperienced SSD user. The use of knowledge engineers, naive in SSD, was more likely to lead to the successful elicitation of the required knowledge. In addition, the Aston members of the team did have some practical experience of building KBSs (EDW88) which BIS did not possess, and so the bulk of the knowledge engineering was done by Aston rather than BIS.

Secondly, the paper-based SSD methodology was subject to various internal reviews within BIS around the time the project started. Also, there appeared to be some inconsistency of view between different BIS consultants on particular aspects of the SSD methodology. Thus it was necessary to identify a version of SSD which could serve as a basis for the KBS tools, and again the "independent" view of the "outsiders" helped in this process.

Thirdly, BIS is not primarily a research and development (R & D) company. Its strengths lie in the application and management of established DP techniques to administrative and financial systems within commerce and industry. The lack of experience in R & D was compounded by the particular difficulties inherent in KBS development, which are absent in conventional DP systems development projects. This made those of the BIS personnel whose experience

153

was solely in conventional DP, a trifle uneasy. At the start of the project, the potential use of BIS's *MODUS* techniques for the management of KBS development was recognised as an important area for investigation. In fact, it had already been agreed by the project team that, if possible, the applicability of conventional DP development techniques to KBS design and development should be addressed at some point during the *Intellipse* project. This book is testimony to the fact that this aim was indeed achieved, but that it also required a considerable amount of work.

We feel that all three of these factors are typical of problems likely to arise in KBS development:

•Human experts are not always good at communicating their own knowledge; indeed, some are not even all that well aware of what knowledge they possess.
•Different human experts in the same field do not always agree.
•KBS is at present less well-defined than conventional DP, and perhaps inherently more complex.

The combination of these factors meant that BIS and Aston had to work more closely than was originally envisaged on most aspects of the project, instead of each partner having discrete areas of responsibility. In particular, Aston had to take a more active role in the technical management of the project. The proximity of BIS and Aston facilitated this closer co-operation. This situation proved successful and the project was reputedly one of the more successful examples of university/industrial collaboration within the Alvey programme (DIG87).

7.4 The Concept of *Intellipse*

The initial feasibility study already referred to in the previous section involved not only BIS and BSC, but other organisations including ICI, the NCC and the attendees at two of BIS's SSD training courses. After considering the results of this study and the outline specification of the proposed tools in the project proposal to the Alvey Directorate, it was concluded that *Intellipse* should, if it proved to be technically possible, exhibit the following five features:

> support for a particular structured design methodology, SSD, which did not require the user to be an expert in that method for the support to be effective;

- the ability to provide expert support for specific design tasks within the overall development life-cycle;

- knowledge about design procedures and past design practices which could be made available to the user;

- the usability, robustness and reliability demanded in an industrial or commercial environment;

- the ability to integrate successfully with current support tools, like BIS/ IPSE, and existing DP development practices.

Four initial phases of development were identified in order to investigate the potential for building a knowledge-based support tool which would exhibit these features:

(i)   The definition of a functional specification for the system.

(ii) The identification and classification of the individual tasks performed within SSD and their precise relationship within the overall SSD method.

(iii) The establishment of a unified system architecture possessing a high degree of modularity and allowing for incremental development over a period of time.

(iv) The adoption of a suitable, umbrella knowledge representation schema for the system.

The succeeding sections will expand on each of these phases and explain why each of them was identified as being necessary.

7.5 Functional Specification

A functional specification was required, in order to provide a framework for developing some prototype tools. This specification was not intended to be a detailed list of functions or actions which the system should perform in precisely defined circumstances (the meaning of "specification" in section 4.2).

This latter type of specification is the necessary basis for the development of a conventional DP system, but not for one whose mode of operation was still undetermined.

Four potential forms of support were identified for a tool intended to help a designer perform a task in SSD:

(i)   remove the decision-making from the designer by completely automating the task - AUTOMATION;

(ii)   share decision-making with the designer by using the tool to offer advice about procedures and techniques, *and their specific application to a design problem being considered,* but leaving the ultimate design decision to the designer - ACTIVE SUPPORT;

(iii) general advice about procedures and techniques for a specific task *which does not offer specific advice in relation to a particular design problem* - PASSIVE SUPPORT.

(iv)   facilities for *recording decisions* made by the designer and for aiding diagram and word processing, but excluding any advice (general or specific) on design procedures or techniques - MECHANICAL SUPPORT.

Most current tools, such as the BIS/IPSE, fall into the last category. The first three forms of support correspond to the KBS roles of *automaton, expert consultant* and *tutor* respectively, identified in section 1.2.3. Bearing this categorisation in mind, two basic modes of operation were devised for *Intellipse*; Advisor-mode and Designer-mode - hereafter referred to as Advisor and Designer respectively. The split between the two modes is closely related to the idea of *passive* and *active* support. Advisor and Designer will be described in more detail in sections 7.10 and 7.11.

Accordingly, the *informal* functional specification devised was for a system which would:

(i)   advise a designer about the SSD method in general, by answering specific questions about *objects* and *activities* which are relevant in the domain (Advisor);

(ii)   offer *active* support to the designer in the form of intelligent advice about a specific task within design. This advice should actively assist the designer to make design decisions and perform specific design tasks - for example, how to choose keys during data analysis (Designer);

(iii)   where appropriate, automatically execute tasks within the design phase of SSD which are currently executed manually, for example, optimizing a set of normalized relations;

(iv)   build and maintain a unified project database and data dictionary which could be linked to any existing systems and proprietary data dictionaries appropriate to a particular DP environment.

7.6 The Tasks Comprising SSD

7.6.1 Objects and activities

ACTIVITIES	OBJECTS
DATA ANALYSIS	DATA, PRIME KEY
STRUCTURE PROCESSES	PROCESS SHEET
IDENTIFY BASIC-LEVEL ACTIVITIES	ACTIVITY, ACTIVITY SHEET

Table 7.1: Examples of related activities
and objects in SSD

SSD consists of a number of tasks or *activities* to be performed in a certain order, and the SSD standards precisely specify the pre-requisites and the output for each activity. The output from an SSD activity is usually an item of documentation, an *object*, which must conform to a pre-defined structure and content. It was decided, therefore, to classify all "things" in the SSD domain as either *activities* to be performed, or *objects* which were the subject or focus of a particular activity.

A general example of this classification would be that *cooking* is an activity and *ingredients* and *meal* are the related objects. In the context of SSD, Table 7.1 illustrates some examples of related objects and activities; other objects include data relations, keys and transaction profiles, while data analysis, normalization and sizing are examples of other activities.

7.6.2 Phases within SSD

Although SSD is only one part of the whole process of software engineering, as we have already pointed out, it may itself be split up into smaller parts. Six phases of design are defined in the SSD method, as shown in Figure 7.2, namely:

•structuring data
•structuring processes
•logical design
•physical design
•detailed design
•system testing

Structuring data

The specified input, output and stored data are reviewed and analyzed in order to establish the basic logical components involved. These act as "building blocks" for the system. A set of techniques called relational analysis is used to produce basic data components in Third Normal Form.

Structuring processes

The processing requirements for the system are examined and broken down into small units. These units, together with the components of the data, will be used to create a model of the system. One of the strengths of this model is that the components may be rearranged later if necessary to meet the physical constraints on the system.

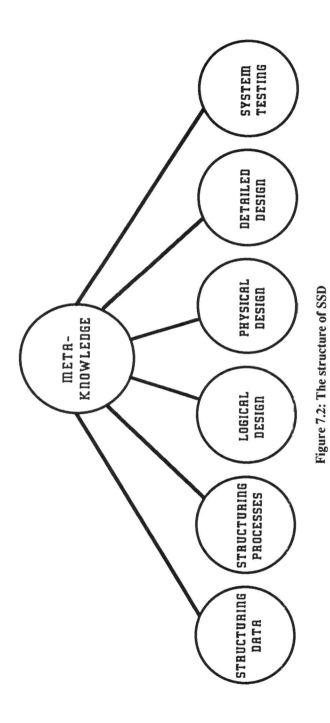

Figure 7.2: The structure of SSD

159

Logical design

A transaction profile is produced for each system input. This links together data and processes, and shows all the events in the life of the system input. Major processing dependencies between different data elements are also identified. From the transaction profiles an "ideal" design of the complete system, ignoring processing constraints, is assembled. This is checked by both the systems analyst and the user. A set of rules and conventions guide the designer in establishing the logical structure of each transaction profile.

Physical design

This is an iterative process in which the logical design is refined to fit within the physical constraints imposed by the hardware and software to be used, on aspects such as response times, run times and use of resources. *MODUS* aims to produce a physical design which is as close as possible to the logical design, in order to make maintenance as easy as possible. The design will cover identification of programs, access methods, physical records, security, etc.

Detailed design

The basic component descriptions identified earlier are used as a basis for the specification of each program. This reduces the amount of documentation to be produced and interfaces easily with whichever programming techniques are used. Procedures are provided to enable the designer to take account of existing data files, installation standards and practices, utilities and common routines.

System testing

Checklists of test conditions are compiled by using the transaction profiles and their associated processes. A series of steps based on these and on the physical design chart produces a documented test plan in terms of runs required, inputs and main files data, and conditions to be tested.

7.7 *Intellipse* Architecture

The architecture of the *Intellipse* system is illustrated in Figures 7.3 and 7.4.

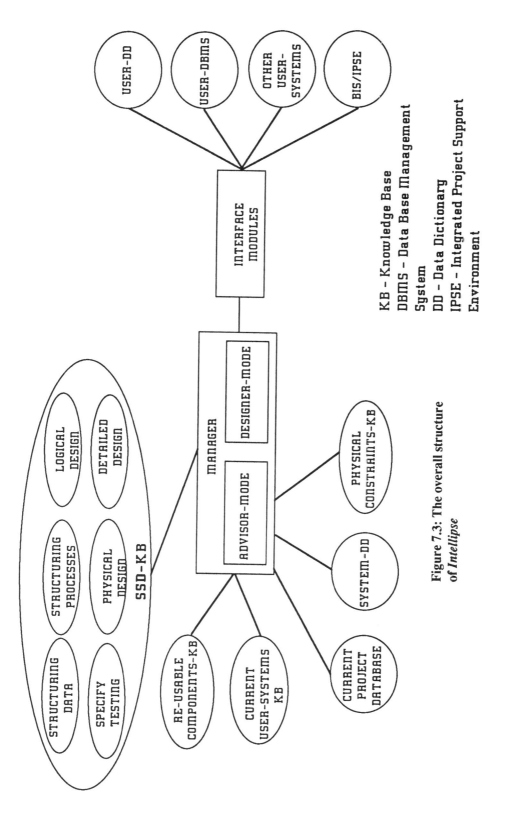

Figure 7.3: The overall structure
of *Intellipse*

KB – Knowledge Base
DBMS – Data Base Management
System
DD – Data Dictionary
IPSE – Integrated Project Support
Environment

161

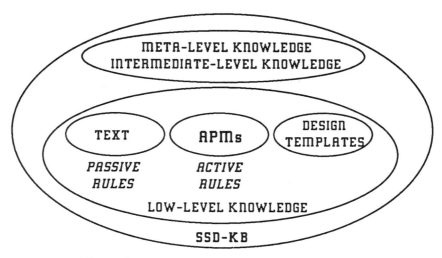

Figure 7.4: The content of an SSD knowledge-base

7.7.1 Activity program modules

The architecture of *Intellipse* has been designed with the maximum degree of modularity allowing development of the system to take place in an incremental fashion. Incremental development ensures that discrete elements of the system can be prototyped, evaluated and implemented without waiting for the system as a whole to be completed. In addition, the modular architecture enables individual components of *Intellipse's* knowledge bases to be revised as developments take place in the SSD method.

Central to the modular architecture are the Activity Program Modules (APMs). The APMs will be executable modules which, together with the meta-level knowledge base, will govern the operation of *Intellipse* in Designer-mode. They will be either KBS modules embodying the facts and rules governing a specific design task, or algorithmic programs, if the particular task can be automated. An APM may also be an existing tool such as an editor or compiler which could be invoked by the system.

The integration of KBS and non-KBS modules is another key feature of the *Intellipse* design. This concept makes explicit the need for support tools in complex domains like DPSD, to encompass both heuristic and conventional approaches under one umbrella. This type of integration is an increasingly important aspect of *operational* KBSs.

The ability to develop *Intellipse* incrementally is crucial. Section 7.6.2 indicated that SSD is a very wide domain containing a large number of distinct tasks and the *Intellipse* concept envisages an integrated system of KBS tools capable of supporting a large number of these tasks. The integration of the system will be through the exchange of data between different tools and by managing the tools under one umbrella environment. Due to the large number of tasks in SSD, the construction of such a system is likely to be unmanageable unless a rigorous *logical* separation between modules is maintained.

Integration of the individual APMs could also be achieved through the use of a project database and data dictionary which would contain details of all design decisions made during a particular project. This concept is used in the BIS/IPSE which generates a *system model* for each project being supported by the system.

7.7.2 External links

All of the DP practitioners interviewed during the initial feasibility study stressed the importance of support tools being able to link easily to existing systems and target environments. A *target environment* is the hardware system that will run a particular application. The term is used to distinguish it from the *development environment* which can be a separate system used to build the software. There are three main reasons why these external links are important.

- Most proprietary data dictionaries and similar systems used by installations to store data about their system designs and databases run in a mainframe environment. CASE tools, on the other hand, usually run in a PC or minicomputer environment, although these tools can often produce files of data in the appropriate mainframe format. If these files cannot be transferred directly to the target, manual keying of the data is required which can be a very time-consuming and error-prone exercise.

- Certain tasks in SSD may require the exchange of data between the target environment and specific *Intellipse* tools. It is also important that this can be done automatically to avoid manual keying of data.

- The BIS/IPSE provides mechanical support for several tasks in SSD. It is sensible therefore for *Intellipse* to supplement these IPSE facilities with active tools, rather than re-implementing the IPSE support and then adding on active tools.

163

7.8 Knowledge Bases

The SSD domain was divided into six separate knowledge bases. This not only corresponded with the six phases of design identified by SSD, but in addition it was expected that when Advisor came to be implemented, the separation of the knowledge bases would make it easier to fit the system into a personal computer (PC) environment.

The last point indicates that decisions about physical implementation of the *Intellipse* tools had been taken early in the project. Ideally, this is not the way things should be done; we would wish to see logical design precede physical design for systems of all kinds. However, pragmatic considerations can and do severely limit the options available from the "ideal" theoretical world.

Each of the knowledge bases is made up of several distinct components.

- Meta-level knowledge describing the objects and activities within a domain and their inter-relationships;

- Intermediate-level knowledge describing the types and categories of knowledge recorded for a specific object or activity;

- Low-level knowledge corresponding to the facts, heuristics, procedures and techniques for a given topic, stored in the system as text or Activity Program Modules (APMs);

- Partially instantiated design templates appropriate for specific activities within SSD and based on past applications, or the design experience of BIS experts. This KB exploits the commonality which exists between the designs of systems built for different application areas but whose functionality is similar.

It was thought by BIS that some of the difficulties users experienced when first using SSD arose because they failed to appreciate the context within which many of the SSD activities were performed. This failure was partly the fault of the manual which often did not justify the necessity for a particular activity or method. The manual also obscures the hierarchical relationship of the SSD activities, and it is difficult to appreciate the position of a particular activity within the overall design method. It was therefore decided, within each of the six knowledge-bases, to classify knowledge about activities in SSD into five categories.

Descriptive	*what* are the activities that must be performed?
Justificational	*why* is the activity important?
Conditional	*when* should the activity be performed and what is its relationship to other activities?
Procedural	*how* is the activity performed? - procedures and techniques.
Illustrative	*example* of the techniques used for the activity applied to a particular case.

A similar classification is used for knowledge about the objects in SSD, except in this case only the *what* and *example* categories are normally employed. The distinction between activities and objects was explained in section 7.6.1.

7.8.1 The choice of a frame-like representation schema

SSD is a domain consisting of a large number of "events" (activities) which follow each other in a strict chronological sequence. Therefore a frame-like representation schema seemed an appropriate choice for representing the knowledge in Advisor. We refer to it as frame-*like* because it exploits only some of the features normally associated with frames (see section 3.1.1). In particular, Advisor does not make use of the concept of *inheritance*, whereby a frame which is a 'child' of a frame at a higher level, inherits the properties of the higher-level frame. The representation schema used also has some similarity to the concept of *scripts* described by Schank and Abelson (SCHANK77), a structure related to frames but more appropriate to the description of knowledge about "events" such as activities in SSD. Scripts have found their best application in systems for understanding news stories written in natural language.

We shall use the term *frame(s)* for the representation schema throughout the rest of this chapter, but it should always be qualified by the proviso made in the last paragraph. One of the main reasons for choosing frames was that they formed a useful conceptual schema for facilitating discussion and communication amongst the project team, during the knowledge engineering for the Advisor system. Other features of frames which seemed appropriate for Advisor and which led to this choice of conceptual schema are summarised in Table 7.2.

SSD KNOWLEDGE	FRAME-LIKE SCHEMA
hierarchical structure	network of frames
different topic- types	slots
several knowledge types per topic	multiple slot categories
sequential description of procedures	scripts

Table 7.2: Knowledge representation
schema used in Advisor

Three types of frames were defined. They are related directly to the description of the *Intellipse* knowledge-bases given above.

Meta-level frames - "knowledge about knowledge", that is, the topics in SSD about which Advisor contains information.

Slots   Domain: e.g. structuring data, logical design...
        Topic: e.g. data analysis, record data...
        Is: e.g. activity, object...

Intermediate-level frames - knowledge about the sub-activities, related objects and knowledge-types for a particular topic.

Slots   Sub-activities: e.g. record data, select key...
        Related objects: e.g. data, prime key...
        Knowledge-type: e.g. what, why...

Low-level frames - the text corresponding to a specific knowledge-type for a particular topic.

Slots   Text: Data analysis/what. Data analysis is
                      an activity.

Examples of a meta-level and an intermediate-level frame are given in Figure 7.5.

166

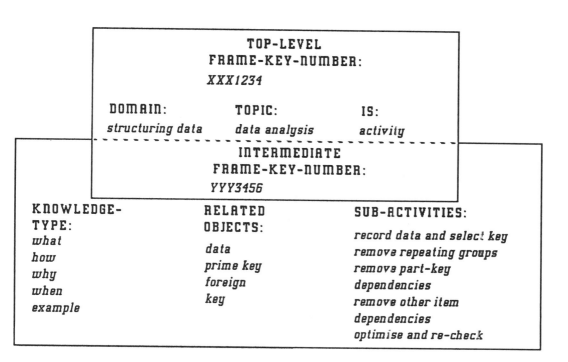

Figure 7.5: Examples of a top-level and an intermediate frame

The frame-key-numbers shown in the diagram are the *physical* means by which the frames were linked together at the implementation stage. They are not an essential element in the *logical* schema and are not therefore listed as slots above. The values of the frame-key-numbers are assigned automatically by Advisor's knowledge acquisition module (KAM), as part of the process of creating and maintaining the links between frames at the different levels, and cannot be entered directly by the knowledge engineers. The meta-level and intermediate-level frames together represent the hierarchical relationship between the SSD activities.

The Advisor system allows a user to navigate and interrogate the six knowledge-bases covering SSD. However, a separate system was required to enable the knowledge engineers to create the knowledge-bases in the first instance, and also to edit them when necessary. The KAM is a system for creating the meta-level and intermediate-level frames. It also allows text to be entered into the low-level frames. The KAM automatically assigns frame-key numbers and provides a number of other house-keeping facilities for managing the knowledge-bases.

The KAM and Advisor were designed in such a way that very little knowledge specific to SSD is built into the code. This means that, in principle, the KAM and Advisor could be used in domains other than SSD. In this respect Advisor/ KAM can be regarded as a "shell" system which could be filled with knowledge about another domain. Of course, the system would only be appropriate for hierarchical domains like SSD, which could be represented using the knowledge representation schema described above.

The structure described so far applies to both Advisor and Designer. However, the active support which Designer is intended to provide requires not only <u>more</u> knowledge about each topic within the existing knowledge-bases than the 5 categories shown in the Advisor example, but also <u>further</u> knowledge-bases. The other knowledge-bases which the Designer system requires are the Current Systems KB, the Physical Constraints KB and the Re-usable Components KB. The first two will contain knowledge about the particular DP environment in which *Intellipse* is installed. This includes data about the storage and processing constraints which the design has to meet. The Re-usable Components KB, which will be linked directly to the Current Systems KB, contains knowledge about programs and other modules available to the designer in their installation.

The knowledge bases identified in the last paragraph are one of the key features of the *Intellipse* concept. It is essential that KBS design-support tools, intended for use in a commercial DP environment, have the facility to take account of pragmatic issues, such as available disk storage and performance constraints, when making design recommendations. Many of the AI environments mentioned in chapter three emphasise the role of *abstract design* knowledge, and appear to give relatively little attention to *concrete target environment* and *application domain* knowledge.

7.9 Is SSD a Suitable Domain for KBSs?

It is useful at this stage to make some observations on the suitability of the SSD domain for KBS support, before describing how the proposed *Intellipse* architecture has actually been implemented in practice. This is most definitely a "how <u>not</u> to do it" section, since from a problem-driven perspective the domain suitability <u>must</u> be determined before any analysis is attempted! However, the *Intellipse* project did include the solution-driven task of tackling the SSD domain using KBSs. In section 2.2 we identified a list of factors which should be considered when assessing the suitability of a problem for a KBS approach. In this section these factors are considered in relation to the SSD domain as a whole.

Narrowness of the domain: SSD is a very wide domain and many of the tasks performed early in the design process involve significant general knowledge about the application environment. The width of the domain is evidenced in the first two SSD phases, structuring data and structuring processes, which contain over thirty different activities. The width of SSD is a key reason why a structured approach to knowledge engineering was required.

Complexity of the problem: SSD is a highly complex domain involving large quantities of data. However, the structured nature of the method means that the activities are performed in a highly ordered manner. This natural structure can be exploited when defining problem-solving strategies in the domain.

Nature of the problem: SSD tasks are cognitive in nature and do not require visual or sensory skills. Many of the tasks are executed manually using a pencil and paper technique.

Nature of the experts: In principle, BIS were prepared to make available domain experts who were not part of the immediate project team. However, this political support for the project had to be balanced against the client work-load at any particular time. This indicated that the involvement of individual BIS consultants would have to be planned well in advance and knowledge engineering sessions organised for maximum efficiency. Since BIS consultants spend a great deal of time working with clients who are having problems with SSD or who require tuition, it was likely that their ability to articulate their knowledge would be good.

Training: BIS have well-established training courses for SSD. The courses make extensive use of *syndicates*, where small groups of course attendees work on case studies illustrating various SSD techniques. This suggested that SSD had evolved well-established approaches to specific design problems; this was likely to make knowledge elicitation easier.

Speed of solution: None of the SSD tasks have to be solved in real-time and, although some tasks are dependent on data from other tasks, there are no specific time constraints for individual tasks.

Sensitivity of the problem: Legal and ethical issues are not relevant in SSD.

Conventional solutions: The existing mechanical support for some aspects of SSD could be regarded as conventional solutions to specific SSD problems. The research objectives of the project dictated that KBS approaches should be the focus of attention. The important issue for the *Intellipse* work was to identify which tasks could be, or were already, supported algorithmically, and which ones needed KBS support - and to integrate both types of support into a single environment.

Written material: The training courses and standards for SSD meant that a large amount of written material was available on many aspects of SSD. The availability of written material enables knowledge engineers to "do their homework" prior to the initial knowledge engineering sessions. This can greatly enhance the credibility of the knowledge engineers in the eyes of the experts, who do not then feel as if they are talking to people ignorant of their field of expertise. Similarly, from the knowledge engineers' point of view, the expert does not appear to be talking a foreign language. Thus the written material can speed up significantly the early stages of knowledge elicitation.

The main advantages of SSD with respect to KBS support can therefore be summarized as:

- SSD is a highly structured methodology;
- the domain experts are likely to be articulate;
- a large quantity of training/written material is available.

The main disadvantages of SSD with respect to KBS support appeared to be:

- the width and complexity of the domain;
- the extensive use made of general knowledge;
- the uncertainty regarding the availability of domain experts.

The last of these points was of course a characteristic of this project, rather than of the domain itself, but it was just as important in practice.

The most difficult potential problem seemed to be the use of common sense knowledge. In the DPSD domain common sense can be taken to mean general knowledge about different application domains (finance, manufacturing, banking, insurance etc.) or different target hardware/software environments (IBM, Honeywell, DEC etc.). Only a closer examination of individual SSD activities could resolve this question, which entailed starting to construct Advisor without knowing how much of it it would be possible to build. This is the classic problem of specifying a KBS, and is a key reason for the existence of the "secondary feasibility" stage in the methodology to be described in chapter 9.

7.10 Advisor

Advisor is a passive, knowledge-based, question-answering system dealing with the SSD domain. It is *knowledge-based* because it contains knowledge about the design process which reflects the expertise of expert human designers not to be found in the SSD manual or standards. It is *passive* since it offers advice about SSD in general, and not in relation to a specific application. It is a *question-answering* system because its mode of operation is intended to model the actions of a BIS/SSD consultant answering general questions about SSD for inexperienced SSD designers. An alternative way to describe Advisor is as a thesaurus of the SSD domain, which enables the user to traverse the knowledge-base(s) in a series of steps or jumps.

7.10.1 Who were the intended users of Advisor?

Advisor was intended to be a more accessible version of the SSD training manual as well as presenting SSD in a more structured and logical manner than the manual. It was to contain knowledge of procedures and techniques which could not be found in the manual, or in any other documentary form. The manual is designed to support the training course and is organised to reflect the way the material is presented on the course. It does not, for example, contain an index. Many attendees of the courses complain that, while the manual is a very good support for the week-long course, it is a very unsatisfactory guide or tutor, once the course is over and the new SSD practitioner is back in their own environment facing real design problems. It followed from this that two basic categories of potential user for Advisor were important:

- *the naive SSD user* - course attendees whose only practical experience of the method is the syndicate work during the training course, and whose only support after the course is the SSD manual;

- *the rusty SSD user* - someone who has attended an SSD course in the past and has significant practical experience gained on actual development projects, but who has not used the method for some time and needs reminding of some of the techniques.

7.10.2 Advisor as it was implemented: structure

Advisor has three basic components, as shown in Figure 7.6:

- a human interface, incorporating a natural language query analyzer;
- a set of knowledge bases containing facts, rules, procedures and techniques relating to the objects and activities in SSD;
- the "core system" , comprising a knowledge base representing the hierarchical relationship of all the activities within SSD, and a mechanism for navigating the SSD domain.

Figure 7.6 also includes the KAM, which has already been described above; although not strictly a part of Advisor, it enables the knowledge engineer to perform the function of the learning system, as discussed in chapter 3. Figure 7.6 has been drawn in the style of Figure 3.1, to emphasize such similarities, and also the differences between Advisor and a typical stand-alone rule-based KBS. The most obvious of these is that Advisor has a "navigation mechanism" rather than an inference engine.

The structure of the knowledge bases and the core system was as we have described in sections 7.7 and 7.8, with extra layers of hierarchy within the activities and objects where necessary. The human interface operates in two modes: a multiple-level menu system, intended for the naive user, and a natural language query analyzer intended for the user who is already familiar with either SSD or Advisor itself. The latter is a simple, pattern-matching interpreter which enables the user to enter free-form queries in English. Examples of the sort of queries which can be processed by the system are:

•What is a prime key?
•When do I start the physical design stage?
•How do I perform first normal form analysis?
•Show me an example of a transaction profile.

The query analyzer is designed to detect only key words or phrases in the input text, rather than being a full natural language capability based on a sophisticated set of grammar rules and so on. It had been established that this was the limit

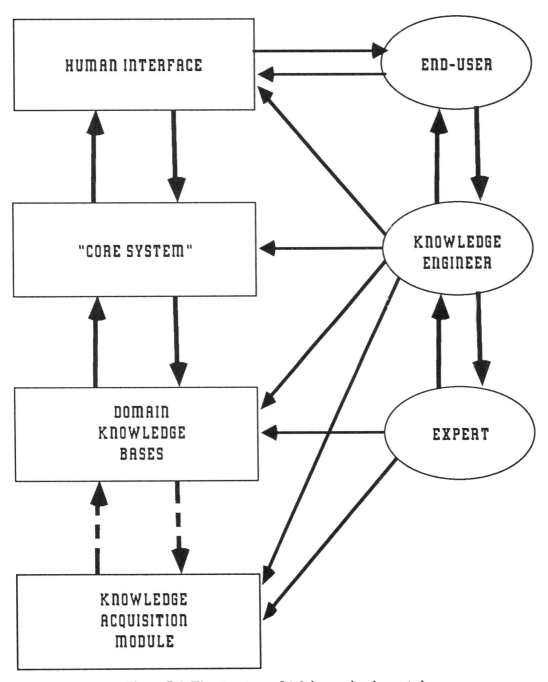

Figure 7.6: The structure of Advisor as implemented

of the capability required (see section 7.3.1). A particular benefit is the ability of the query analyzer to accept ungrammatical and/or incomplete sentences. This enables a user who is familiar with the system to access the knowledge-bases by a "fast path", by using queries which only contain the appropriate key words.

The menu-driven interface mode is based on a standard set of functions permitting the user to step or jump between frames and retrieve the relevant text. Figure 7.7 shows the main screen display in this mode.

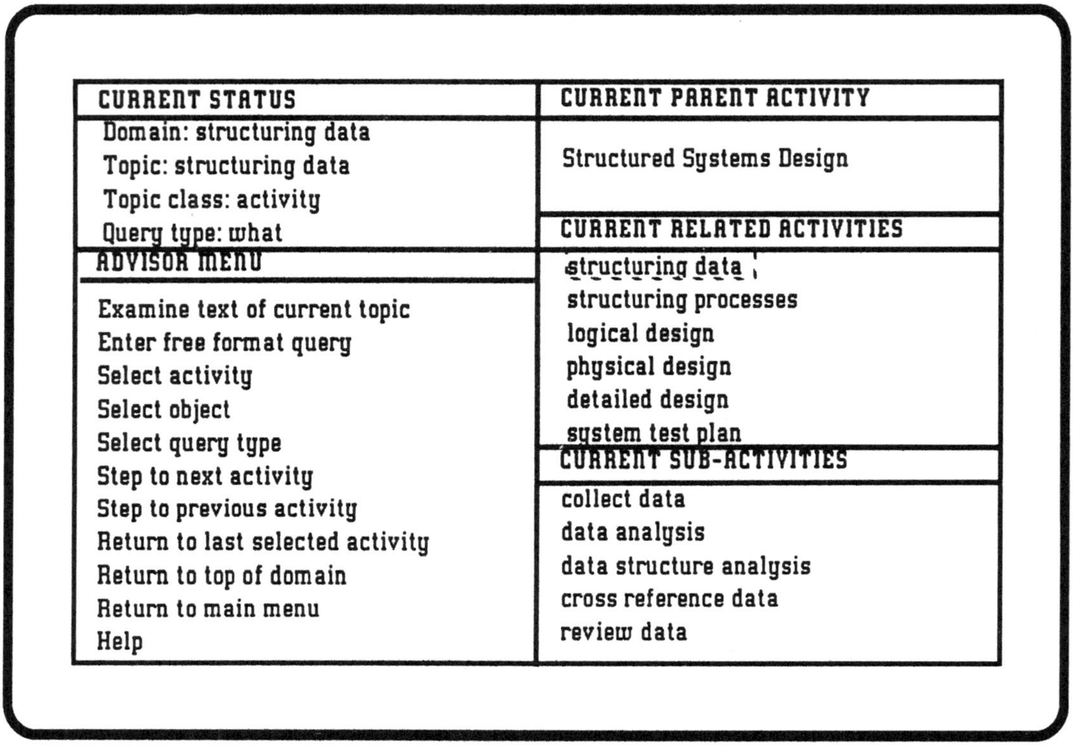

CURRENT STATUS	CURRENT PARENT ACTIVITY
Domain: structuring data Topic: structuring data Topic class: activity Query type: what	Structured Systems Design
	CURRENT RELATED ACTIVITIES
ADVISOR MENU	structuring data structuring processes logical design physical design detailed design system test plan
Examine text of current topic Enter free format query Select activity Select object Select query type Step to next activity Step to previous activity Return to last selected activity Return to top of domain Return to main menu Help	
	CURRENT SUB-ACTIVITIES
	collect data data analysis data structure analysis cross reference data review data

Figure 7.7: Advisor main menu screen

The screen is divided into five windows:

• Current Status
• Current Parent Activity
• Current Related Activities
• Current Sub-activities
• Advisor Menu

Current Status shows the current position of the system within the SSD knowledge-bases. Current Parent Activity shows which activity is immediately "above" the current activity in the hierarchy of frames. Current Related Activities lists all activities with this parent which are at the same level as the current activity. Current Sub-activities lists all the activities which make up the current activity, i.e. have it as a parent.

The Advisor Menu consists of eleven functions:

• Examine text of current topic
• Enter free format query
• Select activity
• Select object
• Select query type
• Step to next activity
• Step to previous activity
• Return to last selected activity
• Return to top of domain
• Return to main menu
• Help

A few of these require further explanation. The "Examine text of current topic" function enables the user to browse through all the text relating to the current topic, beginning with that for the current query type. The two options for stepping through activities apply to those in the three "Current......activities" windows. "Return to last selected activity" is relevant only when the current topic is an object, since objects never have activities below them in the hierarchy, although they may have other objects. The structure of the system is based around the activities, and therefore Advisor's various menu screens normally display related activities but not related objects. The exceptions to this are when "Select object" is chosen from a menu, in which case the system offers the user a further menu of the objects related to the current topic, and when the current topic is itself an object.

7.10.3 Advisor as it was implemented: environment

The Advisor system was implemented in Prolog on IBM-compatible PCs running under DOS. The choice of delivery hardware was principally governed by the desire to make the *Intellipse* tools as widely available as possible. The selection of any particular mini or mainframe environment would have restricted access to Advisor considerably, and the use of a workstation would have been vastly more restrictive. Hardly any workstations were to be found outside research organizations at the time the work on Advisor began to take place (1986). In addition, the PC offered much more scope for the use of windows and a mouse in the human interface. (Note that the Macintosh, which would have offered even better interfacing possibilities, was ruled out during the feasibility studies when it was discovered that most DP departments had never even <u>seen</u> one, let alone bought one!) Development was also done on IBM PCs; access was again important, as was the avoidance of any need to port the system to a different machine before delivery, and the portability of a PC-based system made the testing and demonstration of Advisor much easier. The "downside" of using a PC was that it added the extra problem of linking to whatever mini or mainframe the DP workers were using SSD to develop their systems for. This was not a particular difficulty for the passive Advisor, but would be an issue for the "active" Designer.

As far as software was concerned, Prolog was chosen in preference to a shell because the PC shells available at the time were unable to cope with the desired structure based on frames rather than rules. Conventional languages were also rejected for a similar reason. This left Prolog and LISP, and Prolog was chosen simply because those involved in the project preferred it! It was however also probably true that the Prolog systems available at the time for PCs were faster than the LISP systems. It was found during the development that Prolog could not cope easily with the large amounts of text involved, and this problem was solved by interfacing with a word-processing package for text entry and editing. One or two of the shells would have avoided this problem, but had no facilities for over-riding their rule-based inference engines.

7.10.4 Evaluation of Advisor

Advisor has been evaluated in detail in tests by the industrial partners in the project, and on a development by BIS Banking Systems, a sister company of BIS Applied Systems. In addition, general evaluations were performed by experienced DP personnel from several other installations. The reaction was generally very positive, especially for the induction of new staff. The main improvements needed were identified as the inclusion of far more example problems - several on each topic instead of just one or two - and the ability to tailor the Advisor knowledge bases to fit variations to the BIS SSD standards, or indeed "local" methodologies. This would entail making an improved version of the KAM available to the user organization as well as the Advisor system, to cover the wider function of a Knowledge Base Manipulator (KBM). At the time of writing, this work has not been completed, and Advisor's knowledge remains restricted to "standard" SSD.

7.11 Designer

The objective of Designer is to provide *active* support for the designer carrying out activities in SSD. Designer should not only be able to execute some design activities itself but, where the latter is infeasible, it must provide sufficient advice to allow the human designer to make appropriate design decisions. That is, Designer enables the user to work on a specific design problem by actively invoking the rules and procedures which are passively described in the Advisor knowledge bases.

(In Advisor, the designer is able to interrogate the knowledge bases about any of the objects or activities in the SSD domain, but Advisor cannot actively execute, in relation to a specific application, any of the design activities which it knows about. However, the Advisor knowledge bases can act as an explanation facility while the user is in Designer-mode.)

Looking at Designer concept in comparison with other current support tools, where current tools simply *record* the decisions taken by the designer, or facilitate the mechanical tasks of diagram and document production, Designer should contribute its knowledge of the design process, thereby actively promoting good design on the part of the human designer.

It was pointed out in section 7.9 that DP systems design is an extremely broad domain; progress on Designer has therefore been correspondingly slow. Many tasks are difficult to support effectively with current KBS techniques. For example, putting a list of data items into Third Normal Form is an activity which is largely algorithmic, but requires a high level of understanding of the specific business problem being tackled and the business world in general, in order to perform the task effectively. This is the common sense knowledge problem also identified in section 7.9. Work on Designer has therefore concentrated on the area of physical design within SSD, which is based on a well-defined set of information and requires relatively little general knowledge about the business. It does however require considerable expertise in order to produce a design which meets performance requirements, is necessary in every system development, and is often performed inadequately at present because of a lack of expertise.

This was therefore the first area of Designer to be developed, and led to work concentrating on physical design for one particular database management system. By this time, the proposed methodology for KBS development was taking shape, and hence the system is described in chapter 9, <u>after</u> the methodology itself.

7.12 Summary

This chapter has described the *Intellipse* project as it took place (from 1985 to 1988), warts and all. (We trust we have indicated all the important "how not to do it" points!) When we have finished outlining our proposed methodology for building KBSs, we shall return to the *Intellipse* project and re-evaluate our experience.

References

(DIG87) A.Dignan, The Alvey Directorate. Personal Communication, 1987.
(EDW88) John S.Edwards and Jon L.Bader, "Expert systems for university admissions", *J. Opl Res. Soc.*, Vol.39, No.1, pp.33-40, 1988.
(SCHANK77) R.C.Schank and R.P.Abelson, *"Scripts, Plans, Goals and Understanding"*, Lawrence Erlbaum Associates, 1977.

Chapter 8: Measuring the Success of a Knowledge-based System

8.0 Introduction

All changes to organizational systems should be evaluated. Computer systems particularly need evaluation, as they often represent a drastic change in working practice, one with a substantial initial capital outlay, and a redirection of expenditure from labour to equipment.

Most early KBSs were not evaluated as potential commercial systems, because they were intended solely as research and development tools, i.e. built from an exploratory perspective. This has caused some confusion as to what makes a successful KBS.

Measuring the success of KBSs is in fact a harder task than for conventional systems, and raises new issues. In this chapter we shall consider the problems of performance measurement as a whole, look at what has been done in other areas, and then address the specific issue of measuring the success of KBSs.

This chapter also constitutes the start of our description of the POLITE methodology, since measuring the success of the KBS involves considering all the organizational issues relevant to the KBS, and this is where the methodology must start.

8.1 Why Measure the Success?

We have already stated that all changes of any kind to organizational systems should be monitored, so that their success (or otherwise) may be measured. Indeed, monitoring of all activities is, or at least should be, a key element of managing the organization (see, for example, Humble (HUM73)).

Nevertheless, many managers, whether their responsibilities lie in computer systems or elsewhere, seem to be content with "getting the change working" without ever sitting down afterwards and looking at precisely what the new system has achieved. In particular, the transition from a manual to a computer system is often so disruptive and chaotic that short-term considerations, such as simply ensuring that the new system discharges its basic functions at all, override everything else.

Why, then, are we interested in measuring the success of a new system? There are three principal reasons:

    (i)   to monitor the extent to which the system meets its predicted performance objectives;

    (ii)   as justification for the actions which were taken;

    (iii)   to enable the organization to learn from what happened.

In the complex, rapidly-changing commercial world of today, it is almost inevitable that any action will have slightly different consequences from those originally intended. The more far-reaching the changes, the harder they will be to predict precisely. It is therefore essential to carry out explicit monitoring of a new system, rather than relying on ad hoc or informal feedback on its performance.

Justification should not be seen here purely in the narrow sense of "guarding your back", or as a paper exercise in creative accounting. Whatever type of organization they run, the managers are responsible for the way in which they run it. Whether this responsibility is to the shareholders of a limited company, to the local population served by a local government department, or to each other as the firm's co-owners, the managers should be in a position to justify the time, effort and money spent on organizational changes.

Most managers would admit the need for monitoring and justification, albeit sometimes rather grudgingly, but organizational learning is often completely forgotten. This may be because it doesn't show directly on the balance sheet! However, it is at least as important for the long-term viability of the organization.

Three components of the organizational learning are worth distinguishing here:

- lessons about the particular system being changed;

- lessons about the type of "solution" which was tried;

- improved skills and expertise on the part of those involved with the change.

Example (non-KBS): a company wishes to improve its system for taking customers' orders. In the old paper-based system, all orders are processed on the basis of written information, either from the customer or taken down over the telephone in a somewhat haphazard manner. The new computer system, based on interactive use of VDUs by telephone staff, allows all orders to be phoned in. For such a change, specific benefits under the three headings mentioned above might include:

• a better understanding of how customers' orders are distributed across different times of day and different days of the week;
• practical knowledge of how the response time of the computer used varies with the number of simultaneous users;
• more expertise in database work in the data processing department, job enrichment for the order processing clerks (who now speak directly to customers), more knowledge of telecommunications from setting up the answering system.

Bearing in mind all the considerations we have just outlined, it is clear that measuring the success of a new system is a very broad concept, which can only be done in relation to a particular organization and its needs.

Unfortunately, when the change involves a computer system, this concept has often been confused with the narrower issue of whether or not the system meets its specification. One historical reason for this was the traditional insularity of DP departments, leading to exactly the "guarding your back" style of justification mentioned earlier. ("We've built the system we think you asked for, so stop complaining.") Whilst it is important to be able to assess the performance of a system in this sense, it is not enough for a commercial system, since the specification is itself only an interpretation of the original commercial need.

We will therefore distinguish three levels of measuring the success of a system, following the terminology used by O'Keefe *et al* (O'K87): evaluation, validation and verification. (See Figure 8.1)

Evaluation is the highest-level concept, and thus the broadest. It's the one which we have been addressing so far - "has the system contributed towards the organization's overall success?"

Validation is part of evaluation, though a very important one; O'Keefe *et al* refer to it as "the cornerstone of evaluation". It is concerned with the performance of the system as constructed, i.e. does the system work acceptably, viewed as a computer system for the task envisaged.

Verification is a narrower concept still, being the term we shall use for

181

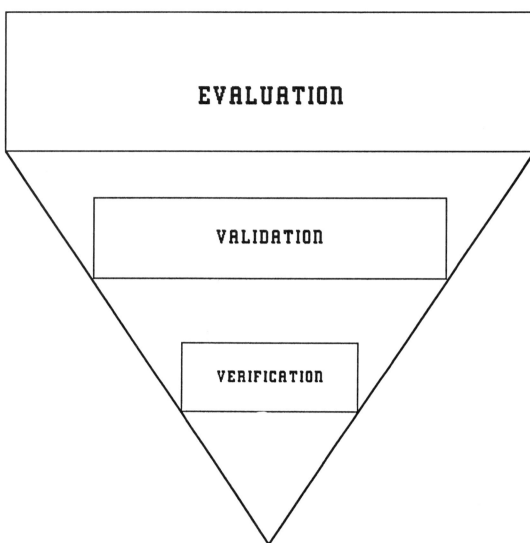

Figure 8.1: Levels of measuring the success

assessing whether or not a system meets its specification, irrespective of how that specification was produced or its relevance to the task or to the organization.

It is important to realise that these *are* three different concepts. Examples abound of systems "built to spec", i.e. successfully verified, which do not function in practice because crucial elements were omitted from the specification. The systems thus fail at the validation level. Similarly, a system may be perfectly valid, and yet not able to be used properly in the organization, for example because of developments elsewhere, or circumstances not directly connected with the computer system. The author encountered an example where a conventional computer system "failed" overall because of the lack of a telephone in the office where the terminal was situated; this made it impossible to integrate the system into the normal working routine of the people who were expected to use it.

When we look specifically at knowledge-based systems, which by their very nature are more closely concerned with human knowledge and behaviour than a conventional system such as a general ledger system, the gap between evaluation and validation is likely to be wider. One reason for this is the greater difficulty of judging whether or not a KBS is an appropriate way to respond to an organizational need. Another is the general lack of experience of what makes a KBS successful in practice as opposed to "in the lab".

The gap between validation and verification is also likely to be wider at present, but not solely because of the nature of KBSs. One feature of the literature on KBSs is that many of the lessons which DP systems builders learned painfully over a long period of time have been ignored by KBS builders. These include the need for proper project management, and the benefits to be gained from the use of structured methods, both of which we have already mentioned in this book. Another "forgotten lesson" is that of involving the user in the development of the system; making incorrect assumptions about the end-user is a potential disaster at the validation level. Yet many reported KBSs have been built with the expert "representing" the user, even though the expert is not the intended user of the system. We ran into problems of this kind ourselves, even with what seemed a relatively straightforward expert system.

The system was intended to help an undergraduate admissions tutor (the author) by allowing straightforward applications to be dealt with by the admissions assistant (a clerical worker). The prototype expert system was constructed by the expert with little reference to the proposed user; to be honest, we weren't entirely sure it could be done at all, it being the first "real" expert system we had tried to develop. As originally constructed, it required the user, among other tasks, to read the reference written by the applicant's head teacher (or equivalent) and then input information about various aspects of it. This the admissions assistant was unwilling to do. She was happy to input information requiring no judgement on her part, for example predicted examination results when these were clearly given, but not for example to give an assessment of what the head teacher had said about the applicant's motivation, even as a menu choice between descriptions such as 'less than satisfactory', 'satisfactory' and 'very encouraging'. Such subjective impressions, she argued, were after all the tutor's responsibility, and she was quite correct. The system therefore had to be redesigned to operate (somewhat less effectively of course) with input restricted to elements which she did not regard as requiring judgement. In addition, in order to avoid other similar problems, the author's further participation in the development was restricted to the role of expert. For a fuller account of this see Edwards and Bader (EDW88). As we have said, we didn't always get it right first time either - but we hope we have learned from our mistakes!

Another interesting difference where KBSs are concerned is the question of the relationships in the reverse direction, i.e. "up" the levels. For a conventional DP system, it is difficult to conceive how a system which failed at the validation level could be rated a success at the evaluation level, or how a system could be valid if it failed the verification against its specification. However, it is less clear that these restrictions apply to KBSs: if we consider a human expert, it is possible that the expert could be making a successful contribution to the organization overall (evaluation) without entirely fulfilling either their original job specification or any modified version of it (verification). This is possible for the human because specifications of human jobs tend to be imprecise by DP standards. For example, a secretary's job description may include "deal with personal callers", with no further indication of *how* to deal with them (offer them a cup of tea? shoot them?). Indeed, in many "expert" jobs, part of the expertise involved is precisely the ability to cope with novel situations. These, by definition, could not be pre-specified.

Current commercial KBSs do not possess expertise relating to novel situations, and so it is unnecessary for us to address this situation yet. We shall therefore proceed on the basis that successful verification is a necessary part of successful validation, and successful validation is in its turn a necessary part of successful evaluation, for KBSs as well as for conventional DP systems. The point about specification of KBSs will however be very relevant to the verification of KBSs, and we shall tackle this in a later section.

8.2 What Needs to be Done?

The basic tasks involved in measuring the success of a KBS can be described very simply: establish the objectives which the organization has for the system, at all levels, and set up a programme of testing related to these objectives.

However, like our secretary's job description in the previous section, this isn't precise enough for commercial use. We need to look more closely at the four key elements, namely objectives, tests, metrics and judgements.

Objectives mean many different things to different people; the term is applied to statements as diverse as:

- "be the U.K.'s No.1 software house";

- "increase our market share";

- "put a PC on the desk of every manager by the end of the year";

- "calculate the payroll for up to 2000 weekly-paid employees".

These examples vary both in the organizational task which they address, ranging from the strategic to the week-by-week operational, and in their precision. Probably only the third example would be sufficiently precise to be usable.

Our view of objectives follows that of Moravsky (MOR77); it is typical of the problems of terminology we have mentioned that *he* calls them goals! He identifies four characteristics which the goals/objectives must exhibit:

-       be manifest statements (i.e. available in a written form for later reference);

-       be specific enough to permit objective interpretation;

-       focus on the receiving system (i.e. the clients/customers/users, not the providers/developers);

-       specify a time dimension.

These objectives need to be set at all levels, since they must cover evaluation, validation and verification.

For a DP system, we need to address commercial and computing issues; there is usually a reasonably close match between the levels, what needs to be assessed, and the people responsible for the assessment, as seen in Figure 8.2. We have labelled the objectives at each level as performance objectives, system requirements and detailed specification respectively, to fit in with common DP terminology. For a KBS or for a hybrid system, i.e. one with both conventional

185

and KBS components, we will need to address commercial issues, computing issues, *and* issues relating to the domain of knowledge/expertise. There will still be a rough matching of the levels, what is being assessed, and the people, but it is certainly not a one-to-one relationship, as Figure 8.3 shows. The setting of objectives for KBSs is thus more complicated than for DP systems.

Evaluation	**Commercial issues**
Validation	**Computing issues (system)**
Verification	**Computing issues (detail)**

Figure 8.2: Issues at each level for a conventional system

Metrics and the measurement activity associated with them are probably the least contentious of our four terms; everyone will realise we mean assessing the quantifiable aspects of the system's performance. Thus for once there is no difference between KBSs and other types of computer system. The only points to highlight are that defining what is to be measured includes choosing the metrics (i.e. the units of measurement) *and* deciding on the method to be used for measuring - including who is to do it.

Judgements are relevant in two different ways where KBSs are concerned; judgements made of the system, and judgements incorporated in the system. As with metrics, there is little controversy about the general meaning of the term, and as far as basic qualitative aspects of the system and its performance are concerned, there is again no difference between KBSs and other computer systems. There is, however, a vital difference in as much as most KBSs are actually intended to embody human judgement, whereas DP systems generally are not. For a DP system, it is feasible to assess most of its operations

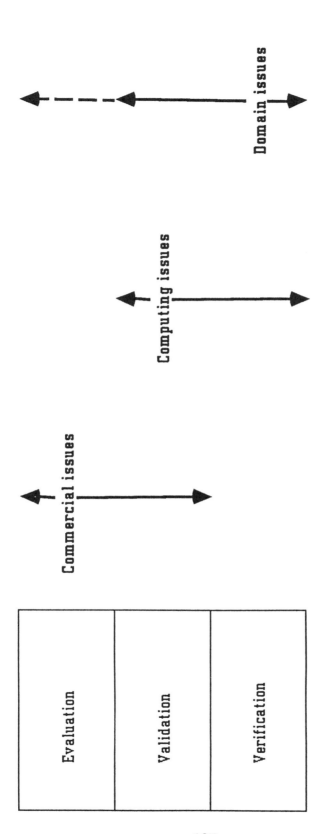

Figure 8.3: Issues related to levels for a KBS

objectively: different, equally competent observers are unlikely to disagree about whether or not the results of a calculation are correct, or the desired record has been retrieved, or the output starts at the stated place on the VDU screen. (We are working at the verification level here).

However, for a KBS, the correctness of the system's judgements may have to be related to those of the humans whose knowledge it contains. This may be the only reference available, as in our admissions tutor system or in credit scoring systems; there is no universally applicable right decision. In such cases, the problem owner must set the appropriate criteria of performance. After all, if the task requires judgement, then by definition it cannot be completely specified in an objective algorithmic manner. Another typical possibility is that it may be possible to check some of the system's recommendations, but not others. PROSPECTOR's reputation was based on the discovery of a molybdenum deposit which human geologists had overlooked; this being confirmed by subsequent drilling (DUDA79). However, this approach can only work for *positive* recommendations; it would not be possible to drill everywhere that a geological KBS suggested was not worth trying, just to make sure there were no deposits of value there. The test here would thus have to be by reference to the human geologists. Even then we would not know how many (if any) deposits both PROSPECTOR and the human geologists missed.

This need to rely on the human expert's performance in measuring the system's performance thus raises difficulties related to the meaning of human performance, which we shall explore in later sections.

The reader may feel that there is a slight contradiction between our comments here and our earlier requirement that objectives must be specific enough to permit objective interpretation. This is not in fact a problem; the statement of objectives should only permit one interpretation, but any part of the assessment calling for a judgement is necessarily subjective. For example, one of the objectives for a KBS which advises customers about a company's life assurance policies may be to explain clearly and accurately the reasons for recommending a particular type of policy. "Definitions" of clarity and accuracy could be added if necessary, so that the objective itself was unambiguous to those specifying it. However, different customers might still disagree about the clarity of the same explanation, and different experts might disagree about its accuracy.

Tests are the last of our four aspects. Hardly anyone would doubt the need for some kind of test of the operational KBS before it is put into commercial use, but there are problems not only with how to carry out the tests, but with what can reasonably be concluded from the test results. These problems are not confined to KBSs; they apply also to conventional DP systems, to decision support systems, and to models such as simulations.

Conventional DP in particular has produced a considerable amount of literature on software testing (e.g. Myers (MYERS79)). One school of thought - allied to the formal methods school which we mentioned in chapter 4 - is that the only way to ensure the production of error-free software is to use languages for specification and coding which permit the correctness of the software to be proven mathematically. This is a worthy goal, and still the focus of considerable research effort, but relatively little of this work has been taken up by data processing departments so far.

Even if such a method is eventually perfected, it cannot address all the levels of performance measurement. Verification would be taken care of, as would the validation of those systems where general agreement exists as to precisely what that system should do (cf. Partridge's idea of a completely specified problem, mentioned in chapter 6) - for example, one which performs calculations which themselves are based on a mathematical model, such as a linear programming package. By its very nature, however, this program proving approach cannot address either the evaluation level, or the validation of systems where some flexibility of definition exists. Validation of most KBSs will fall into this category.

In the absence of methods based on formal proof, the principal issue in testing is to balance the effort expended on testing against the resultant improvement in the quality of the system produced. Even for conventional systems, it is not unusual for testing to consume 40% of total development effort/costs, rising to as much as 80% for some safety-critical systems such as flight control and the monitoring of nuclear reactors. Despite this expenditure of effort, the combinatorial explosion which results from the loops and branches in all but the most trivial of programs means that exhaustive testing, i.e. trying all possible combinations of inputs, is impracticable given the size of commercial systems. The testing strategy thus needs to be developed very carefully, covering how the testing is to be carried out (almost always on more than one level), the bank of test cases to be used, and the people who are to carry out the testing. All three of these facets are potentially more difficult for KBSs than for other types of system: the first because of the relative lack of experience of testing such systems; the second because cases may be harder to generate and evaluate; and the third because the nature of the interaction between the user and the system is less constrained for KBSs than for conventional DP systems.

8.3 How to Measure the Success: Sources of Inspiration

We have already referred to the existence of a considerable amount of literature on the testing of conventional software. One of the key points in this literature is that many of the lessons learned only emerged from considerable experience of testing actual systems, which revealed the inadequacies of the approaches then in use, especially the ad hoc ones.

Our philosophy therefore is to look first at methods for measuring the performance of other types of system, in order to see the extent to which they are suitable for KBSs. We believe that this is a far more fruitful approach than concentrating solely on the properties of KBSs themselves, since the overall similarity of purpose (evaluating a system in relation to a given commercial need) between different types of systems is more important than any differences in the nature of the systems themselves. Also, where the system developed is a hybrid system, i.e. one with some knowledge-based components, the methods to be used for measuring the success of these components must integrate with those for the other parts of the system, which may be conventional computer systems (data processing or technical) or indeed paper-based systems (e.g. training manuals). In most cases, *evaluation* can only sensibly be done for the whole system rather than its component parts, whereas some validation and/or verification may be done at the component level. We shall therefore draw extensively on methods for setting objectives which come from the fields of operational research and the systems approach; on methods for managing change from general management theory; and on methods of validation from data processing and from mathematical and simulation modelling.

8.3.1 Operational research and "soft" systems analysis

One of the major contributions from operational research and soft systems is the realisation that activities are going on at two levels - the organization's commercial needs, and the project itself, which is intended to meet one or more of them. Managing the project must therefore concentrate on both of these levels, and on the interface between them, in order to improve the chances of a successful outcome. This has already been implicit in the earlier sections of this chapter.

Another significant contribution is that there has for many years been research into the success of OR projects in practice. This stemmed from an element of doubt about the effectiveness of some OR work, especially that involving sophisticated mathematical models. The division between the "commercial"

The Analyst's view

The Manager's view	UNSUCCESSFUL	SUCCESSFUL BUT NOT IMPLEMENTED	SUCCESSFUL AND IMPLEMENTED	TOTAL
UNSUCCESSFUL	3	3	5	11
SUCCESSFUL AND NOT IMPLEMENTED	5	7	16	28
SUCCESSFUL AND IMPLEMENTED			10	10
TOTAL	8	10	31	49

Figure 8.4: Perceptions of analysts and managers regarding OR projects

view of the project and the "technical" view of the project was as apparent here as it used to be in conventional DP; only the nature of the technical expertise differed. Wedley and Ferrie took the interesting step of seeking two views about each OR project - those of the analyst and the manager (WED78). The differences involved are salutary, both for their magnitude and their direction (see Figure 8.4). This supplies us with yet more justification for paying attention to the people who are carrying out any part of an evaluation. The situation is of course further complicated for KBSs by the presence of the human experts as a *third* "interested party".

As a result of such studies, the work done under the heading of "OR methodology", or "the process of OR" has concentrated quite heavily in recent years on the "problem structuring" phases of the project, which precede (and lead to the commissioning of) any technical element which there may be.

Most of these activities are concerned with translating the commercial need into a specific project, and thus may be seen as a process of specifying the appropriate objectives against which the success of the project overall, i.e. at the evaluation level, should be measured. Many of these activities are equally necessary in the production of a computer system, and their messy nature may open a few eyes amongst those readers concerned solely with technical matters.

Because of the different technical nature of some of the solutions, OR methodology itself has little to contribute at the levels of validation and verification, although OR people and their philosophy (including the author!) will have an influence. One specific OR technique of close relevance to KBSs is simulation modelling, and we shall look at that aspect in a later section.

8.3.2 Conventional software engineering

We have already covered conventional software engineering in some detail in chapter 4. As far as measuring the success of its systems is concerned, then in contrast to OR, conventional software engineering has looked mainly at verification and validation, with relatively little about the evaluation issues which we mention here. However, in recent years many authors (of whom Gladden's contribution was both early and thought-provoking) have at least begun to recognise the existence of evaluation, and some influence on conventional software engineering has been seen. Validation and verification are usually combined under the heading of testing; a good summary of current practice is the one edited by Ould and Unwin on behalf of the British Computer Society (OULD86). This does cover some evaluation issues, and indeed devotes more space to validation than to verification. It is based on 4 different views of testing, namely those of the manager, the user, the designer and the programmer respectively, and a life-cycle approach in which the following "products" are produced: the requirements expression, the system specification, the system for trial and the delivered system.

8.3.3 Monte Carlo simulation modelling

One operational research technique which does have lessons to offer is that of Monte Carlo simulation. Monte Carlo simulation models are intended to forecast the behaviour of systems with some uncertain elements, so that "what if?" analyses may be carried out. Merely creating a model which runs successfully (verification) is therefore inadequate; in order to be useful, the model must capture the relevant features of the real system accurately enough to be of value as an experimental test. The considerable reliance on statistical techniques also means that there are potential similarities between the way a simulation model functions and the way in which a knowledge-based system handling uncertainty will function.

As far as testing is concerned, the properties of the statistical techniques used to handle uncertainty are only helpful at the validation level, except for issues relating to the speed at which the simulation model runs. At the validation level, the overall structure of the model is far more important than its statistical properties. Indeed, simulation models are often constructed by building a deterministic version of the structure first and "slotting-in" the variability later, using modules which have been verified separately. (See for example Pidd (PIDD88).)

Other specific lessons emerging from simulation modelling include:

• the problems of judging the adequacy of the model's behaviour in rare or novel cases;

• the gap between identifying incorrect behaviour in a complex model and being able to correct it;

• the importance of displaying the process, rather than just the outputs, to enable users to judge when the model is inadequate.

One advance addressing the first and last of these three issues was the development of visual interactive simulation, whereby the operation of the model system is animated graphically on the VDU screen. (See for example P.Bell (BELL86).) In the best of such systems, the model may be stopped, modified, run backwards, run faster or slower, allowing much closer investigation by both developers and users. This bears some similarities to Gladden's proposed approach to software development already referred to in the previous section.

8.3.4 Other literature on KBSs

At all three levels, testing of existing KBSs has tended to be by *ad hoc* methods. No generally accepted methods have yet emerged, and the literature is noticeable for considerable disagreements about what needs to be tested and how to do it. In our view, many of these difficulties again stem from the R & D/ commercial system dichotomy. It is only realistic to evaluate a system against a commercial need. Since the majority of reported systems were not built in response to a commercial need, it is not surprising that confusion has resulted. Nevertheless, there have been some useful "theoretical" contributions, a few of which we shall now review. An early contribution was that of M.Bell (BELL85), who considered why expert systems fail at the validation and verification levels, without apparently seeing the difference between validation and evaluation.

The work of Connell and others at Southampton (CONN87), by contrast, concentrated on evaluation, and was one of the first to clarify two key differences: those between research and development systems and commercial systems, and those between small and large KBSs.

O'Keefe et al, whom we have already mentioned, looked particularly at validation issues for expert systems, again drawing upon one or two ideas from OR. Their work is particularly important as being a comprehensive look at the question of finding suitable metrics for KBSs. Many have mentioned this question, but few others have contributed much towards answering it.

Broadening the issue even further, Beerel (BEER87) produced the first book on KBSs which was primarily addressed to the management issues, rather than those of a research or technical nature. As such, it therefore covers not only evaluation and validation, but more general objectives still, i.e. those of the whole organization.

More detailed advice to be borne in mind includes the recipe of Hayes-Roth to "seek problems that experts can solve via telephone communication", and

White's criticisms (WHITE85) of the handling of uncertainty in PROSPEC-TOR and those shells which are descended from it. White's work has a particular bearing on the distinction between validation and verification for KBSs.

To close this section, we give examples of the evaluation of two very different KBSs, to demonstrate that the evaluation must be tailored to the particular problem which the KBS addresses. The first is that of a KBS developed by Lockheed for fault diagnosis of electronic systems (GIL87). After six months of use by Lockheed technicians, during which time the system was updated more than once, an evaluation took place. This consisted of a formal evaluation of the performance of the KBS "on the job" over a period of time. The KBS correctly identified the fault(s) in 41 of the 43 cases which occurred during the evaluation period, and time spent troubleshooting the faulty systems was reduced by a factor of 5. This gives a clear evaluation in quantitative terms; such an approach to evaluation is likely to be attractive where the "correct" performance in a given case is relatively easy to establish, as in this example.

The second KBS, GESPI, is used by the French railway company SNCF to plan the movements of trains in and out of the Gare de l'Est station in Paris (INT89). The commercial goals for this system are clearly stated as "increasing the regular traffic flow" and "facilitating the introduction of new daily traffic conditions such as supplementary trains or track repairs". However, precise quantitative assessment is not so straightforward. Although it is possible to obtain quantitative measures relating to the achievement of these commercial goals, such as the average delay to train departures, or the number of changes to regular platform allocations, these are affected by many factors, several of them seasonal ones. It would thus be extremely difficult to know how much of any change observed in these measures was actually due to the use of GESPI. A further complication arises from GESPI's use almost as a decision support system, the final platform allocation plan being produced by the human operators after GESPI has resolved the more straightforward conflicts. What the system is required to produce is a workable solution, in time to avoid de-laying the trains concerned; there is no point in seeking some theoretical optimum. For example, which would passengers prefer - a departure 5 minutes late from the advertised platform, or an on-time departure from a different platform? Not all passengers would agree. Thus much of the evaluation of this KBS has to be done subjectively by those humans performing the task of allocating trains to platforms at the station (now with the aid of GESPI) and their bosses, and this is how GESPI was evaluated in practice. We would argue that in addition some survey of passenger opinions should form part of the evaluation of such a system, as the passengers are the Customers for the system.

These two contrasting examples bring us back once again to some of the issues raised in chapter 5. Where we are dealing with a domain relating to a designed physical system, like an electronic circuit, it is often possible to state with a reasonable degree of certainty what the performance of the KBS should be. However, with a human activity system such as the train management one, there will be no general agreement on what the "best" outcomes are, so there can be no appeal to an external mechanism to decide what the KBS should ideally have done.

8.4 How to Measure the Success of a KBS: Our Recommendations

The first step is to start with the organization's commercial need, which must be translated into a set of performance objectives for the outcome of the project. Only then is it possible to decide whether *any* computer system, let alone one with knowledge-based components, is likely to provide an adequate "solution". The difficulty of this translation should not be underestimated, as was stressed in the chapter on operational research/soft systems methodology. The decision to commission the building of a system must be taken by the problem owner(s); unless they are committed to the KBS, it is almost certain to fail at the evaluation level. Once the decision has been made, these objectives must be cast into a form which is appropriate for a KBS or, more likely, for a hybrid system with some knowledge-based components. In order to formulate the objectives for the system, we need to determine the tasks to be performed and the criteria of performance for each task.

The process must start at the evaluation level, then go down to the validation and verification levels, with the appropriate expansion of detail. It is vital to realise that this cannot all be done at the start of the project, or even at the same time. It may well be that only after some of the knowledge acquisition has been carried out will it be possible to specify the system precisely enough to determine criteria of performance at the validation level. Equally, the metrics to be used for verification will depend to some extent on the exact hardware and software being used for the operational system; these will not be determined until the emphasis shifts from the logical design of the system to the physical design of the system.

It is inevitable that there will be some iteration between the levels, but this process needs to be controlled very carefully. In the rest of this chapter we will

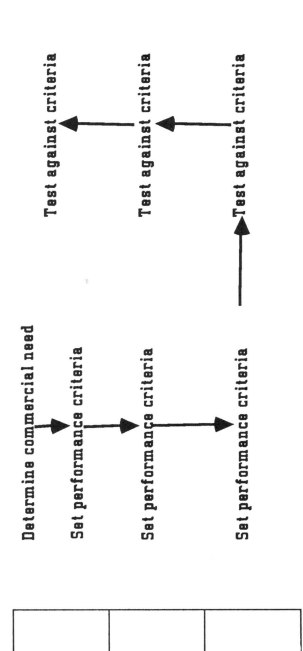

Figure 8.5: A "one-shot" view of evaluation

treat performance measurement and testing as if it were a simple "once down the levels and back up again" process for clarity, as shown schematically in Figure 8.5, but the issue of managing iteration will be a central one in the methodology we propose in chapter 9.

At each of the levels, we must define the factors to be assessed in order to judge the system's performance, define who are the assessors, define metrics, timescales, measuring instruments, etc.

8.4.1 At the evaluation level

Begin by establishing the commercial need which the system must meet. This process is as much an art as a science. An appropriate analogy is perhaps that of a doctor (general practitioner) seeing a patient; the system builder/knowledge engineer is the doctor, the managers in the organization are the patients. The patient arrives with some symptoms; he may or may not understand what they are; he may or may not have his own diagnosis of the illness causing the symptoms; he may even have some idea of the treatment he wants/needs/ expects! The doctor will try to establish how accurate the patient's descriptions are (does he merely feel hot, or is his temperature really higher than normal?). She will use her own observations, and if necessary and possible, carry out further tests. She may need to call for yet more tests, either by herself or by others, to be carried out at some stage in the future. Pursuing the analogy, the goal at this stage is to establish what the disease or illness is, NOT to prescribe treatment (yet). The additional difficulty faced with by "organizational doctors" is that of deciding what constitutes a "healthy" organization as opposed to an "ill" one.

Our suggestions for carrying out the process of being an "organizational doctor" are that system developers should follow one of the "soft" approaches outlined in chapter 5, for example Checkland's SSM or Robins's OR methodology. Neither is "better" than the other; the choice between them is partly a question of "horses for courses", and partly one of personal preference. It may be that the diagnosis of the commercial needs and the type of system called for is clear-cut, with a correspondingly well-specified path to building the system, but from our own experiences we suspect that in most cases it will not be that straightforward.

Above all, please remember that whilst we can present guide-lines for what needs to be done, we cannot teach you the "bedside manner" of how to do it! It should be clear then that we see the problem of deriving criteria of performance at the evaluation level as being inextricably linked to commercial needs. This link is so close that the process required in this section must aim at establishing BOTH the need and the criteria of performance. It would be a serious mistake to see this step as merely consisting of deriving appropriate criteria of performance from commercial needs which have already been well-established and clearly articulated. Even for conventional computer systems this is comparatively rare. For systems where knowledge/expertise is involved, three factors combine to make a joint investigation by the problem owner(s) and the potential system builder(s) imperative:

- the fuzziness of the issues involved;

- the novelty of trying to systematise them;

- the lack of familiarity of managers with the capabilities of KBSs.

Even where the basic commercial need is comparatively clear, for example where the organizational system concerns manufacturing process control, and the overall aim is to produce improvements in response to criticisms of operational performance, the need may have to be "fleshed out" considerably before the project objectives can be agreed. In our example, the operational needs will have to be refined into the precisely the sort of operational gains which are anticipated.

Although it would be nice to completely separate the consideration of the commercial need from the potential solutions, in reality this will not be the case. We have to convert the commercial need into a specification for the overall project task. This involves having at least a tentative idea about the sort of system to be constructed, in order to ensure that the managers are being advised by the right experts - there's little point in consulting a plumber when you really need an electrician! Several other aspects of this system will also need to be decided before we can accomplish this, for example:

- what is the target hardware?

- who are the hands-on users of the computer system?

- who are the beneficiaries of the organizational system (i.e. the Customers in a Checkland root definition)? (May not be the same group of people.)

To clarify the distinction between the last two aspects, suppose that we are considering a system to assist in the management of beds in a hospital ward. The hands-on users will probably be nurses, but the beneficiaries/Customers are neither the nurses, nor the doctors, nor the hospital administrators; they are the patients!

Specific performance objectives at this level may be divided into three categories:

Direct financial and organizational

Return on Investment. In many books and articles on KBSs, particularly the "evangelising" ones, return on investment is the only criterion mentioned in this category. It is indeed an appropriate criterion, but only for a revenue-earning system. Most organizations will be able to decide on appropriate levels for return on investment for particular types of project, but the problem can be in determining what to include as initial investment and what to count as earnings. This applies to all projects (and is one of the reasons why organizations need accountants), but KBSs raise especial difficulties in terms of costing the time of the human experts involved.

Operational effectiveness. Improvements in the way in which operational activities are carried out may have other direct benefits than purely financial, in terms of ability to accept orders, offer shorter delivery times, introduce new products, etc. It is under this heading that the major part of the considerable benefits attributed by DEC to the use of R1/XCON come.

Cost-saving. Many organizational activities are administrative, rather than directly earning revenue. Such systems support the primary activities of the organization rather than carrying them out. Financial improvements may result from improved efficiency or by changing the cost structure.

Cost-minimising. Some organizational activities cannot be directly related to the organization's outputs at all, such as various statutory duties, social facilities for employees, etc. In this case the likely choice would be the cheapest adequate system, either in terms of the initial investment or in net present value terms.

Assessment against these financial and operational criteria should be carried out by the managers responsible for the system and their financial advisors.

Quality of decision-making

Does the KBS function well enough for the organization's commercial need? In other words, is it working in the real environment, as opposed to any tests which might have been carried out at the validation level? This will include both the question of whether it is adequately knowledgeable, and whether it is usable by the people for whom it was intended. It does not matter how many decisions an expert system gets "right" in tests, if the organization lacks the confidence to trust its recommendations in real-life. (This has been a particular problem with medical KBSs and decision support systems.) Thus some of the measures under this heading will be quantitative metrics, and others qualitative judgements. As with a human advisor, we are asking not just "do they know enough to do the job?", but "do they fit in?". The difference between this and the similar aspect at the validation level corresponds to the difference between judging a human's job performance and assessing their qualifications.

Quantitative assessment against this type of criterion should be by the managers responsible for the organizational system and by the domain experts, advised by the KBS builder where necessary. Qualitative assessments should be by the managers, the domain experts, and the hands-on users, and perhaps by other staff who interact with the KBS indirectly. The assessment should, when appropriate, include confirmation from the intended beneficiaries of the system.

Indirect (Opportunity) benefits

Current KBSs do not know very much about the world as a whole, and in that sense are considerably inferior to humans. Thus it is not realistic to think in terms of KBSs as replacing humans, but rather as supporting them by freeing their time or improving the quality of their performance. Evaluation of the KBS must therefore include an attempt to assess these opportunity benefits. This is NOT in terms of time freed - that is a validation issue; the system may give a manager more time, but cannot guarantee that anything useful is done in that time. At this level, we must look for actual "useful" activities which the humans are carrying out which they did not do before, or new skills which have been acquired as a result of the KBS. We would recommend that the approach to this aspect is qualitative/subjective, rather than quantitative. Anything with even a hint of work study or job evaluation is likely to sour the climate for the implementation of the KBS, which involves quite enough problems as it is!

Assessment against this criterion should be by the managers responsible, with the assistance of the hands-on users.

The three categories are summarised in Figure 8.6. All units of measurement and measuring instruments should be those which are determined by the organization's commercial needs, such as standard financial indicators, market research methods and human performance appraisal techniques. At this level, the fact that we are using a KBS does not affect the nature of the measurements. Specific details of such techniques are beyond the scope of this book, but may be found in any good management text.

Financial	Quantitative, but with some subjectivity over what to include
Quality of Decision-making	Both quantitative and qualitative
Opportunity benefits	Qualitative

Figure 8.6: Measurement factors at the evaluation level

8.4.2 At the validation level

As with the evaluation level, we must define the factors to be assessed in order to judge the system's performance. The difference at this level is that the system requirements must be much more detailed than the performance objectives, and that computing and domain issues play a much larger part.

What to validate?

Is the concentration to be on the process or on the end-result? For some types of KBS, for example "intelligent" tutors or co-operative question-answering systems, there is only a process to assess, since no definite decisions are reached. It might be thought, at the other extreme, that if a system does produce a definite decision or recommendation, as in the classic standalone expert system, then that alone should suffice for validation, but this is not the case. Good expert systems produce intermediate advice and justification, as well as the "final answer", and it makes sense to assess all of these if possible. After all, an expert system which produces the decision like the proverbial "rabbit out of a hat" is unlikely to be acceptable unless it is of the automaton type.

Who are to be the validators?

Any trials of the whole system for the purposes of validation are meaningless unless carried out by the people who are to be the end-users of the system. The knowledge engineers will of course need to be closely monitoring the trials, but the element of judgement involved where KBSs are concerned renders it vital that we use the "right" people for the tests. In addition, it is important that where there are many potential users, as wide a range as possible are incorporated in the trials.

Where the KBS can be separated into parts for the purposes of validation, some of which do not involve the end-users, then it may be possible for the system builders alone to validate such parts. For example, this may include checking that the system correctly uses graphics when required. We would expect that, as with this example, parts which can be validated in this manner would be those which are more similar to conventional DP. The nearer we come to the judgement of humans, the more careful we must be to involve the end-users.

Example (due to Hugh Dorans): an expert system for classifying rock samples was being developed, with the intention of aiding geology students. Geologists have developed many terms to describe the appearance of different rock samples under the microscope. However, new geology students cannot relate these terms to what *they* see. Thus the standard classifications could not be used as the basis of the system's knowledge unless they were first taught to the students.

Where judgements have to be made about the system, then obviously humans who are knowledgeable about the domain must be involved. No-one else, even the manager who commissioned the system, is qualified to do the job. Ideally, validation judgements should be made by a different expert from the one who provided the knowledge-base for the system, but it must be accepted that circumstances may sometimes preclude this:

- there may be only one expert available;

- different experts may not agree;

- the expert whose knowledge is embodied in the system may resent judgements on it (and thus by implication on them) being passed by others.

Because of the judgements involved, the manager must also be involved at the validation level as the final arbiter who resolves disagreements. This would not normally occur with a conventional DP system.

Timescales

The KBS literature leaves us with a contradiction of views between those who feel that a KBS must immediately perform at levels close to those of a human, and those who feel that it takes time to achieve such levels of performance. This issue overlaps evaluation (which can only be done once the system has been delivered) and validation. Our view is that validation tests should begin as any working version of the KBS exists. This is one of the aspects where properly-managed iteration is essential. It is much easier for knowledge engineers and domain experts to refine the knowledge in a KBS than to work entirely in the abstract.

Measuring instruments

At this level, the units of measurement are determined principally by domain issues and general issues about expertise. Unfortunately, neither of these is without problems: consensus in measuring human knowledge is rare, and methods for validating KBSs are in their infancy. A brief discussion of the problems of validating the knowledge of humans will help to clarify this.

Many professions (domains) require the passing of certain examinations before membership is granted. Yet the pass-mark is nowhere near 100% (at least in those cases with which we are familiar). Similarly, few organizations would fire a human expert for the occasional mistake; such action is more likely for "errors" at the organizational level or involving human interactions. Indeed, even establishing that a domain expert has made a mistake may be a difficult task for the beneficiary of his/her services, or his/her non-domain expert manager, since it frequently involves reference to *other* domain experts. As an aside, our earlier point about assessing the process is backed up by the way in which most examination papers are marked for the quality of the argument or method and not just the "right" answer or conclusions.

Our advice here is to concentrate on the beneficiary's view of the KBS, and of other ways of carrying out the same task (e.g. human expert, other computer system, paper-based system). Metrics and judgements should be related primarily to the outputs provided for the beneficiary. Note that where the requirements of the system relate to ease of maintenance, or amendment of the knowledge-base, the effective beneficiary will be the maintenance programmer, the system developer and perhaps the end-user.

Metrics (quantitative validation)

Here we are comparing the performance of the KBS (usually in terms of final decision or recommendations) with known performance. We have already discussed how the "correct" answers may themselves rely on judgement; alternatively we may be able to assess the right decision independently, say in the case of a prediction. It is up to the manager to decide on the "pass-mark" for these tests, which will normally be less than 100%, as we argued earlier. As with any performance comparison, the sampling implicit in the deliberate or chance selection of test cases makes it essential to use statistical methods to compare actual and desired performance. Any good statistical textbook will give an introduction to such methods.

Judgements (qualitative validation)

O'Keefe *et al* list seven methods of qualitative validation, including four which have been reported in the KBS literature (face validation, predictive validation, Turing tests and field tests), one which involves validating sub-systems, and two suggestions inspired by OR (sensitivity analysis and visual interaction). Again it is necessary for the manager and the domain expert to agree on the appropriate standards which the KBS is expected to reach.

8.4.3 At the verification level

In principle, there is no difference at the level of modules between the verification of KBSs and that of any other type of system. We are dealing with functionality against specification, looked at in information technology terms. The key difference concerns the specification itself. Those aspects of a KBS, or those components of a hybrid system, which can be specified at the level of detail required of a conventional DP system may be, and should be, tested in a similar way. However, those parts which specifically relate to the *cognitive* tasks, i.e. to know-how, knowledge and expertise, cannot in our view be specified in sufficient detail for verification testing. If this were possible, then the specification itself would serve as the (paper) base for an algorithmic approach to the task, and we would be back to a conventional DP system.

One consequence is that a KBS will not be completely specified in the DP sense, as Partridge would have it (see chapter 6). Thus there may be elements of its behaviour which need to be studied first in order to be understood. This feature has also been observed in simulation models: the question of whether the unexpected behaviour is desirable or undesirable is one which should be answered at the validation level.

For those parts which can be specified, it is worth bearing in mind that considerable effort has been expended on developing test harnesses and test data banks for common DP languages and applications. By and large, this "testing equipment" is much less well developed for AI languages such as LISP and Prolog and for knowledge-based applications. This may affect decisions taken about which software is to be used for the system, back at the validation level.

8.5 Summary

Unless your concern is solely with research and development KBSs, then your KBS must be built in response to a commercial need in the organization. Its success (or otherwise) should therefore be measured on that basis.

This involves comparing the system's performance with its objectives at each of three levels: evaluation, validation and verification.

We have set out our recommendations as to how to do this, drawing on our experience and on lessons from related fields. On the whole, there is still comparatively little experience of measuring the success of KBSs, and so these ideas may yet need modification in the future, particularly when it comes to methods for validation. Nevertheless, this forms the "top and tail" of our methodology; the part in the middle is described in chapter 9!

References

(BEER87) Annabel C.Beerel, *"Expert Systems: Strategic Implications and Applications"*, Ellis Horwood, Chichester, 1987.

(BELL85) M.Z.Bell, "Why expert systems fail", *J. Opl Res. Soc.*, Vol.36, No.7, pp.613-619, 1985.

(BELL86) P.C.Bell, "Visual interactive modelling in 1986", pp.1-12 in *"Recent Developments in Operational Research"* (eds. V.Belton and R.M.O'Keefe), Pergamon, Oxford, 1986.

(CONN87) N.A.D.Connell and P.Powell, "Success and failure in the commercial implementation of expert systems", Working paper, Department of Accounting and Management Science, University of Southampton, 1987.

(DUDA79) R.O.Duda, J.Gaschnig and P.Hart, "Model design in the Prospector consultant system for mineral exploration", pp.153-167 in *"Expert Systems in the Micro-electronic Age"* (ed. D.Michie), Edinburgh University Press, 1979.

(EDW88) John S.Edwards and Jon L.Bader, "Expert systems for university admissions", *J. Opl Res. Soc.*, Vol.39, No.1, pp.33-40, 1988.

(GIL87) J.F.Gilmore and K.Gingher, "Diagnostic Expert Systems", pp.305-312 in *Proceedings of the Third International Expert Systems Conference*, London, 2-4 June 1987.

(HUM73) J.W.Humble, *"Management by Objectives"*, British Institute of Management, London, 1973.

(INT89) "French railways' train management system improves planning and efficiency at Paris station", *intelligence*, No.15, pp.1-3, April 1989.

(MOR77) R.L.Moravsky, "Defining goals - a systems approach", *Long Range Planning*, Vol.10, pp.85-89, April 1977.

(MYERS79) G.J.Myers, *"The Art of Software Testing"*, Wiley, New York, 1979.

(O'K87) R.M.O'Keefe, O.Balci and E.P.Smith, "Validating expert system performance", *IEEE Expert*, Vol.2, No.4, pp.81-90.

(OULD86) M.A.Ould and C.Unwin (eds), *"Testing in Software Development"*, Cambridge University Press, 1986.

(PIDD88) M.Pidd, *"Computer Simulation in Management Science"* (second edition), Wiley, Chichester, 1988.

(WED78) W.C.Wedley and A.E.J.Ferrie, "Perceptual differences and effects of managerial participation on project implementation", *J. Opl Res. Soc.*, Vol.29, No.3, pp.199-204, 1978.

(WHITE85) A.P.White, "Inference deficiencies in rule-based expert systems", pp.39-50 in *"Research and Development in Expert Systems"* (ed. M.A.Bramer), Cambridge University Press, 1985.

Chapter 9: A Methodology for the Practical Engineering of Knowledge-based Systems

9.0 Introduction

This chapter summarises the core of our methodology for building knowledge-based systems, which is intended to be a structured engineering approach. Much of the detail of the methodology has been covered in earlier chapters, and is only repeated here if absolutely necessary. The use of the methodology in a practical example is discussed, in order to shed further light on it. We do not claim that our methodology is perfect, nor that this is the final version of it. There is in general little experience of building KBSs compared with that of other types of computer system, and less still of building them explicitly to meet the standards of robustness demanded of commercial applications. Our methodology is, therefore, our best attempt so far - it never will be perfect, but the only way to improve it is by us and, we hope, others using it in practice.

9.1 A POLITE Engineering Methodology for KBSs

In chapter 4 we concluded that conventional development models such as MODUS, itself based on the waterfall model, were the best available basis for evolving an engineering model for KBS development. It follows therefore that we should attempt to combine the RUDE paradigm, as described in section 6.2, with the waterfall model. In short, the RUDE cycle must be augmented, so that it becomes POLITE:

Produce Objectives - Logical/physical design - Implement - Test - Edit.

The central feature of conventional development methodologies for commercial software development, which provides the basis for a *controllable framework,* is the definition of detailed design tasks and procedures, with accompanying checkpoints and documentation standards for carrying out those tasks. The proposed POLITE model, based on this type of approach, is described below.

A schematic view of the proposed POLITE life-cycle is shown in Figure 9.1. Each of the development phases is divided into two. The left side is related to conventional components and the right to the knowledge-based or cognitive

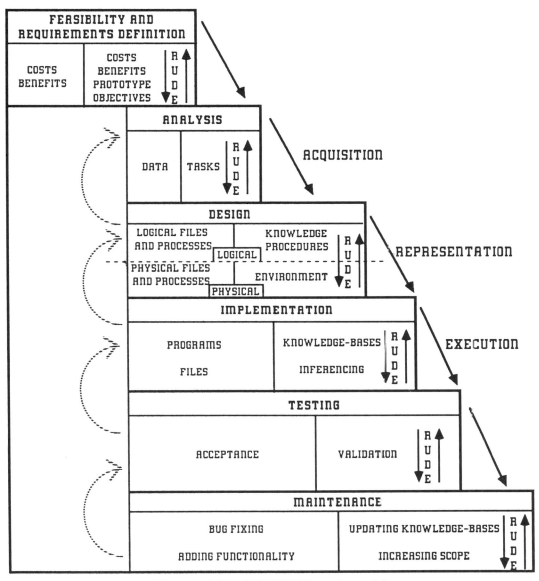

Figure 9.1: The POLITE life-cycle model

elements in the system. The following sections will give an overview of the tasks associated with each of the development phases identified. For maximum clarity, each phase in the POLITE model is illustrated with a diagram. Two points should be noted:

- The tasks identified reflect the experience gained during the *Intellipse* project (see chapter 7) and other KBS projects, as well as the methods for KBS development described in chapters 2 and 6.

- To avoid unnecessary repetition, the level of detail is restricted.

The description of the POLITE model which follows deals with the development of hybrid knowledge-based systems, i.e. systems comprising both conventional and knowledge-based components. In the diagrams illustrating each phase of the model, those aspects mainly associated with knowledge-based components appear in the bolder shapes. Conventional tasks are not discussed in detail as it is assumed that models like SSD (see chapters 4 and 7) are being used in these areas.

9.1.1 Performance objectives

A key feature of the POLITE model is the production of performance objectives at the start of any project intended to produce an *operational* KBS. Performance objectives are a statement, in the problem owner's terms, of how the KBS should operate in the chosen domain.

A clearly stated set of performance objectives is essential, in order to facilitate evaluation of the KBS. Performance objectives are a complete statement of requirements for a KBS *at a particular time* and they provide a framework within which any RUDE development (see section 6.2) can be controlled. The performance objectives should be used as the basis for evaluation, validation and verification at each stage in the POLITE cycle where RUDE development is appropriate. Thus the process for producing objectives described in chapters 5 and 8 provides not only the initial impetus for developing the system but also the means for evaluating what is produced.

It is worth stating once more here that the difficulty of obtaining a usable set of performance objectives for all but the smallest of systems should not be underestimated.

9.1.2 Feasibility and requirements definition

Figure 9.2 identifies the main issues that need to be considered during a KBS feasibility study and those people involved in the exercise.

Tasks and procedures for this phase are not given here, as these have been covered in earlier chapters; problem selection, human factors and prototyping

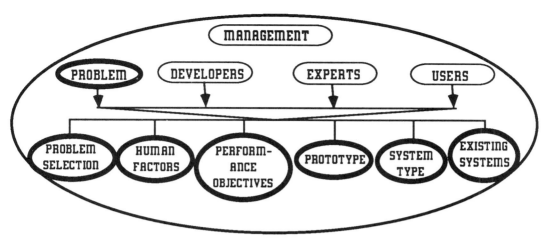

Figure 9.2: Feasibility and requirements definition

in sections 4.6 and 4.7, and the type of system and its relationship to existing systems as early as chapter 1. The diagram also illustrates the fact that co-operation between several (often discrete) parts of an organisation is crucial to the successful completion of this phase. It is particularly important that management oversee the feasibility exercise, since they will have to take the decision on whether to proceed to a full operational system at the end of it.

9.1.3 Analysis

Figure 9.3 shows the tasks and people involved in the analysis phase of the POLITE life-cycle. The main tasks during this phase are domain and task analysis, secondary feasibility, cognitive task analysis (CTA) and data analysis. (Tasks begun in the CTA phase may overlap into the logical and physical design stages - see chapters 2 and 3.) There are many parallels here with conventional systems analysis. The main differences arise when the task being examined is a cognitive activity carried out by a human expert. A crucial point here is that not all of the tasks which a human expert performs are best computerized by means of a knowledge-based component rather than a conventional one. Much effort in this phase must therefore be devoted to establishing which components of the hybrid system should be knowledge-based, and which conventional.

Domain and task analysis

The first stage of this activity is to take a broad look at the application domain, in order to identify and label the main tasks which the expert performs. This high-level picture is successively refined by analysing each of the high-level activities. Finally, a sufficient level of detail is reached to provide an accurate guide to the expert's approach to the problem domain. The resulting description can be represented using a network structure, showing the hierarchical relationship between the activities, as was done for SSD in chapter 7. This exercise is particularly useful in familiarising the knowledge engineers with the application domain. This early analysis may not require much involvement of the expert, since a great deal of the information needed can often be obtained from existing manuals or text-books. In addition to the high-level description of activities obtained, a domain taxonomy can be produced, which identifies and describes the key terms and concepts in the domain.

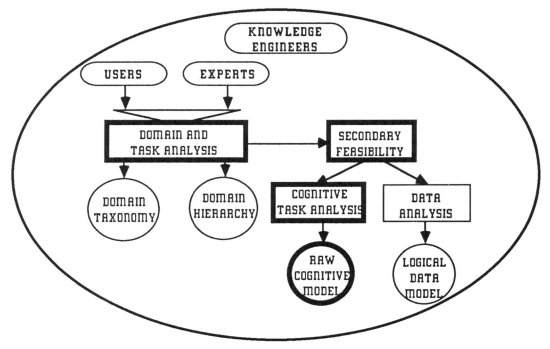

Figure 9.3: Analysis

Secondary feasibility

Depending on the nature and the level of complexity of the problem being studied, a varying proportion of the list of tasks identified will be non-heuristic and could be modelled using conventional procedural algorithms. For example, a financial analyst may begin the examination of a company by calculating various ratios based on financial data. The calculation of the ratios is algorithmic; it is only the analysis of them which is heuristic. Since the machine execution of conventional algorithms is relatively well understood, these tasks should be subjected to conventional analysis. Only those tasks which appear to rely on judgemental reasoning or cognitive analysis by the expert should be the subject of cognitive task analysis.

Cognitive task analysis and conventional analysis have been described in chapters 2 and 4 respectively.

9.1.4 Logical design

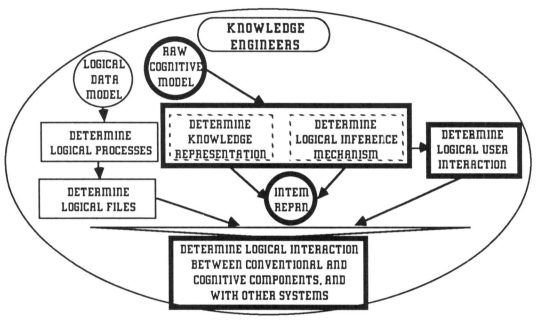

Figure 9.4: Logical design

The logical design phase is shown in Figure 9.4 and is concerned with transforming the raw knowledge, obtained from the analysis stage, into a particular knowledge representation schema. At this stage it will also be necessary to devise an inferencing mechanism which reflects the expert's approach to problems in the application domain. A *logical* representation is required at this stage, which does not depend on any specific implementation environment. This will provide flexibility in the choice of hardware and software at the physical design stage, as well as providing the basis for maintaining the knowledge bases in the future. In an operational or commercial environment this logical or *intermediate representation* (INTEM REPRN in Figure 9.4)) should be paper-based (or held as machine-based documentation within a project management environment) - another important maintenance consideration. Without an intermediate representation, validation and verification of the machine-based representation of the knowledge base can only be carried out with reference to the human expert(s). This process will certainly be time-consuming and (if the expert(s) cannot understand the machine representation) probably unsatisfactory. Indeed, if the knowledge base is intended as an archive for the knowledge of an expert who is leaving the organization, it may be impossible. The broad options available for the representation schema and inference mechanism were described in section 3.1.

9.1.5 Physical design and implementation

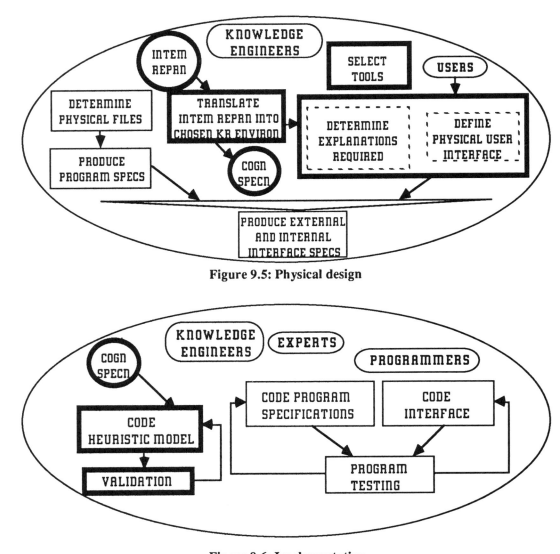

Figure 9.5: Physical design

Figure 9.6: Implementation

The physical design and implementation phases are shown in Figures 9.5 and 9.6 respectively. This is the stage when the intermediate representation is translated into the chosen implementation environment - the *cognitive specification* (COGN SPECN in Figure 9.5). Sections 2.4.3, 3.1.3, 3.5 and 3.6 have discussed the tasks involved - in particular, the need to define the user interface and explanation facilities required - and some of the pros and cons of the available tools. Extensive RUDE development is likely here and the logical representation of the system, obtained during the last phase, allows this iterative process to be kept under control.

Three components will require coding: the cognitive specification, conventional program specifications and any programs needed to provide interfaces with external computer systems. If KBS shells or AI toolkits/environments are used to implement the system, it is both possible and desirable for the expert(s) and users to be involved at this stage. Incremental validation of the executable model and interface can then be performed. The use of other tools may postpone this involvement until the testing stage.

9.1.6 Testing and maintenance

Testing of a KBS or hybrid system was discussed at length in chapter 8, while the maintenance phase in KBS development was considered in sections 3.7 and 4.6. Formal acceptance testing of the KBS, including all external interfaces, will differ from the testing which is performed on a DP system. The probable absence of a DP-style statement of requirements means that the performance objectives, defined at the outset of the project and refined and expanded to lower levels of the system at the feasibility and analysis stages, must be used as a basis for measuring the system's performance.

If the rules and procedures in the application domain of the KBS are subject to regular change, a maintenance regime is needed which ensures that experts and management periodically review the performance of the system. The adoption of a structured methodology to build the system should ensure that additions or changes to the cognitive model, and to the overall functionality of the system, can be made and documented relatively easily.

9.2 Standards for the POLITE Engineering of KBSs

The proposed POLITE life-cycle model is a synthesis of two existing development models (*waterfall* and *RUDE*). It was formulated by the author and others while building KBSs as part of the *Intellipse* project. A sound life-cycle model, based on a structured methodology, is a necessary, but not sufficient, first step towards engineering KBSs. In addition to identifying the key phases and tasks required to design and implement an operational KBS, it is also necessary to identify a *practical* method of executing each of the development phases. These methods need not be totally novel; in many cases, what is required is to formalize already existing methods for performing individual tasks, and integrate them within a standard framework. To mix metaphors, the framework of the POLITE model has to have appropriate "hooks" on which to attach techniques which have already proved their usefulness for specific tasks.

The evolution of KBS *development standards*, based on the POLITE model, is thus required to assist developers in the practical construction of KBSs. It is important to bear in mind that these standards need to cover all aspects of system development - including for example project management as well as the purely technical tasks involved. Two project management tasks where standards are of critical significance are *documentation* and *change control*.

The production of consistent and reliable documentation is one of the corner-stones of structured methods for conventional systems development such as BIS's *MODUS*. Indeed, in some cases the whole life-cycle is driven by the production of successive documents of different types, the completion of each document marking the end of a stage in the life-cycle. The problems of documentation for systems with knowledge-based components are even more substantial than those for conventional systems, with the need to deal with considerable amounts of input documents such as manuals, codes of practice and interview transcripts. It is likely that in many cases a computer-based document management system will be needed to handle this task.

Change control procedures will also be even more important for knowledge-based components. Most changes in conventional systems result from a change in the requirements which the users have of the system, or perhaps it would be more accurate to call it a mis-match between the requirements as currently perceived and the system as currently implemented. A knowledge-based component may need to be changed for these reasons, but may also need to be changed because of "knowledge drift" over time. Where the system is operating in the role of expert consultant, with relatively inexpert users who may also be geographically separate both from each other and from the experts whose knowledge was used in creating the system, formal procedures for review as well as implementing change will be essential.

We cannot, unfortunately, present detailed POLITE standards yet. The PO-LITE model at present has the status of a hypothesis, based on some empirical evidence and limited theoretical foundations. Substantial effort is therefore required, over an extended period of time, to evaluate and validate the proposed model, and to <u>evolve</u> the standards vital for its practical application in an industrial or commercial environment. It should be noted that conventional DPSD models, and their accompanying standards, have evolved to their present state only after many years of use in the commercial DP environment. The succeeding sections describe one evaluation of the POLITE model, in the context of the ITAM investigation first mentioned in chapter 7. The standards which are currently used to support the structured development of DP systems are the product of practical experience of many hundreds of projects. POLITE standards, *and the validation of the POLITE model itself*, can only be achieved through the use of the model on something approaching a comparable number of KBS or hybrid system development projects. Figure 9.7 summarises the origins of the POLITE model and its potential evolution in the future.

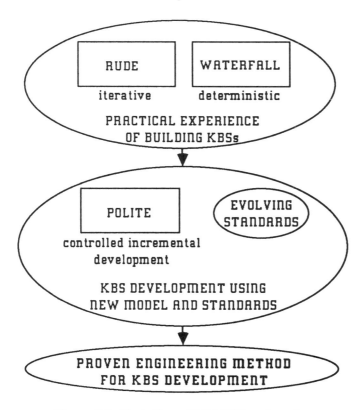

Figure 9.7: Evolution of POLITE engineering

9.3 An Example of the Use of the POLITE Methodology: the ITAM investigation

The ITAM (Intelligent Total Advisory Module) system arose from the feasibility study into the Designer mode of *Intellipse* (see chapter 7). Note that it was later renamed "the Total system" in the light of our worries about using the adjective intelligent, expressed in chapter 1; we shall continue to refer to it as ITAM here.

ITAM was intended as a knowledge-based tool for the physical design areas within BIS's SSD, based on the proprietary *Total* database management system available from Cincom Ltd., which was in use by our project collaborators at BSC.

9.3.1 The general objectives of the ITAM investigation

The initial objectives of the ITAM investigation were as follows:

- To confirm the initial findings of the Designer feasibility study in the domain of DB design.
- To specify and design a KBS tool for supporting the design, optimisation (tuning) and maintenance of DBMS applications in the *Total* environment.
- To begin the evaluation and validation of the POLITE model.
- To begin the evolution of practical development standards for the POLITE model.

The second of these served as the initial statement of performance objectives, as required by the POLITE model.

9.3.2 Approach adopted for the ITAM investigation

The first step taken was to conduct two separate knowledge engineering sessions with physical design experts at BIS and at BSC. These were intended to confirm the initial findings of the Designer feasibility study, and to establish an overall set of functional requirements for a KBS support tool, including the terms in which more detailed performance objectives should be defined. As a preliminary exercise, the knowledge engineers had studied the extensive documentation available on DB design in general, and the *Total* DBMS in particular. Some early domain hierarchy sheets were prepared on the basis of these sessions.

Initial observations

The points which emerged from the first two KE sessions are summarised below:

- Acceptable performance of *Total*-based applications is achievable, in principle, using information available in the Cincom manuals, data from appropriate hardware and operating system manuals, and heuristic knowledge about database design in general, and *Total* in particular.

- In practice, installations do not usually achieve optimal performance from their *Total* applications. Those installations which can afford it resort to Cincom or other external consultants to sort out their performance problems. It is possible for a *Total* expert to identify and recommend a solution to a performance problem in a few hours, on average. The use of consultants for this purpose is nevertheless very expensive.

- The failure of installations to achieve optimal performance unaided is due to five main factors:

    (i)   The complexity and size of the paper-based manuals.
    (ii)   The reluctance of database administrators (DBAs) and others to grapple with the mathematical and statistical content of the Cincom tuning manual.
    (iii) The absence of a disciplined or structured method for designing database applications and tackling optimization problems.
    (iv)   Insufficient understanding of the general mode of operation of Cincom's products. This undermines the ability of installations to relate performance problems to potential solutions.
    (v)   The absence of the required heuristic knowledge in the installation. This knowledge accumulates over extended periods of time and an individual end-user of *Total* is unlikely to have the experience of a database consultant or Cincom expert.

- There is an absence of mainframe or PC-based tools to support the design and optimisation of *Total* applications.

219

- Significant improvements in the performance of *Total*-based applications can be achieved through relatively simple techniques. In addition, it is clear that, if a few simple design principles were adhered to at the 1st and 2nd pass physical design stage, many installations could avoid most of their performance problems.

Conclusions

Optimization problems with *Total* can be solved by a human expert in a few hours, using a small set of heuristic rules. The heuristic knowledge is well understood and could be represented in machine form.

A tool for optimising *Total* applications, able to simulate the function of a Cincom expert or external consultant and usable by a typical *Total* installation, would be a cost-effective solution to a problem which occurs in a very wide user-base. The design, optimization and maintenance of DBMS applications is a key operational problem in commercial DP.

It appeared at this stage to be technically feasible to represent the heuristic knowledge of the expert, the inferencing techniques employed and the external data required. The support tool would need to be a hybrid system which contained both knowledge-based and conventional components. The main problem would be to acquire the knowledge and structure it ready for transfer to the machine environment.

Detailed objectives

The general objectives for the ITAM investigation stated earlier were re-defined as follows:

- To produce a KBS tool which could assist a typical *Total* installation to achieve significant performance improvements in a live *Total* application, without resorting to external expert support.

- To assist *Total* database designers to achieve an optimal physical design, from a normalised logical model, prior to the installation of the database, using a KBS support tool.

- To design ITAM so that it integrated conventional and knowledge-based components.

- To ensure that the knowledge-based components in ITAM required the minimum amount of keyboard input on the part of the user.

- To conduct the knowledge engineering for ITAM, with a view to generalising the knowledge about database design, so as to lay down a basis for KBS support tools for other proprietary DBMSs.

- To determine task-lists, documentation standards, check-points and deliverables enabling the ITAM investigation to be conducted as closely as possible to the approach envisaged in the POLITE life-cycle.

The prospective users of ITAM were determined as:

- Database administrators in *Total* installations.
- Database designers in *Total* installations.
- Cincom product consultants.

9.3.3 The main functional requirements for ITAM

The following is a high-level set of functional requirements determined for the ITAM system based on the initial knowledge engineering sessions with the BIS and BSC experts:

- Passive, advisory support on translating a logical database design into an optimised 1st and 2nd pass *Total* physical design. This advice should help the user check that the logical design does not contain any obvious errors or inefficiencies.

- Facilities for displaying graphs of the values of the various statistical formulae used for *Total* tuning which are described in the Cincom manuals. This function should also allow the user to interpolate values from the graphs, and to invoke the formulae when using other ITAM functions.

- A facility to download the output from the Cincom statistics package and other mainframe statistics packages to the PC enabling the data to be used by various ITAM functions.

- A knowledge base containing data about various proprietary hard-

221

ware (e.g. disk capacities, transfer rates, block transfer sizes etc.) which can be accessed by the appropriate ITAM facilities.

- Facilities for creating user-definable "warning files" which could be used in conjunction with the *Total* statistics to check for specific problems arising in the database.

- Facilities for determining the optimum values for *Total* system parameters, based on a given logical data model, and a set of expected user-queries, prior to the installation of the application.

- Facilities for supporting the tuning of live *Total* applications using a combination of conventional and heuristic analysis of the *Total* statistics. This facility should recommend changes to system parameters with explanations of why particular changes are being suggested.

- Facilities for storing and retrieving data on specific applications or projects which have been partially designed or tuned using ITAM. This function should allow the user to analyse historically the performance of a specific *Total* file and the changes which have been made to it over a given period of time. It should also be possible to annotate this historical data with comments, indicating the reason for changes which have been made.

As the main purpose of this discussion is to give some results of, and reflections on, employing the POLITE model, further details of the ITAM system, such as the quantitative performance objectives set for the system at lower levels, are not discussed here.

9.4 POLITE in Action

The activities described above constitute the POLITE life-cycle's feasibility and requirements definition phase, the result of which was a detailed set of objectives for the ITAM investigation, together with a statement of high-level functional requirements for the proposed KBS support tool. In addition, a start had been made on the analysis phase, with the production of an overall domain hierarchy sheet which identified nine high-level tasks, to be supported by ITAM. The overlap in this case arose because those most involved in specifying the requirements were also domain experts; the manager at BIS was also knowledgeable about the domain, and the management at BSC were happy to

SCHEDULE	Project: ALVEY		Sub-Project: ITAM	
Phase: Analysis	Initials: BIS2	Date:		Page: 1 of 3
		Time Intervals: Weeks		Units: Days

Description	Total Effort	Staff																	
Discuss and agree initial domain analysis																			
Task analysis for tasks 1 to 9																			
Consolidate task analysis																			
Expert review of task analysis																			
Determine KB or not (secondary feas.)																			
Define logical rules for KB																			
Conventional analysis for non-KB tasks																			
QA of analysis																			
Review meeting																			

Figure 9.8: Schedule for analysis phase of ITAM

rely on the views of their expert. Such overlaps are likely to be typical of KBS development; managing the performance of an expert skill is very different from managing the performance of a procedural task. Thus a waterfall-style fixed endpoint to a phase is inappropriate; RUDE cycles may occur even during feasibility!

The next step was to produce a plan and schedule for the remainder of the analysis and design phases of the investigation, based on the POLITE model.

It was important for the credibility of this early test of the POLITE model that people other than those who developed it attempted to employ it in a practical context. Any development methodology must be usable by a DP environment, without the constant support of those who formulated the method in the first place; BIS expect users of SSD to be able to employ it successfully after a one week training course and some additional consultancy. Of course, chapters 4 and 7 have shown that SSD does need at least some tool support to be successfully used. However, the principle that an engineering methodology should be usable by different people, in a variety of installations, with the minimum of human expert support, is a valid one.

Thus, BIS staff not involved in formulating POLITE took the main responsibility for drawing up a detailed schedule of tasks and checkpoints, which were required to complete the analysis and design phases, based on the POLITE model. A part of this schedule, for the analysis phase, is shown in Figure 9.8 (the numerical details have been omitted from the diagram). Similar schedules were prepared for the logical and physical design phases.

The analysis phase involved four further knowledge engineering sessions with the expert at BIS and one session involving three BSC experts. The basic procedure followed that evolved during work on the Advisor project and the Designer feasibility study, namely a form of protocol analysis (see section 2.4.2). The interviews were recorded and transcribed; extensive domain and task analysis was carried out and the resulting paper-based documentation was iteratively refined (RUDE again) in close consultation with the experts. Since BIS's expert was heavily committed to other work, careful planning and preparation was essential to ensure that the knowledge engineering sessions were productive, and that the expert was given the maximum notice of dates for the sessions. One of the main objectives of using a structured approach is to allow this type of planning and scheduling to be done. Figures 9.9 and 9.10 show how the planning and scheduling of the knowledge engineering were accomplished.

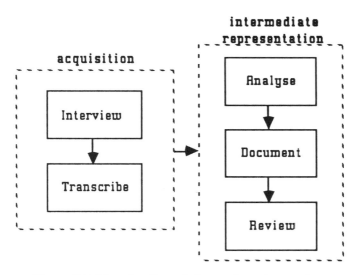

Figure 9.9: Planning knowledge engineering sessions

TASK	KE(s)	CLERICAL	EXPERT(s)
preparation	1/2	-	-
interview	1/2	-	1/2
transcription	-	1	-
analysis	2-3	-	-
documentation	1-2	-	-
review	1/2	-	1/2

(units of days)

Figure 9.10: Scheduling knowledge engineering

Figure 9.10 illustrates the need for metrics to enable knowledge acquisition effort to be estimated. The metrics employed are based on empirical evidence gained during the *Intellipse* project and elsewhere. Much further work on metrics for KBSs and hybrid systems is required, and Aston University, BIS Applied Systems and Expert Systems Ltd. have just begun to pursue this avenue in a spin-off project from the original *Intellipse* project, sponsored by the UK Department of Trade and Industry and Science and Engineering Research Council.

The design phases were based around diagrammatic analysis and presentation, as has already been indicated. The system was effectively divided into three modules: Build Database, Tune Database, and Monitor Performance. Work concentrated initially on Monitor Performance, as carrying out this activity for over 400 database files was a task which BSC were conscious they were failing to perform fully. "Tune" followed, with "Build" last.

Implementation of the system was on IBM-compatible PCs, the system being written in C to allow easy integration of the conventional and rule-based parts of the system. Testing was carried out by reference to the POLITE model. On the basis of these it was estimated by BSC that, for example, full use of the system to monitor the performance of their database files would save at least a half day per week of staff time, as well as checking many factors which were not being checked before. Unfortunately, before operational testing could be undertaken over a sufficiently long period for maintenance issues to arise, higher-level management in BSC decided to convert the DP systems concerned from *Total* to Cincom's relational database product *Supra*. Accordingly, further work on the *Total* system ceased at this point, but we feel that the investigation was a useful test of all aspects of POLITE except long-term maintenance. Work on systems for use with *Supra* continues.

9.5 Evolution of POLITE Standards

The sessions with BIS's expert involved the extensive use of case studies to determine the accuracy of the diagrammatic representations produced. The sessions necessarily overlapped with the logical design phase during which rules, explanations and potential user-interactions were identified and documented. Figure 9.11 shows an example of the documentation used to record the decomposition of a high-level task, identified during the analysis phase.

The document illustrated in Figure 9.11 makes use of notation recommended in the BIS *MODUS* standards for *Structured Systems Analysis*. Martinez and Sobol (MART88) have reported on the use of conventional systems analysis techniques for expert systems development. They commented that the use of these techniques "...provide a way to document processes so that the experts can review them to see if they have accurately described what they do." This is in line with the experience of using these techniques throughout the *Intellipse* project, and with the approach advocated by Keller, described in section 6.3.4.

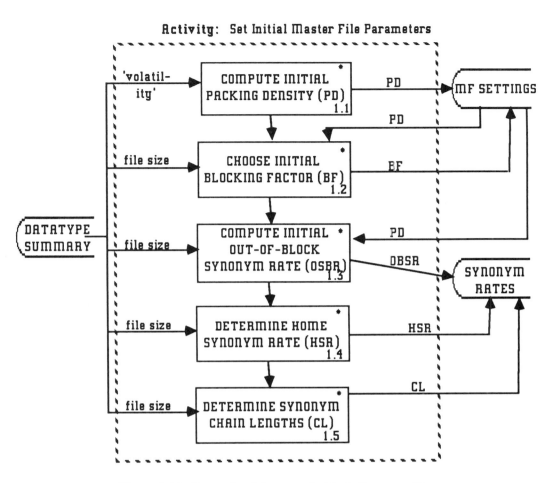

Activity: Set Initial Master File Parameters

Figure 9.11: Example of documented task decomposition

Addis (ADDIS85) has also discussed the use of conventional relational data analysis techniques (RDA) for AI systems. His discussion is mainly concerned with a comparison of conventional database theory and AI. Although techniques from RDA theory are identified, which could be used for knowledge representation in KBSs, Addis does not relate his work to the requirements of an operational KBS development methodology.

Figures 9.12 and 9.13 give examples of the documentation which has evolved for recording activity descriptions and rules. This documentation was based on existing *MODUS* standards, although they have had to be amended to meet the particular needs of KBS development. This adaptation of conventional standards to create POLITE KBS development standards is the process which was envisaged in section 9.2.

```
┌─────────────────────────────────────────────────────────────────────┐
│  ACTIVITY SHEET      No.   1.2.3        Name     Calculate file size  │
├─────────────────────────────────────────────────────────────────────┤
│  For Each:      Primary file                                          │
│                                                                       │
│  When:                                                                │
│  - - - - - - - - - - - - - - - - - - - - - - - - - - - - - - - - - -  │
│  Input:        Number of records in file                              │
│                                                                       │
│  Output       File size in blocks                                     │
│  - - - - - - - - - - - - - - - - - - - - - - - - - - - - - - - - - -  │
│  Explanation:                                                         │
│                                                                       │
│   Block size can be anything up to 16k.                               │
│   Select 8k to start with unless file is so small that it can fit into a smaller │
│   block.                                                              │
│                                                                       │
│  - - - - - - - - - - - - - - - - - - - - - - - - - - - - - - - - - -  │
│  Procedure:                                                           │
│   Number of records per block = block size / physical record size     │
│   (total is rounded down)                                             │
│                                                                       │
│   Total blocks = total number of records / number of records per block │
│                                                                       │
└─────────────────────────────────────────────────────────────────────┘
```

Figure 9.12: Example of documentation for an activity

It should be noted that the adapted *MODUS* documentation illustrated has been developed by BIS independently of the author. This is an important observation, as it adds credibility to the proposition, advanced earlier in this chapter, that the use of the POLITE model on live KBS development projects is necessary to evolve the required practical development standards.

9.6 Lessons from the ITAM Investigation

The ITAM project is a relatively small exercise by typical DPSD project standards. Caution is therefore necessary in drawing any firm conclusions. However, the following is a list of initial observations made on the basis of the ITAM work:

- The findings of the Designer feasibility study in the area of DB design were confirmed. The technical feasibility of designing KBS tools to support the building, optimisation and maintenance of a DBMS application was demonstrated.

```
┌─────────────────────────────────────────────────────────────────┐
│ RULE DESCRIPTION                    RULE NO  6                     │
├─────────────────────────────────────────────────────────────────┤
│ System: ITAM                                                      │
│                                                                   │
│ Activity Name: Analyse statistics        Activity Ref: 2.1.1      │
├─────────────────────────────────────────────────────────────────┤
│ Data required:                                                    │
│   Statistics files                                                │
├─────────────────────────────────────────────────────────────────┤
│ Rule context:    Primary files only. 13 other rules for this activity. │
│                                                                   │
│ Rule:        IF (physical reads / logical reads) > 1.05           │
│              THEN out-of-block synonym rate may be getting too high │
│              AND OUTPUT warning                                   │
│                                                                   │
│                                                                   │
│ Source:        MC9                                                │
│ - - - - - - - - - - - - - - - - - - - - - - - - - - - - - - - - - │
│ Explanation:                                                      │
│                                                                   │
│        Warnings are output where performance is (potentially) poor. │
│        User has option to let system continue to reach recommended │
│        actions.                                                   │
│                                                                   │
│                                                                   │
└─────────────────────────────────────────────────────────────────┘
```

Figure 9.13: Example of documentation for a rule description

- Complex design tasks involve both heuristic and conventional elements necessitating the use of hybrid support tools in this type of domain.

- The methods used for structuring the knowledge engineering again proved successful, as they had on other developments. The diagrammatic representation of the results of the expert task analysis was also found to be valuable, not only for recording the results, but also for confirming the accuracy of the analysis with the expert. The diagrams and accompanying documentation were also useful as a basis for iteratively refining the analysis with the expert. It should be noted, however, that the experts used were familiar with the techniques of conventional systems analysis, which also makes extensive

229

use of diagrammatic techniques. Thus, the usefulness of this type of documentation with experts who are unfamiliar with such approaches needs to be investigated further. This cautionary note applies only where it is intended to make use of the diagrammatic material as the basic means of communication with the expert.

- The POLITE life-cycle model provided a basis for planning and scheduling the feasibility, analysis, design and testing phases of the ITAM investigation. The model enabled BIS to draw up detailed task lists and check-points for managing the work.

- Practical standards and documentation have begun to emerge from the ITAM work, continuing work using *Supra*, and other projects. Much of this has been adapted from existing *MODUS* standards. This indicates that conventional software engineering does have something to give to KBS "engineering", but also confirms that conventional techniques do need to be *adapted* to suit the particular requirements of KBS development.

If we look back at the differences between ITAM, which was carried out using the POLITE life-cycle, and the construction of Advisor (see chapter 7), which was not, the clearest difference concerns the task-lists and checkpoints mentioned above. In Advisor, we had none (at least in any formal sense), until after we had determined the structure to be used for knowledge representation (a logical design task). After we had accomplished that, a fair amount of backtracking was involved in order to make what we had already done consistent with the logical design. Fortunately, we had previously realized the value of a paper-based intermediate representation!

The other clearest difference was the use of a special-purpose language (micro-Prolog) for Advisor and a conventional language (C) for ITAM, but this arose from the nature of the two systems being developed rather than the different development processes. Advisor had hardly any conventional components, and dealt mainly with words, whereas ITAM involved a considerable amount of statistical calculations and more elaborate graphics.

9.7 Summary

This chapter has described the central part of the POLITE life-cycle model, and the initial results of applying POLITE to developing hybrid systems for physical database design. This investigation suggests that the model will be able to achieve the intended level of practical applicability in the future. Development standards have also begun to emerge, adding extra weight to the validity of the POLITE model. BIS are satisfied with the results to the extent that they will continue to pursue the development of commercial standards for operational KBS development based on the POLITE life-cycle. One avenue for this is continuing work on database design by the original *Intellipse* project partners, Aston, BIS and BSC.

We believe that the POLITE methodology will be useful not only for hybrid knowledge-based/conventional systems, but also for stand-alone knowledge-based systems where the development process concerns more than one or two people.

References

(ADDIS85) T.R.Addis, *"Designing Knowledge-Based Systems"*, Kogan Page, London, 1985.
(MART88) D.R.Martinez and M.G.Sobol, "Systems Analysis Techniques for the Implementation of Expert Systems", *Information and Software Technology*, Vol. 30, No. 2, pp.81-88, March 1988.

Chapter 10: Conclusions

10.0 Introduction

In this concluding chapter we shall summarize and bring together the various aspects of our thoughts about building knowledge-based systems (KBSs).

Our intention throughout has been to take an applications-driven viewpoint, looking at KBSs as one of many tools which can be used to solve problems which arise in the management of organizations or in specialized tasks within them. This implies also that we should not regard KBSs as a field in isolation, but one which must be integrated with other problem-solving approaches such as conventional software engineering, operational research and "soft" systems analysis.

CONTRIBUTIONS TO PRACTICAL KBS DEVELOPMENT
• FROM SOFT OR/SYSTEMS 　　　　- Problem structuring 　　　　- Choice between approaches 　　　　- Managing the process(1)
• FROM CONVENTIONAL SOFTWARE ENGINEERING 　　　　- Managing the process(2) 　　　　- Standards/documentation 　　　　- Testing
• FROM AI 　　　　- Internal aspects of KBSs
UNRESOLVED QUERY: Where to put credit/blame for use of prototyping?

Table 10.1: Contributions to practical KBS development

One of the views we have put forward is that much of what has been written on the subject of building KBSs <u>does</u> look at KBSs in isolation, whether as a subset of AI or not, and as a result is only relevant to KBS applications which are equally isolated. An example of this would be a small stand-alone expert system which is only intended for use by a single user. However, we believe that relatively few KBS applications are likely to be of this kind, and therefore the approach to building KBSs needs to be correspondingly broader. Our approach therefore draws not only upon work done on knowledge-based systems in themselves, but also on conventional software engineering and soft OR/ systems. The contributions of the various fields are summarized in Table 10.1.

10.1 Tackle the Right Problem

In section 2.1 we identified three types of approach to building KBSs: exploratory, solution-driven and problem-driven. Their characteristics are summarized briefly in Table 10.2. We believe that a problem-driven perspective is essential when KBSs are being considered as just another competing solution technology. When the possibility of building a KBS is simply one of various solution technologies, one of the key questions to be tackled is how to choose between a KBS and the other available candidates. This entails being very clear about the business objectives which the solution system is supposed to address. (We use the phrase "business objectives" throughout, but similar considerations apply to public sector and not-for-profit organizations.)

We suggest that these objectives - and hence the purpose for which the KBS is required - should be clarified and indeed made explicit using the methods of soft operational research and/or soft systems analysis. Precisely which approach of this kind should be used must in the end be a matter of the personal preference of those carrying out the investigation. Our own preference would be for Checkland's SSM or a soft OR approach (both described in chapter 5), given that a solution is usually sought in relation to a problem or opportunity occurring in a particular part of the organization. It is, however, occasionally possible to take a really wide approach, at the level of the whole organization; for example, a complete re-design of the organization's information systems to include knowledge-based components. In such a case it would be best to consider the use of management cybernetics. Space does not permit us to describe that topic in this book; the interested reader should consult Beer (BEER85) for details of the theory and Espejo and Harnden (ESPE89) for some examples of applications.

TYPES OF APPROACH TO BUILDING KBSs:
EXPLORATORY - Typical of "Research" - Results from roots in AI - Inward-looking perspective can be misleading
SOLUTION-DRIVEN - Typically "Buy a Shell for our PC" approach - Limits potential for development - Can lead to concentration in wrong areas
PROBLEM-DRIVEN - Could also be called "Business-driven" - Must acknowledge other 'Solution technologies' - Not specific to one tool or technique

Table 10.2: Types of approach to building KBSs

Once the characteristics of the desired solution system have been clarified, the next step is to see whether a KBS solution is both necessary and desirable. To some extent this may already have been accomplished during the previous stage. For example, if Checkland's SSM (see section 5.4) is being used, it will be necessary to have defined one or more root definitions of the organizational system concerned. The Transformations (T in the CATWOE mnemonic) identified in these root definitions may shed some light as to whether or not a KBS would be the best choice of solution "technology".

For example, consider the different organizational systems whose root definitions contain the following statements about their transformations:

•"a system to record the information required about each order received"

•"a system to perform payroll calculations for weekly-paid employees"

•"a system to forecast demand for the company's products"

•"a system to determine the creditworthiness of loan applicants"

•"a system to enable sales staff to configure computer hardware orders".

Building a KBS becomes a more plausible option as we move toward the bottom of the list, although perhaps only in the last of the 5 examples is it clear that a KBS is likely to be the best choice.

The comparison of KBS solutions with those produced by other types of approach is a very under-developed area at the moment. We have been involved in some theoretical speculations on this point which have appeared elsewhere (ROD89), but much more experience of the long-term operation of KBSs is needed before any general lessons may be drawn. Configuring computer systems is probably the only task for which building a KBS would at present be universally accepted as the best approach! Although there is a shortage of comparative studies, there is nevertheless a considerable body of work on the suitability of KBSs, looked at in isolation. Some of the factors which need to be taken into account in looking at the suitability of a domain for a KBS were discussed in section 2.2. The TRESSA expert system developed by Touche Ross (see chapter 6) also examines the feasibility of using an expert system solution in any particular problem, and thus represents a further step toward formalizing the process.

10.2 Developing the KBS

Once it has been decided that a KBS is definitely what is required (or perhaps we should say "is definitely what is going to be built"!), then the business objectives need to be translated into objectives for the KBS, which will be used to guide the development of the system and then to assess the system produced, as described in chapter 8.

The process of constructing the KBS itself should be carried out according to the POLITE methodology as set out in chapter 9 and summarized in Table 10.3.

This will necessitate, amongst other things, careful management of iteration wherever it occurs. A vital element in the management of iteration will be the development of appropriate standards and checkpoints. These must evolve over time, as the corresponding standards for conventional systems development have done.

THE POLITE METHODOLOGY

Produce
Objectives

Logical and physical design

Implement

Test

Evaluate (and if necessary Edit)

Table 10.3: The POLITE methodology

Many of the specifically knowledge-based aspects of the system will involve activities which have been discussed in earlier chapters, particularly chapters 1 and 3. Table 10.4 shows some of these activities, together with the stage of the POLITE methodology at which they first become relevant.

10.3 Another Potential Area for Development

In addition to its use in building hybrid and stand-alone KBSs, we feel the POLITE life-cycle may perhaps also be useful for building decision support systems, by providing a framework for controlling the prototyping essential to DSS development. Existing approaches to conventional systems development do not usually cater for this. The phases of the POLITE model apply just as well to decision support systems as they do to KBSs. However, a complete POLITE model for DSSs would require additional development work, on the lines we shall now set out.

POLITE effectively contains a conventional methodology based on BIS's SSD, consisting of the activities shown in Figure 9.2 and the non-shaded parts of Figures 9.3 - 9.6. For decision support system development, this would need to

ASPECTS OF KBSs RELATED TO POLITE STAGES	
Mode of operation (Figure 1.3)	Feasibility
Style (section 1.2.3)	Analysis
Tools (sections 3.2 - 3.7)	Physical Design
Knowledge acquisition (section 2.4.2)	Analysis
Knowledge representation (sections 3.1.1 and 3.3)	Logical Design
Knowledge execution (sections 3.5 & 3.6)	Physical Design
Human interface (section 3.1.3) (as it should be considered)	Logical Design
Human interface (as conventionally understood)	Physical Design
Inferencing mechanism(s) (section 3.1.2)	Logical Design

Table 10.4: Aspects of KBSs related to POLITE stages

be augmented by the addition of certain tasks - often similar to, but not quite the same as, those in the KBS part of POLITE - in the analysis, design and testing phases. For example, the user interface of a DSS will need to be carefully and explicitly considered in the physical design phase, but the detailed criteria may well differ from those applicable to a KBS. As a second example, whereas for a hybrid KBS the activity Secondary Feasibility is concerned with deciding which parts of the system should be built as knowledge-based components and which as conventional components, for a DSS the corresponding activity is deciding which tasks should be performed by the computer system and which by the human user/decision-maker.

This last example reveals what at first glance might appear to be a most important difference between POLITE as applied to decision support systems and POLITE as applied to hybrid, conventional or knowledge-based systems. The overall requirements for a DSS must initially be specified not in terms of what is desired from the computer system, but in terms of what is required from the combined human/computer system. Only in the analysis phase will the actual requirements for the support provided by the computer system become clear, and POLITE permits these to be determined iteratively (at least to some extent) by the user/decision-maker.

In fact, this is <u>not</u> a difference between DSSs and other types of system; it is precisely the reason why so much fuss has been made about business objectives throughout this book! No computer system, of whatever kind, should be viewed in isolation, because in isolation it can achieve nothing. It must be looked at in the wider context of the business objectives, the attainment of which the system is supposed to be assisting with. Development approaches which miss this point and are based on a set of unchanging requirements fixed at the outset of the project are almost certainly doomed to run into problems as a result.

10.4 Summary

In this book we have attempted to put forward our ideas about building knowledge-based systems. We hope it is not too fanciful to call them a methodology, even if we would not yet claim that our ideas are either complete or fully tested. We have been motivated particularly by considering KBSs which are more complex than the straightforward stand-alone expert system, in which the process of building the system often involves only two people - one expert and one system builder. This extra complexity might come from any or all of the following sources:

•More than one user
•More than one developer
•Need to think carefully about relationship between KBS and business objectives
•Need for a robust, maintainable system
•Need to integrate with other computer systems
•Need to choose between KBS and other potential solution technologies

In time, we hope that the use of knowledge-based systems, or the inclusion of knowledge-based components within other types of computer system, will cease to be seen as something which is exclusively the prerogative of AI workers, but become a part of the mainstream in both software engineering and operational research. If our speculations in the section above prove correct, this may even help to integrate those other "lost sheep", decision support systems, into the mainstream fold as well.

References

(BEER85) Stafford Beer, *"Diagnosing the System for Organizations"*, John Wiley, Chichester, 1985.
(ESPE89) Raul Espejo and Roger Harnden (eds.), *"The Viable System Model"*, John Wiley, Chichester, 1989.
(ROD89) M.A.Rodger and John S.Edwards, "A Problem-driven Approach to Expert System Development", *J. Opl Res. Soc.*, Vol.40, No.12, pp.1069-1077, December 1989.

Glossary of Terms

(Indicated as applying to knowledge-based systems (KBS), "soft" operational research/systems analysis (ORSA) or conventional software engineering (SE) where appropriate.)

Agenda (KBS) List of current and pending goals to be investigated by a knowledge-based system.

Analysis (SE) Construction of detailed description (often called the specification) of the functionality of proposed system, by modelling the relevant areas of business activity.

Artificial intelligence "The science of making machines do things which would require intelligence if they were done by a human" (Marvin Minsky).

Backward chaining (KBS) Method of inference which proceeds backwards from the potential goal(s) to the data by investigating whether or not the necessary conditions for a particular goal are satisfied.

Cognitive task analysis (KBS) The process of transferring knowledge from a human expert into machine-executable form.

Decision Support System Computer system intended to assist a human to make better decisions about semi-structured problems.

Design (SE) Expansion of specification produced by analysis (q.v.) to include full details of all programs, files, records, etc.

Environment (KBS) Software package providing a wide range of facilities for the building, testing and debugging of knowledge-based systems, usually offering a choice of approaches and often requiring specialised hardware.

Environment (ORSA) Everything outside the boundary of the particular organizational system being examined which interacts with it, either directly or indirectly.

Evaluation Establishing whether or not a system has contributed to an organization's overall success.

Expert system (KBS) Computer system intended to mimic the performance of a human expert in a well-defined domain.

Feasibility (SE) Investigation whose purpose is to establish whether there is a need for a computer system and, if so, the general nature of the tasks the system is to perform. The latter are usually specified in the form of the requirements definition (q.v.).

Forward chaining (KBS) Method of inference which proceeds forwards from the data to the potential goal(s) by making any conclusions which can be made from the current state of the knowledge-base, and continuing iteratively until no further inferences are possible.

Implementation (ORSA) Putting the chosen "solution" into place in the real organizational system.

Implementation (SE) Transformation of the detailed design (q.v.) into machine-executable code.

Inference engine (KBS) Part of a knowledge-based system which carries out inference, search and matching operations on the knowledge-base.

Knowledge-based system (KBS) A computer system which attempts to represent human knowledge or expertise.

Knowledge drift (KBS) The process by which knowledge gradually becomes out of date (e.g. incomplete or incorrect) over a period of time. More common in applied domains than in theoretical ones.

Knowledge engineer (KBS) The person responsible for constructing a knowledge-based system.

Knowledge representation schema (pl. **schemata**) (KBS) Method by which knowledge is represented in the computer system's knowledge-base, for example frames, rules or semantic nets.

Learning system (KBS) System by which the knowledge in a knowledge-based system is acquired and updated. May or may not be computer-based.

Machine learning (KBS) Computer-based learning system, normally based on "training" by correctly classified examples.

Maintenance (SE) Making sure that a computer system continues to run in operational use for as long as it is required, by correcting errors, adding functionality which is lacking, etc.

Problem structuring (ORSA) Finding out about a situation in which someone has perceived there to be a problem. The aim is to gain as broad an appreciation as possible of the true causes of the problem (as opposed to its symptoms).

Requirements definition (SE) A summary of the tasks which a computer system is required to perform, set out in the users' (i.e. "output") terms.

Rich picture (ORSA) A description of an organizational problem situation which is both broad and highly detailed. Often literally in the form of pictures or diagrams.

Root definition (ORSA) A statement about a system in an organization, which attempts to define what that system is for, as seen from a particular viewpoint.

Rule induction (KBS) A particular type of machine learning (q.v.) in which the training set of examples is used to produce a rule-base in the form of a decision tree.

Secondary feasibility (KBS) Examination of the tasks performed by the human expert to see which should be represented as a knowledge-based system and which as a conventional computer program.

Shell (KBS) A software package intended to facilitate the building of knowledge-based systems, by providing a built-in knowledge representation schema and inference engine (usually only one of each), leaving "only" the task of adding the domain knowledge.

Soft methodology (ORSA) An approach to tackling organizational problems which acknowledges that many such problems are either caused or worsened by the different opinions of the people making up the organization. "Solving" such a problem is not a question of deciding on "the right answer", but (for example) of producing some measure of agreement as to what constitutes "right".

Toolkit (KBS) Set of software routines intended to assist a knowledge engineer in building and testing a knowledge-based system.

Validation Establishing whether or not a computer system works correctly for the task(s) it was envisaged to perform.

Verification Establishing whether or not a computer system meets its specification.

Workstation (KBS) A special-purpose computer specifically configured to run artificial intelligence/knowledge-based system software efficiently. Often based around the language LISP.

Index

Judgements   186–188, 205

KADS   118, 139–141
KBS development methodology
  current/"classic"   135–136
KEE   11, 14
Knowledge acquisition   77–78, 144. *See also* Acquisition
Knowledge base   60–65
Knowledge drift   90, 91, 241
Knowledge engineer   241
Knowledge engineering   45–47
Knowledge representation   78–82, 213–214. *See also* Representation
Knowledge representation schema   241
Knowledge-based system
  "definition" of   241
  styles of   16–18
Knowledge-based systems
  modes of interaction   19–20
KnowledgeTool   12

Le_Lisp   13
Learning system   70–71, 74–75, 91, 241
Leonardo   9, 11, 80
Linkman   18
LISP   1, 2, 12–14, 14, 15, 21–22, 81, 84–85, 105, 145, 176, 206
LSDM   93

M.1   80
Machine learning   241. *See also* Rule induction
Machine vision. *See* Pattern recognition
Mainframe systems. *See* Mini/mainframe systems
Maintenance   90–91, 99, 113–114, 215, 242
Management cybernetics   233
Metrics   186, 194, 196, 205, 225
Mid-range KBS products   80
Milestones   100
Mini/mainframe systems   11–12, 15, 15–16, 20, 75, 80, 85, 86–87
Models of human cognition   25
MODUS   93, 149–150, 154, 160, 208, 226–228
MYCIN   7, 9, 79

Natural language understanding   3, 20–21
Neural networks   23, 71
Nexpert Object   80
NOEMIE   17

Objects   53, 80, 84
Operational KBSs/ESs   39–45, 94, 96
Operational research   117, 120–125, 126, 190–192, 198
  "soft"   117, 125–126, 233
OPS5   15
Organizational learning   180, 180–181

Pascal   13
Pattern recognition   23
PC-based systems   8, 9, 10–11, 12–13, 15, 20, 58, 80, 85–86, 123–124, 175–176
Performance objectives   109, 127, 180, 184–199, 188, 194, 196, 200–202, 210, 220–
    221, 222, 233. *See also* Business objectives
Personal Consultant   79, 80
Personal Consultant Plus   11
Polapres   11, 18
POLITE methodology   152, 179, 208-231, 235–238
Problem selection   108
Problem structuring   242
Problem-driven perspective   32, 34, 36, 39, 44, 145, 151, 168, 233
Project management   144–146, 216
Prolog   1, 12–14, 21, 65, 81, 84–85, 105–106, 144, 175–176, 206
PROSPECTOR   79, 188, 195
Protocol analysis   50–51, 224
Prototyping   93–94, 101–106, 109–110, 114, 129, 131, 136, 139, 210–211, 236

R1. *See* XCON
Repertory grids   51
Representation   48, 53, 60–68
Rich picture   129, 242
ROMC approach   103–104
Root definition   127, 129–130, 234–235, 242
RUDE cycle   136–139, 208, 210, 215, 224
Rule induction   51, 70, 74–75, 77–78, 242
Rules   10, 35–36, 45, 47, 48, 53, 60–61, 79, 80, 105–106

SAGE   13, 79
SAVOIR   79
Scripts   165
Secondary feasibility   171, 211, 237, 242
Security   89
Semantic nets   53, 64, 84
Semi-formal methods. *See* Structured methods
Shells   9–12, 20, 33–34, 35, 36, 53, 58, 79–80, 82–84, 168, 176, 242
Simulation modelling   14, 18, 27, 189, 193–194, 206
Soft methodology   242. *See also* Operational research: "soft"; Soft systems
    analysis; Soft systems methodology